POTTERY & PORCELAIN

Frontispiece. Tucker & Hemphill Vase, ca. 1835. One of a Pair Owned by the Philadelphia Museum of Art. Photograph by A. J. Wyatt, Staff Photographer.

POTTERY AND PORCELAIN

OF

THE UNITED STATES

AN HISTORICAL REVIEW OF AMERICAN
CERAMIC ART WITH A NEW INTRODUCTION
AND BIBLIOGRAPHY

EDWIN ATLEE BARBER

1971

CENTURY HOUSE AMERICANA
WATKINS GLEN/NEW YORK

PRINTING BY VALLEY OFFSET, INC.

PREFACE

During his lifetime Dr. Edwin AtLee Barber (1851-1916) explored many fields. A trained scientist and archaeologist, he accompanied the geologist Hayden in the capacity of Assistant Naturalist during his famous survey of the West from 1874-1875. He dabbled in politics until 1885 and then spent the final years of his life studying ceramics and working for the Philadelphia Museum and School of Industrial Art; from 1901 he was its curator and its director from 1907 until his death. Even in his own time, however, it was his fifteen books on ceramics that made him this country's leading authority on pottery and porcelain, and it is for these that he is still remembered, in particular his 1904 *Marks of American Potters* (Chamberlain *Art Reference Book* number 1779) and his 1893/1901/1909 *Pottery and Porcelain of the United States* (Chamberlain *Art Reference Book* number 1780). John Spargo, a leading twentieth-century authority writing in 1926, says "The well known works of Dr. Barber . . . are virtually indispensable to the student of American ceramics . . . His principal book, *Pottery and Porcelain of the United States* . . . is one of the most important source books that we have." More recently, Dr. Barber was cited in the important catalogue to the great 1957 exhibition of *Tucker China, 1825-1838* held at the Philadelphia Museum of Art: ". . . much of our knowledge of the history of Tucker china is due to Dr. Barber's research . . ." Two years ago, Herbert Peck, in his masterful *Book of Rookwood Pottery,* cited Dr. Barber again and again as the first authority to give Rookwood national recognition; his *Marks of American Potters* is, in several instances, the only means we have of identifying Rookwood decorators. In 1886 Rookwood approached him at the Philadelphia Museum and School of Industrial Art; two years later in 1888 the annual Pottery and Porcelain Exhibition held in Fairmount Park's Memorial Hall, sponsored by the Museum, and organized by Dr. Barber honored Rookwood with the two first prizes. It was the first major prize the firm had ever won and preceded by one year the gold medal won at the 1889 Exposition Universelle.

The preceding is recorded here to document the most astounding feature of Dr. Barber's work, *i.e.,* its durability. His *Pottery and Porcelain of the United States* continues to be a standard authority after nearly seventy years of active use by three generations of scholars in the field of American decorative arts. More than a pioneer study of American ceramics, it was also the first, major scholarly history to be devoted exclusively to one aspect of American decorative arts. It is the only historical survey of American ceramics (and, for that matter, of *any* American decorative art) from the nineteenth century that has remained useful in spite of later scholarship. Few books, in fact, from the twentieth century can make such a claim. At this moment, its greatest strength resides in those sections devoted to the pottery and porcelain of the latter half of the nineteenth century. Recent scholars have explored a few of the manufacturers, such as Rookwood, Chelsea, and Phoenixville, yet none have succeeded in producing a general historical survey that can surpass Dr. Barber's book. Broad in scope, temporate in opinion, and articulate in thought, his *Pottery and Porcelain of the United States* remains the standard, single-volume authority on Victorian ceramics.

G. L. Freeman
August 1971

CONTENTS

INDEX

CHAPTER I

INTRODUCTORY REMARKS

FOREIGN writers would have the world believe that the United States can boast of no ceramic history.

Even our own chroniclers have, singularly enough, neglected a branch of our industrial progress which is not altogether insignificant nor devoid of interest. On the contrary, it can be shown that the fictile art is almost as ancient in this country as in Great Britain, and has been developed in almost parallel, though necessarily narrower, lines.

The need of a history of the Pottery Industry in America has long been felt, and has led to the preparation of the present volume, which, it is hoped, will be found to possess some interest to the student of ceramics, as well as to the collector.

The author claims that his work is not a mere compilation, but has been based almost entirely upon thorough personal investigations. Some of the time-honored fallacies which have been perpetuated by compilers have been omitted from this record, and special care has been taken to avoid the use of statements which could not be substantiated. This result could only be reached by patient and systematic research, by a thorough study of

the products of the potteries of the United States, and
by consultation with intelligent potters in the leading
establishments of the land.   Much of the material contained herein appears for the first time, and will doubtless
form the basis for other histories which will follow later.

It does not come within the scope of this volume to
include the history of every pottery which has been established since the time of Columbus, or which is now in
operation in this country.   Such a detailed review would,
even if desirable, be manifestly impossible in an undertaking of this compass.   The main purpose of the work
is to furnish an account of such of the earlier potteries as,
for any reason, possess some historical interest, and of
those manufactories which, in later days, have produced
works of originality or artistic merit.

I am highly gratified to be able to call the attention of
lovers of art to the remarkable progress which has been
made in ceramic manufacture in our midst within the past
fifteen years, and if my efforts shall result, in any measure,
in the breaking down of that unreasonable prejudice
which has heretofore existed against all American productions, I shall feel that I have been abundantly re-
warded.   America, within the next few decades, is destined
to lead the world in her ceramic manufactures, and the
future student will be entitled to know something of the
earlier struggles of the art in this country.

CHAPTER II

SYNOPSIS

THE history of pottery and porcelain in America, as presented in the foregoing pages, may be summed up briefly as follows :

Building bricks were made in Virginia as early as 1612.

White ware was first manufactured in this country about 1684.

Clay tobacco-pipes of European design were probably first made in America in 1690.

Terra-cotta roofing tiles were made in Pennsylvania previous to the year 1740.

Slip-decorated earthenware was fabricated in Pennsylvania as early as 1760.

The earliest attempt to manufacture white ware (and possibly porcelain) with underglaze decorations was made in Philadelphia in 1770.

William Ellis Tucker, of Philadelphia, was the first to successfully produce hard porcelain, in the year 1825.

The first Rockingham ware was made in the United States at East Liverpool, Ohio, by James Bennett in 1839.

Transfer printing from engraved plates was first applied to pottery in this country at the Jersey City Pottery previous to 1840.

Parian ware was first produced at Bennington, Vermont, about the year 1846.

Inlaid floor-tiles were made at the United States Pottery in Bennington in 1853.

Pottery coat-buttons were manufactured at Norwalk, Connecticut, about the same time.

Architectural terra-cotta was not made in the United States until about 1870.

Ornamental relief tiles were not produced until after the Centennial Exposition.

Belleek or egg-shell porcelain was first made in this country, at Trenton, in 1884.

The Great Exhibition of 1876 marked the ceramic art movement which has since resulted in the wonderful development of the pottery industry in this country.

For more than a century intelligent and public-spirited men and women in Europe have been interested in gathering together, from the four corners of the globe, examples of ceramic manufactures, which, above all other objects of human industry, have been instrumental in recording the history of nations, the customs and manners of peoples, and the artistic progress of races. Sovereigns and subjects have vied with each other in forming collections of the quaint, the curious, the beautiful in art, as exemplified in the handiwork of the potter.

In our own country no serious attempts were made in this direction by collectors until a comparatively recent period, and previous to 1876 but few private or public collections of potteries or porcelains could be found in the United States. Since the Philadelphia Exhibition, however, widespread interest has been awakened among students and collectors in the ceramic art, and to-day many valuable cabinets are to be found in the land filled with rare and costly examples of Old World skill. We have our specialists who confine themselves to the study of Oriental art; our collectors of Grecian and Roman potteries; our ceramists who are particularly interested in the wares of mediæval Europe, of Sèvres, of Wedgwood, and a few general collectors who cover the fictile arts of the world. The one fertile field, however, from which we may expect to reap the most abundant harvest, has thus far been neglected, although a step has been made in the right direction by one of our prominent public institutions, the Pennsylvania Museum, of Philadelphia, which has recently commenced the formation of a collection of American wares to illustrate the history and development of the potter's art in the United States from the first settlement of the country to the present time, which shall serve as a permanent reference collection for the student and the artisan.

The unreasonable prejudice which has heretofore existed against American ceramic production is rapidly disappearing as the discriminating public becomes more familiar with them. One of the foremost pottery concerns in this country, which was a few years ago forced to remove its trade-mark from its goods, in order to insure their sale in the home market, has recently resumed the marking of its wares, because the people have discovered

that they are fully equal, in every respect, to imported
china of the same class.   It has not been more than three
or four years since a leading jewelry establishment in one
of our large cities refused to handle the thin Belleek
china made in Trenton, unless stamped with a foreign or
misleading mark.   To-day these wares are meeting with
an extensive sale on their own merits and through the
domestic marks which are placed upon them.

Our potters are themselves largely responsible for the
ignorance of the American public in respect to the progress
which has been made in this country in ceramic manufacture.   The inquirer is met at the outset by an almost in-
surmountable difficulty in ascertaining where many of the
best wares are to be procured.   Some of the most meritorious productions of prominent potteries are rarely seen
on sale outside of their respective warerooms, and a search
through the crockery shops of any of our cities will bear
but scanty fruit in the discovery of American wares.   Even
in Trenton, the manufacturing centre for the finest American goods, it is impossible to see the various manufactures
of different establishments without visiting some thirty
separate works.   Not until a permanent bourse or exchange shall be established, by a combination of the
potters of this country, can the general public be fully
educated to the knowledge that the best pottery and
porcelain can be purchased at home.   The petty jealousies
which actuate many of our manufacturers must be over-
come, and they must consent to enter into friendly rivalry
before they can hope to successfully present their claims
for popular favor.   Every important city should have its

exchange where the best wares from all sections can be congregated together for examination and comparison. Such a movement would benefit all of our potters and eventually result in the decreased consumption of imported goods and the large increase of exports.

Another means of fostering, to some extent, our home manufactures would be the refusal to admit foreign-made wares to any of our exhibitions of decorative execution. Awards of merit should be confined to work done by our professionals and amateurs *on American bodies*. There is no reason for the selection of imported china by decorators when our own manufactories are producing wares for ornamentation in sufficient variety and of equal, if not superior, excellence to any that are imported for this purpose.

The possibilities of American art should appeal strongly to our art patrons, and our potters should receive the encouragement which wealthy connoisseurs have heretofore confined to foreign factories. Where could their patronage be more worthily and profitably bestowed than upon the artistic conceptions of our manufacturers, which only need proper recognition to insure greater originality and a still higher order of merit?

We cannot but believe that it should be the duty of those high in authority in the National Government to give their support to this branch of our national industry. The un-American sentiment which actuates the ordering of a service of china from abroad for use in State ceremonies should be discountenanced by our patriotic citizens. We are fully capable of producing table services equal to the best that can be obtained from foreign factories, and

our manufacturers are certainly entitled to official recognition.   It is gratifying to know that already some of our
Chief Executives have patronized home manufactures by
commissioning Americans to make special services for the
White House, and the recent example of a cabinet officer
selecting a dinner set for his own table from a Trenton
factory, after considering many which were submitted in
competition, is one which, we trust, may be extensively
emulated in the future.

Thus far our potters have been, in a great measure,
imitative rather than inventive, and the result is that we
have largely reproduced, though in a most creditable manner, patterns and designs, bodies, glazes, and decorations,
of foreign factories.   With some few exceptions, our
commercial manufacturers have been content to copy and
imitate the products of foreign establishments and have,
in consequence, unconsciously assisted in perpetuating
certain offences against good taste, as, for instance, in the
continued production of the ancient style of table plates
with depressed centres and horizontal borders, the modern
use of individual salts, butters, and bread and butter plates
rendering the plate rim no longer necessary.   It should,
therefore, be discarded as being obsolete and inelegant.
The most convenient, useful, and graceful form of plate is
that with the simple, sweeping, curved line, not made, however, except by a few progressive English potters.

Our producers have also yet to learn that modern
table etiquette demands a reduction in the size of many
pieces intended for family use.   It is no longer necessary
to make butter dishes and gravy boats large enough to

serve the purpose of vegetable dishes, nor the latter of a capacity sufficient for an ordinary soup tureen. The increasing refinement of our modern civilization rebels against the continued use of the capacious and clumsy utensils of pre-Centennial times. While the quality of our domestic table wares is not inferior to that of the foreign, the commercial element in design and workmanship must be made secondary to the artistic before our manufacturers can expect the more cultured classes to abandon, to any great extent, the imported for domestic manufactures. We are progressing rapidly in the right direction, however, and some of the designs of a few of our more progressive potteries have been copied extensively by English and German factories. The modelling of pieces for services is receiving more careful attention, and underglaze decorations are gradually superseding the inappropriate and unsubstantial overglaze work in table ware.

One of our acquaintances, who is greatly interested in American china, recently conceived the idea of giving a series of mid-day entertainments to her lady friends, which she christened " American Luncheons," for the reason that not only was the bill-of-fare distinctively American, but the china ware used on the table was entirely of American manufacture. As this suggestion may be followed by others with profit, we subjoin a sample

MENU.

BLUE POINTS ON HALF-SHELL.

(Oyster Plates of Mazarine Blue, made by the New England Pottery Co., East Boston, Mass.)

BOUILLON.

(Two-handled, covered cups, Belleek ware, made by the Willets Manufacturing Co., Trenton.)

CREAMED SALMON.   SARATOGA CHIPS.

(Semi-Porcelain Plates, Clifton shape, underglaze blue " peony " decoration, made by the Chesapeake Pottery, Baltimore, Md.)

BROILED QUAIL, CURRANT JELLY.

(Semi-Porcelain Plates, underglaze Royal Blue decoration, made by
International Pottery Co., Trenton.)

SWEETBREAD PATÉS.

(Fluted China Shells, made by International Pottery Co., Trenton.)

BREADED LAMB CHOPS WITH MUSHROOMS.

(Thin vitreous China Plates, made by the Greenwood Pottery Co.,
Trenton.)

TOMATO SALAD.

CHEESE AND WAFERS.

(Thin China Plates, made by Knowles, Taylor, & Knowles, East
Liverpool, O.)

NESSELRODE PUDDING.

(Ice-cream cups on platters of thin Belleek China, made by Ceramic
Art Co., Trenton.)

COFFEE.

(After-Dinner Coffees of Egg-Shell China, made by the Ott & Brewer
Co., Trenton.)

At the four corners of the centre-piece were Cupid
candelabra, made by the Ceramic Art Co., and in the
centre an artistic *jardinière* from the Burroughs and
Mountford factory, of Trenton, containing ferns.   On
the table were *faïence* almond-shells in underglaze decoration, from the Rookwood Pottery, Cincinnati, with salted

peanuts; *bonbonnières* in underglaze, triangular and heart-shaped, after the Japanese Kioto ware, made at the Pauline Art Pottery, Edgerton, Wis.; individual salts of pink Belleek, in the form of snail-shells, from the Etruria Pottery of Ott & Brewer; bread and butter plates, from the Willets Manufacturing Co., and butter spreaders, with decorated china handles, made by the Ceramic Art Company. Beside each guest was a delicate souvenir consisting of a china shell flower, holding sweet violets, from the American Art China Works of Trenton. No foreign productions could be more dainty and artistic than this combination of domestic wares, though selections from other American potteries could have been made with equally satisfactory results.

Some of the most prominent ceramic artists and artisans of England, France, and Germany are now connected with our American manufactories, contributing their experience and skill in the elevation and improvement of the standards of our productions. The United States have also produced potters, designers, decorators, and modellers who stand in the front rank of progressive workers in this branch of industry, and the art schools and industrial institutions which have been established in many parts of the land are educating our youth in the practical arts, and preparing them for this new field of labor. It is to be hoped that, at no very distant day, a National School of Pottery and Porcelain may be instituted, under the auspices of the Federal Government.

The day is not far distant when the legends, " Made in England," " Made in France," or " Made in Germany "

will not be necessary to insure the sale of ceramic productions in this country.   On the contrary, we are rapidly
approaching that time when the purchasing public will
discriminate in favor of such wares as shall bear the
marks of domestic manufactories, or the words " *Made in
the United States.*"

CHAPTER III

AMERICAN MARKS AND MONOGRAMS.

MANY important facts pertaining to American pottery and porcelain have been allowed to pass into oblivion for the want of a chronicler, and more than one erstwhile prominent pottery has been forgotten, and the unmarked wares, once celebrated, have seemingly disappeared, without leaving a trace to show that they ever existed. We must be content with the bare information that certain products were manufactured by our ancestors, who, when they passed away, carried the knowledge of their works with them. Who is there to-day that can identify a single piece of the white ware or " chiney " produced at Burlington, N. J., in 1688? What collector can positively assert that he possesses a veritable example of the " tortoise-shell," or " green colour " ware made in 1769 at the Boston factory? Where can be found an authenticated specimen from the China Manufactory which was turning out queensware in Philadelphia in the year 1800?

In the older countries of the East, it has been the custom for centuries to place upon ceramic wares, which were considered worthy of preservation, distinguishing marks, monograms, or symbols, by which their origin should be known for all time.   Had such precaution been adopted by our earlier American potters, many a priceless gem would now grace our collections, for many a suspected rarity can be found in our private cabinets and public museums believed to be American, but, alas, unauthenticated.   Before me stands a quaint old porcelain coffee-pot, embellished with bunches of hand-painted roses, which tradition assigns to the city of Penn previous to the Revolution, yet we have no knowledge that polychrome decoration was practised in this country at that period.   Here is a graceful teapot of somewhat similar body, decorated with clusters of minute flowers in natural colors and bronze bands, bought of a dealer on the assurance that it, also, had been made in Philadelphia more than a century ago.

On the other hand, unmarked pieces of undoubted genuineness have been handed down to us carefully from the time of our grandparents, and by means of these the ceramic student may hope to be enabled to penetrate the vail of uncertainty which surrounds others.   Fortunately, we find now and then a specimen bearing a mark among the productions of discontinued factories of the present century.   We can at least commence now to gather together what is still to be procured from the past and to collect material for the history of the potter's art as it exists in America in our own time.   Further delay would seem inexcusable, because it would result in the loss of information, which, while now obtainable, could not be procured a few years hence.

No attempt has ever been made, so far as we know, to compile a list of marks and makers' designs on American wares. That which follows is, therefore, necessarily imperfect, but it will serve as a nucleus for the preparation of a more complete one hereafter. It has not been deemed necessary to include all of the trade marks which occur on the ordinary utilitarian or commercial grades of recent wares, many of which appear in the body of this work.

THE AMERICAN CHINA MANUFACTORY,
PHILADELPHIA, PA.

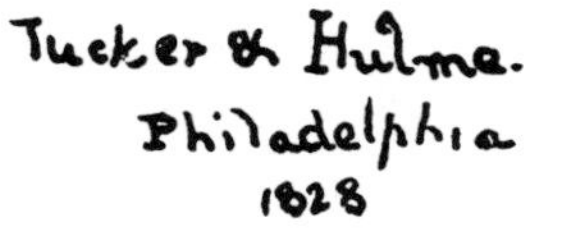

Tucker & Hulme.
Philadelphia
1828

Mark used in 1828, *painted* in red, beneath the glaze. A porcelain vase-shaped pitcher thus marked was presented to the Pennsylvania Museum in Fairmount Park, Philadelphia, by Mr. Charles Henry Hart.

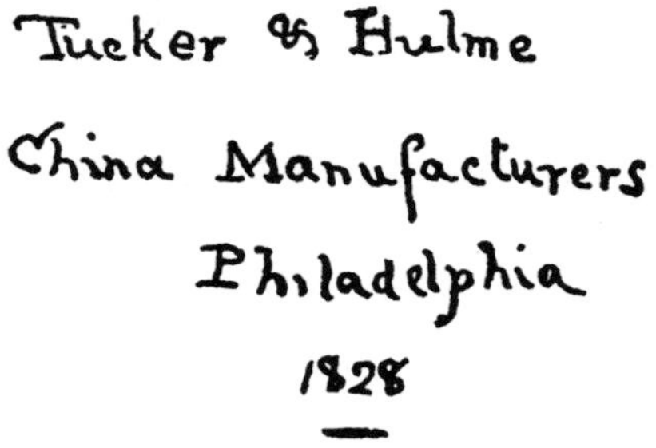

Tucker & Hulme

China Manufacturers

Philadelphia

1828

—

Another mark used in the same year. Three decorated porcelain pitchers are known which bear this inscription, in red.

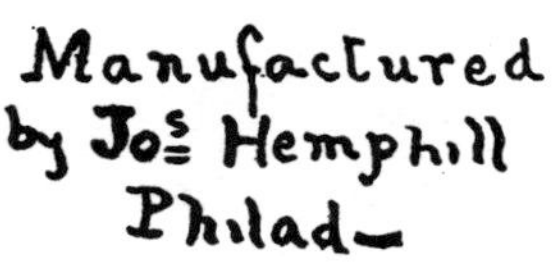

Manufactured
by Jos Hemphill
Philad—

In 1833 and 1834, after the factory had passed into the hands of Judge Joseph Hemphill, this mark was used to a limited extent on decorated pieces. It also was painted in red under the glaze.

Workmen's Marks.

These were scratched in the paste beneath the glaze. They are numerous on Tucker and Hemphill porcelain, but at this late day very few of them can be identified. Only those which have been recognized are given.

This letter occurs frequently on fine pitchers and other pieces, and was used by Andrew Craig Walker, who worked at this factory as a moulder.

The private mark of Joseph Morgan, a moulder.

Mark of Charles Frederick, a moulder.

William Hand, an Englishman and a well-known potter in the old Philadelphia potteries.

The mark of one Vivian, a Frenchman.

Mark *impressed* or stamped in the red body of *Sgraffiato* ware made by Jacob Sholl, near Tyler's Port, Montgomery Co., Pa., in 1831. Two ornate earthenware jars from this pottery have recently been found bearing this mark, which was evidently made with an engraved stamp. Decorated dishes from the same pottery bear the above date.

THE JERSEY CITY POTTERY.

Mark used by D. & J. Henderson of the Jersey City Pottery, about 1830. It occurs on a stoneware "Toby Jug," *impressed* in the body.

Mark used about 1840 by the American Pottery Co. of Jersey City, N. J. This occurs on a cream-colored water-pitcher, with black printed portrait of General William Henry Harrison, and picture of log-cabin. The mark is *printed* in black beneath the glaze.

Mark used at Jersey City Pottery from 1840 to about 1845, impressed in the ware.

Impressed mark used at Jersey City Pottery about 1840 and later. This is found on a many-sided pitcher with Toby head.

THE UNITED STATES POTTERY,

BENNINGTON, VT.

Mark found on a few pieces of parian ware supposed to antedate the establishment of the U. S. Pottery, Bennington, Vt. Letters impressed in a raised panel.

Mark used at the United States Pottery of Lyman and Fenton, Bennington, Vt., on parian and porcelain about 1853. The letters and figures are impressed in a raised ribbon. The figure to the right varies on different pieces and was probably the pattern number.

Mark used on Lyman & Fenton's *Patent Flint Enamelled* ware, in 1849. Impressed.

Mark used on "scrodled" and other ware made at U. S. Pottery. Impressed.

A.P.M. C⁰

Mark of the American Porcelain Manufacturing Co. of Gloucester, N. J., from 1854 to 1857. Impressed in the body of the ware.

Impressed mark used on telegraph insulators, and probably porcelain, by the Southern Porcelain Company, of Kaolin, South Carolina, previous to, and at the commencement of, the Civil War.

THE CHELSEA KERAMIC ART WORKS.

CHELSEA KERAMIC
ART WORKS
ROBERTSON & SONS.

Chelsea (Mass.) Pottery of James Robertson and Sons. This mark was employed to some extent between 1875 and 1880 and was *impressed* in the clay.

Stamped or impressed in art pottery made at the Chelsea Keramic Art Works of Robertson and Sons from 1875 to 1889.

Impressed mark used by the *Chelsea Pottery, U. S.*, at Chelsea, Mass., on art wares, from 1891. Hugh C. Robertson, manager.

THE UNION PORCELAIN WORKS.

First mark used by the Union Porcelain Works of Messrs. Thomas C. Smith & Sons, Greenpoint, Long Island, adoped 1876 and impressed in their commercial hard porcelain. In 1877 the same mark was *printed* in green under the glaze.

Mark used by same factory since 1877, printed in green under the glaze, on commercial porcelain. In a few instances, this mark has been used in raised ornamental form on large exhibition pieces, as a tablet applied to the bottom of the ware.

Decorating-shop mark used at the Union Porcelain Works since 1879 ; printed on decorated porcelain, usually in red, over the glaze.

Decorating-shop mark adopted in August, 1891.

GREENWOOD POTTERY COMPANY.

Mark first used on the Greenwood Pottery art wares, at Trenton, N. J., about 1883 to 1886, *printed* in purple. The *Ne Plus Ultra* art pottery was copied from the Royal Worcester, having an ivory finish and raised gold decoration. The figures in the centre indicate the date of the establishment of this factory (1861), the design having been suggested by the Worcester mark.

Stamp used on hard porcelain body art ware, printed in purple beneath the glaze, from 1886 to the present time.

A modification of the above, also used on art ware.

THE NEW ENGLAND POTTERY CO., EAST BOSTON, MASS.

Mark used on ironstone china by Messrs. Thomas Gray and L. W. Clark, from 1878 to 1883.

Bird stamp, New England Pottery Co., used on a special order of goods made by this company for a purchaser. Stamped or printed on plates, etc., in black, under the glaze.

Used on stone china from 1883 to 1886.

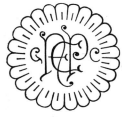

Printed in black on " C. C." or cream-colored ware, under the glaze.

Printed in black, under the glaze, on stone china and white granite wares, since 1886.

Printed in black, under the glaze, on " Rieti " ware, from 1886 to 1888.

Printed in black, under the glaze, on colored bodies, denominated " Rieti " ware, from 1888 to 1889.

Printed in red, above the glaze, on " Rieti " and the finer decorated wares, since 1889.

ROOKWOOD.

Mark used at the Rookwood Pottery, Cincinnati, Ohio, from 1880 to 1882, to a limited extent. This was designed by Mr. H. F. Farny, and *printed* on the ware in black, beneath the glaze. In 1883 a small kiln mark was *impressed* in the ware made during that year.

 Mark used on a few pieces in 1882, *impressed* in the clay.

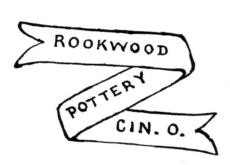

Special mark used only on a trade piece (large beer tankard with raised figures) made expressly for the Cincinnati Cooperage Company, in 1882. The letters are impressed on a raised ribbon.

ROOKWOOD 1882 Employed on art pieces made from 1882 to 1886, the date being changed each year. Impressed in the clay.

 Mark adopted in June, 1886, and used during the remainder of that year, *impressed*.

 In 1887 a flame point was placed above the monogram to indicate that year, and one point has been added each year since, so that the date mark used on pieces made in 1893 possesses seven points.

C   Cream-colored clay.

R   Red clay.

W   White clay.

S   Sage-green clay.

Y   Yellow clay.

G   Ginger-colored clay.

O   Olive clay.

Body marks impressed in the clay.

PHŒNIXVILLE POTTERY.

Mark used by Messrs. Griffen & Smith, at the Phœnixville (Pa.), Pottery, between 1880 and 1890, on majolica ware. *Impressed.*

The central monogram was also used on majolica or C. C. ware, alone. It is composed of the letters G., S., & H., Griffen, Smith, & Hill. The words Etruscan Majolica were sometimes impressed in a straight line.

Mark used on a peculiar vitrified porcelain body with underglaze color effects, the color, glaze, and body being thoroughly incorporated together ; made by Prof. Isaac Broome at Trenton, in 1880, on a throwing wheel. Only about one hundred small vases of this character were produced. These pieces, different from any other ware made in America, are scattered among collectors, and are highly prized for their beauty and rarity. This mark is an arbitrary one, being a modification of the sign of the planet Jupiter, and should not be confused with that used on old Plymouth (England) porcelain, which is somewhat similar.

THE CHESAPEAKE POTTERY, BALTIMORE, MD.

 Mark used to some extent by Messrs. D. F. Haynes & Co., on their "Clifton" ware, belonging to the majolica family. Adopted before 1883.

 Used occasionally on "Avalon" ware, about same period.

 Used on "Ivory Body" ware, same time.

 Used on semi-porcelain ware. These marks, however, were employed only to a limited extent, the greater portion of the ware being unmarked.

ARUNDEL.

POPPY.
DEC.

ARUNDEL.

GLEN ROSE.
DEC.

Marks adopted in 1889 to designate the style of decoration and shape. They were printed over the glaze in the same colors as the decoration. The letters C. P. stand for Chesapeake Pottery ; H. B. for Haynes and Bennett. Other marks, with slight variations, were also used.

Mark used at the Hampshire Pottery of J. S. Taft & Co., of Keene, N. H., printed in red above the glaze, on art ware of an opaque white body.

THE CINCINNATI ART POTTERY.

The earliest mark of the Cincinnati Art Pottery Co. was a little turtle. Later it was discovered that an Indian name for turtle was "Kezonta," which name was added to the device about 1886. The mark opposite was printed on the finer grades of ware, in red.

KEZONTA Mark impressed on the plainer wares, such as the blue and white pottery for decorators.

OTT & BREWER CO., TRENTON, N. J.

Mark used on opaque china table ware.

Mark used on fine egg-shell Belleek ware, printed in red above the glaze.

Another mark in red or brown overglaze.

Willets Manufacturing Co., Trenton, N. J.—Mark printed in red above the glaze, on decorated Belleek ware.

CERAMIC ART CO.

Overglaze stamp, printed on "Belleek" ware, made by the Ceramic Art Co., of Trenton, N. J., in red, since 1889.

Used on art ware of the Pauline Pottery Co. of Edgerton, Wis., since 1888. On the earlier productions this mark was *impressed*. On the later it is *printed*.

Impressed mark used on underglaze art ware made by the Lonhuda Pottery Co., Steubenville, Ohio, 1892. The lower mark is the monogram L. P. Co. On some of the later pieces, after native American designs, the figure of an Indian's head is impressed.

Mark used on decorated *faïence* and porcelain made by the Faïence Manufacturing Co. of New York, 1886 to 1892.

Incised mark used on majolica and so-called barbotine ware by the Faïence Manufacturing Co. of New York.

Printed mark used on thin art porcelain of the American Art China Works, of Messrs. Rittenhouse, Evans, & Co., Trenton, N. J.

Mark of Messrs. Morris & Willmore, Trenton, N. J., manufacturers of art wares, adopted in 1893.

CHAPTER IV

MARKS OF AMERICAN POTTERS

MARKS OF PENNSYLVANIA POTTERIES

Note: See pages 47-52 for key to these marks.

MARKS OF PENNSYLVANIA POTTERIES—Concluded

MARKS OF NEW JERSEY POTTERIES

MARKS OF NEW JERSEY POTTERIES—Continued

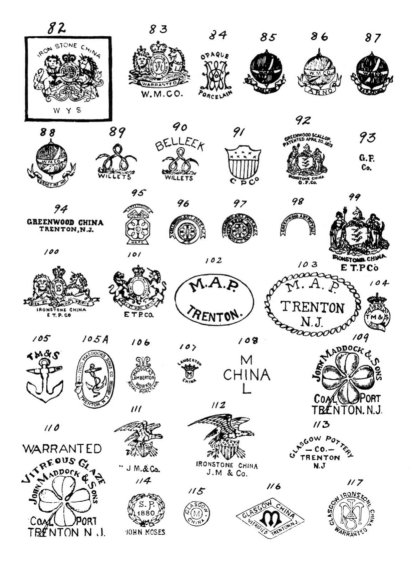

MARKS OF NEW JERSEY POTTERIES—Continued

MARKS OF NEW JERSEY POTTERIES—Continued

MARKS OF NEW JERSEY POTTERIES—Continued

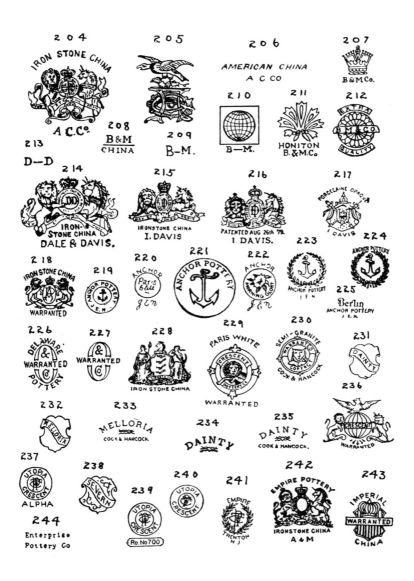

MARKS OF NEW JERSEY POTTERIES—Concluded

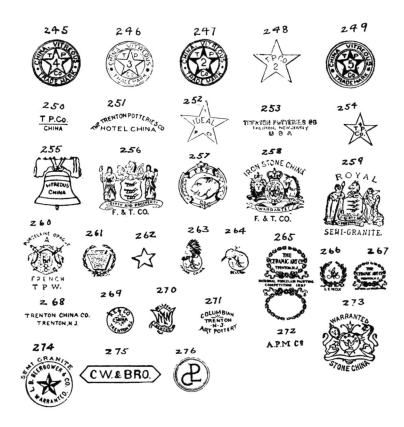

MARKS OF NEW YORK POTTERIES

MARKS OF NEW YORK POTTERIES—Concluded

MARKS OF NEW ENGLAND POTTERIES

MARKS OF NEW ENGLAND POTTERIES—Concluded

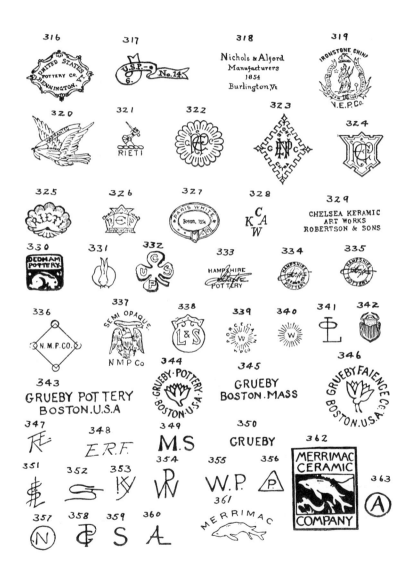

MARKS OF OHIO POTTERIES

MARKS OF OHIO POTTERIES—Continued

MARKS OF OHIO POTTERIES—Continued

469 Nautilus GPC9EL.O.

470 GLOBE GPCO CHINA.

471 Made by GlobePotteryCo. E.L.,O.

472 HOTEL G.P. CO.

473 SIRIUS

474 GPCO REGAL

475 SEMI-VITREOUS CHINAQUE CHINA

476 The Admiral

477 Raleigh

478 Champion

479 E.L.P. CO. WACO CHINA

480 ELP Co IRONSTONE CHINA

481 D. of R. 174.

482 WACO CHINA.

483 ELPCo WACO CHINA

484 Paris 9 C.m.&Co.

485 Manhattan

486 SEMI PORCELAIN

487 MURPHY & CO. VITREOUS HOTEL PORCELAIN

488 EAST END P.CO E LIVERPOOL.O.

489 ROYAL IRONSTONE CHINA WARRANTED

490 Columbus

491 Alaska

492 E.E.P.CO PORCELAIN

493 DEWEY E.E.P CO

494 SEMI-VITREOUS PORCELAIN U.S.A. EAST LIVERPOOL POTTERIES CO.

495 UNION CHINA CORINNE

496 SIGSBEE

497 UNION CHINA

498 UNION CORINNE

499 ELECTRIC

500 BURFORD B.P.Co CORAL CHINA.

501 DEFENDER BURFORD BROS. P CO.

502 Burford Bros CHAMPION

503 VIGILANT BURFORD BROS P CO

504 BB ARTISTIC

505 BURFORD PORCELAIN

506 BURFORD BROS. BEAUTY

507 IDEAL B

508 STONE CHINA CORAL SHAPE BURFORD BROS

509 HOTEL

510 BURFORD CHINA

510 A BURFORD BROS

MARKS OF OHIO POTTERIES—Continued

MARKS OF OHIO POTTERIES—Continued

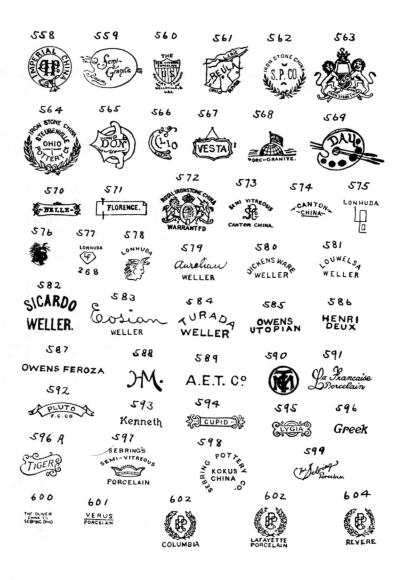

558 IMPERIAL CHINA

559 Semi-Granite

560 THE U.S.

561 BEULA

562 IRON STONE CHINA S.P. CO.

563

564 IRON STONE CHINA STEUBENVILE OHIO POTTERY CO

565 DON

566 L-10

567 VESTA

568 PORC-GRANITE.

569 DAU

570 BELLE

571 FLORENCE.

572 ROYAL IRONSTONE CHINA WARRANTED

573 SEMI VITREOUS S.P. CANTON CHINA.

574 CANTON CHINA

575 LONHUDA

576

577 LONHUDA F 268

578 LONHUDA

579 Aurelian WELLER

580 DICKENS WARE WELLER

581 LOUWELSA WELLER

582 SICARDO WELLER.

583 Eosian WELLER

584 TURADA WELLER

585 OWENS UTOPIAN

586 HENRI DEUX

587 OWENS FEROZA

588 HM.

589 A.E.T. Cº

590 M

591 La Francaise Porcelain

592 PLUTO F.C.CO

593 Kenneth

594 CUPID

595 LYGIA

596 Greek

596 A TIGER

597 SEBRING'S SEMI-VITREOUS PORCELAIN

598 SEBRING POTTERY KOKUS CHINA CO.

599 The Sebring Porcelain.

600 THE OLIVER CHINA CO SEBRING OHIO

601 VERUS PORCELAIN

602 COLUMBIA

602 LAFAYETTE PORCELAIN

604 REVERE

MARKS OF OHIO POTTERIES—Concluded

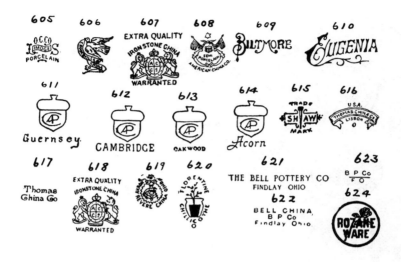

MARKS OF SOUTHERN POTTERIES

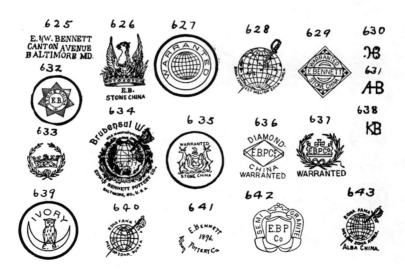

MARKS OF SOUTHERN POTTERIES—Continued

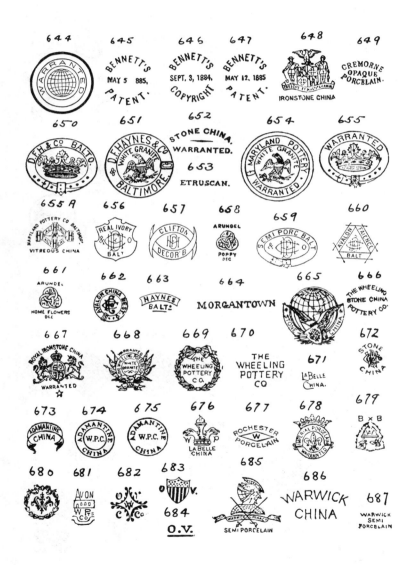

MARKS OF SOUTHERN POTTERIES—Concluded

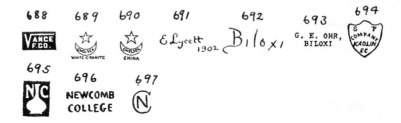

688   689   690   691   692   693   694

695   696   697

MARKS OF WESTERN POTTERIES

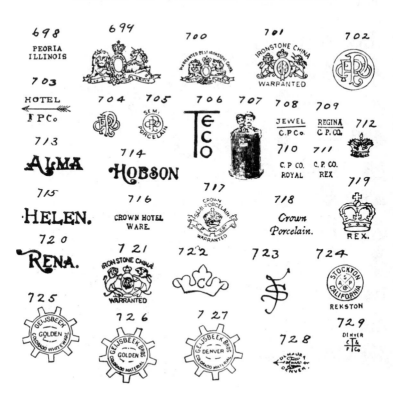

698   699   700   701   702

703   704   705   706   707   708   709   712

713   714   710   711

715   716   717   718   719

720   721   722   723   724

725   726   727   728   729

MARKS OF WESTERN POTTERIES—Concluded

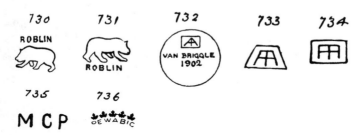

730   731   732   733   734

735   736

PRIVATE MARKS OF ROOKWOOD DECORATORS

MARKS OF PENNSYLVANIA POTTERIES

Plate Nos.   Established.

1. Bonnin & Morris, Philadelphia, Penna.   1770
2. Joseph Smith Pottery, Bucks County, Penna.   1767
3, 4. Henry Roudebush, Montgomery County, Penna.   1811–1816
5. Samuel Troxel, Montgomery County, Penna.   1823–1833
6. George Hubener, Montgomery County, Penna.   1785–1798
7. Jacob or Isaac Tany, Bucks County, Penna.   1794
8. John Drey, Eastern, Penna.   1809
9. Andrew Headman, Rock Hill, Bucks County, Penna.   1808
10, 11. Unidentified marks on German American Pottery.
12. Jacob Scholl, Tylers Port, Montgomery County, Penna.   1830
13. Womelsdorf, Penna.
      John Menner.   1784
      Willoughby Smith.   1864
14. American China Manufactory, Philadelphia, Penna.   1825
15, 16. Tucker & Hulme.   1828
17. Judge Joseph Hemphill.   1832–1836
18–24. Private marks of workmen.
25. Smith, Fife & Co., Philadelphia, Penna.   1830
26. Ralph Bagnall Beach, Philadelphia, Penna.   1845
27. Kurlbaum & Schwartz.   1851
28. Workman's mark.
29. The Phoenix Pottery, Kaolin and Fire Brick Co.,
      Phoenixville, Penna.   1867
30. Beerbower & Griffen, Phoenixville, Penna.   1877
31–34A. Griffen, Smith & Hill, Phoenixville, Penna.   1879
35–37. Chester Pottery Company of Pennsylvania,
      Phoenixville, Penna.   1894
38. The Philadelphia City Pottery, J. E. Jeffords & Co.   1868
39. Galloway & Graff, Philadelphia, Penna.   1810
40–59. The Mayer Pottery Co., Beaver Falls, Penna.   1881
60. Star Encaustic Tile Co., Pittsburg, Penna.   1882
61. The Robertson Art Tile Co., Morrisville, Penna.
62. The Shenango China Co., New Castle, Penna.
63, 64. Moravian Pottery and Tile Works, Doylestown, Penna.
65. The Wick China Co., Kittanning, Penna.
66–70. The Ford China Co., Ford City, Penna.
71. The New Castle Pottery Co., New Castle, Penna.
72. The Derry China Co., Derry Station, Penna.
73. Pennsylvania Museum and School of Industrial Art,
      Philadelphia, Penna.   1903

MARKS OF NEW JERSEY POTTERIES

Plate Nos.		Established
74–81.	The Jersey City Pottery, Jersey City, N. J.	1829
	D. & J. Henderson.	
	American Pottery Manufacturing Co.	1833
82.	William Young & Sons, Trenton, N. J.	1853
83–90.	The Willits Manufacturing Co., Trenton, N. J.	1879
91.	The City Pottery Co., Trenton, N. J.	1859
92–98.	Greenwood Pottery Co., Trenton, N. J.	1861
99–101.	The East Trenton Pottery Co., Trenton, N. J.	1888
102, 103.	Millington, Astbury & Poulson, Trenton, N. J.	1853
104, 105.	Thomas Maddock & Sons, Trenton, N. J.	1859
105A.	Thomas Maddock's Sons Co., Trenton, N. J.	1902
106–108.	The Maddock Pottery Co., Trenton, N. J.	1893
109, 110.	John Maddock & Sons, Trenton, N. J.	1894
111–140.	The Glasgow Pottery, Trenton, N. J.	1863
141–155.	Ott & Brewer, Trenton, N. J.	1863
156–163.	The Cook Pottery Co., Trenton, N. J.	1894
164–166.	Isaac Broome, Trenton, N. J.	1880
167.	Coxon & Co., Trenton, N. J.	1863
168.	Trenton Pottery Co., Trenton, N. J.	1865
169–184.	Mercer Pottery Co., Trenton, N. J.	1868
185.	The New Jersey Pottery Co., Trenton, N. J.	1869
186–203.	International Pottery Co., Trenton, N. J.	1860
204–206.	American Crockery Co., Trenton, N. J.	1876
207–212.	Burroughs & Mountford Co., Trenton, N. J.	1879
213–217.	The Prospect Hill Pottery Co., Trenton, N. J.	1880
218–225.	Anchor Pottery Co., Trenton, N. J.	1894
226, 227.	Delaware Pottery, Trenton, N. J.	1884
228–240.	Crescent Pottery, Trenton, N. J.	1881
241–243.	Empire Pottery, Trenton, N. J.	1863
244.	Enterprise Pottery, Trenton, N. J.	1880
245–254.	Trenton Potteries Co., Trenton, N. J., Organized	1892
255.	The Bellmark Pottery Co., Trenton, N. J.	1893
256–258.	The Fell & Thropp Co., Trenton, N. J.	
259, 260.	The Trenton Pottery Works, Trenton, N. J.	
261.	Keystone Pottery Co., Trenton, N. J.	
262.	Star Porcelain Co., Trenton, N. J.	
263–267.	The Ceramic Art Co., Trenton, N. J.	1889
268.	The Trenton China Co., Trenton, N. J.	1859
269.	The American Art China Works, Trenton, N. J.	1891
270, 271.	Columbian Art Pottery, Trenton, N. J.	

MARKS OF NEW JERSEY POTTERIES—Concluded

Plate Nos.   Established.
272. American Porcelain Manufacturing Co., Gloucester, N. J.   1854
273, 274. L. B. Beerbower & Co., Elizabeth, N. J.   1816
275. Charles Wingender & Brother, Haddonfield, N. J.
276. C. L. & H. A. Poillon, Woodbridge, N. J.

MARKS OF NEW YORK POTTERIES

277. Salamander Works, New York, N. Y.   1848
278–286. New York City Pottery, New York, N. Y.   1853
287–291. Union Porcelain Works, Greenpoint, N. Y.   1876
292–298. Onondaga Pottery Co., Syracuse, N. Y.   1871
299–302. Volkmar Pottery, Greenpoint, N. Y.   1879
303. East Morrison China Works, New York, N. Y.
304–306. The Faience Manufacturing Co., Greenpoint, N. Y.   1880
307. Charles Graham Chemical Pottery Works, Brooklyn, N. Y.
308, 309. Middle Lane Pottery, East Hampton, Long Island,
          T. A. Brouwer, Jr.
310, 310A, 310B. The Chittenango Pottery Co., Chittenango,
          N. Y.   1897
311. American Art Ceramic Co., Corona, N. Y.   1901

MARKS OF NEW ENGLAND POTTERIES

312–314. Norton Pottery Co., Bennington, Vt.   1793
315–317. United States Pottery Co., Bennington, Vt.   1849
318. Nichols & Alford, Burlington, Vt.   1854
319–327. New England Pottery Co., East Boston, Mass.   1854
328, 329. Chelsea Keramic, Chelsea, Mass.   1866
330–332. Dedham Pottery Co., Dedham, Mass.
333–335. Hampshire Pottery Co., Keene, N. H.   1871
336–342. New Milford Pottery Co., New Milford, Conn.   1886
343–347. The Grueby Faience Co., Boston, Mass.   1897
348–360. Artists' Marks.
361, 362. Merrimac Ceramic Co., Newburyport, Mass.   1897
363. The Low Art Tile Co., Chelsea, Mass.   1893

MARKS OF OHIO POTTERIES

Plate Nos.		Established
364–367.	The Harker Pottery Co., East Liverpool, O.	1840
368–372.	The Goodwin Pottery Co., East Liverpool, O.	1844
373–377.	The Smith-Phillips China Co., East Liverpool, O.	
378–391.	The Vodrey Pottery Co., East Liverpool, O.	1848
392–401.	The William Brunt Pottery Co., East Liverpool, O.	1850
402–435.	The Knowles, Taylor & Knowles Co., East Liverpool, O.	1854
436.	D. E. McNicol Pottery Co., East Liverpool, O.	1863
437–443.	C. C. Thompson Pottery Co., East Liverpool, O.	1868
444–452.	The Homer Laughlin China Co., East Liverpool, O.	1874
453–463.	The Potters' Co-operative Co., East Liverpool, O.	1876
464–468.	Cartwright Brothers, East Liverpool, O.	
469–474.	The Globe Pottery Co., East Liverpool, O.	1881
475.	The Wallace and Chetwynd Pottery Co., East Liverpool, O.	
476–478.	The United States Pottery, East Liverpool, O.	
479–483.	The East Liverpool Pottery Co., East Liverpool, O.	1896
484–487.	The George C. Murphy Pottery Co., East Liverpool, O.	
488–493.	The East End Pottery Co., East Liverpool, O.	
494.	The East Liverpool Potteries Co., East Liverpool, O.	
495–498.	The Union Potteries Co., East Liverpool, O.	
499–510A.	The Burford Brothers Pottery Co., East Liverpool, O.	
511–514.	The Taylor, Smith & Taylor Co., East Liverpool, O.	1899
515, 516.	The West End Pottery Co., East Liverpool, O.	1893
517–521.	The Sevres China Co., East Liverpool, O.	1900
522, 523.	The Edw. M. Knowles China Co., East Liverpool, O.	1901
524–526.	The Brockman Pottery Co., Cincinnati, O.	1862
527–540.	The Rookwood Pottery Co., Cincinnati, O.	1879
541–543.	The Cincinnati Art Pottery Co., Cincinnati, O.	1879
544–546.	The Matt Morgan Art Pottery Co., Cincinnati, O.	1883
547.	Avon Pottery, Cincinnati, O.	1886
548, 549.	Miss M. Louise McLaughlin, Cincinnati, O.	1876
550–558.	The Wellsville China Co., Wellsville, O.	1879
559.	J. H. Baum, Wellsville, O.	1897
560.	The United States Pottery Co., Wellsville, O.	1899
561–574.	The Steubenville Pottery Co., Steubenville, O.	1879
575–578.	Lonhuda Pottery, Steubenville, O.	1892
579–584.	S. A. Weller, Zanesville, O.	
585–587.	J. B. Owens Pottery Co., Zanesville, O.	

MARKS OF OHIO POTTERIES—Concluded

Plate Nos.   Established

		Established
588, 589.	The American Encaustic Tiling Co., Zanesville, O.	
590.	The Mosaic Tile Co., Zanesville, O.	
591–596A.	The French China Co., Sebring, O.	
597–599.	The Sebring Pottery Co., Sebring, O.	1887
600, 601.	The Oliver China Co., Sebring, O.	1899
602–604.	The East Palestine Pottery Co., East Palestine, O.	
605.	The Ohio China Co., East Palestine, O.	
606.	The Crooksville China Co., Crooksville, O.	
607–610.	The American China Co., Toronto, O.	1897
611–614.	The Cambridge Art Pottery Co., Cambridge, O.	
615.	The Bradshaw China Co., Niles, O.	
616, 617.	The Thomas China Co., Lisbon, O.	
618, 619.	The Akron China Co., Akron, O.	
620.	The Florentine Pottery Co., Chillicothe, O.	
621–623.	The Bell Pottery Co., Findlay, O.	
624.	Roseville Pottery, Zanesville, O.	

MARKS OF SOUTHERN POTTERIES

		Established
625–647.	The Edwin Bennett Pottery Co., Baltimore, Md.	1846
648–655A.	The Maryland Pottery Co., Baltimore, Md.	1879
656–663.	Chesapeake Pottery Co., Baltimore, Md.	1880
664.	Morgantown, West Virginia.	1785
665–680.	Wheeling Pottery Co., Wheeling, W. Va.	1879
681.	The Wheeling Potters Co., Wheeling, W. Va.	1903
682–684.	Ohio Valley China Co., Wheeling, W. Va.	
685–687.	The Warwick China Co., Wheeling, W. Va.	1887
688.	The Vance Faience Co., Wheeling, W. Va.	
689, 690.	The Chelsea China Co., New Cumberland, W. Va.	1888
691.	Edward Lycett, Atlanta, Ga.	1861
692, 693.	Geo. E. Ohr, Biloxi, Miss.	
694.	Southern Porcelain Co., Kaolin, S. C.	1856
695–697.	Newcomb Pottery, Newcomb College, New Orleans, La.	1896

MARKS OF WESTERN POTTERIES

CHAPTER V.

EARLY POTTING IN AMERICA.

THE potter's art was probably first practised in this country by the earlier emigrants in Virginia. Numerous small potteries sprung up to supply the modest needs of the simple-minded inhabitants, which furnished coarse earthenware utensils for culinary and other purposes. While such crude wares were made to a considerable extent, no record of any one of the primitive kilns, which were insignificant affairs, has descended to us. The older chroniclers seem to have completely ignored, as unworthy of note, the existence of an art in their midst which had already become familiar to them before leaving their native soil. Previous to 1649 there were a number of small potters in Virginia who carried on a thriving business in the communities in which they operated ; and the first Dutch settlers in New York brought with them a practical knowledge of potting, and are said to have made a ware equal in quality to that produced in the ancient town of Delft,—hardly a white ware, but such as could be produced from the natural clays which abounded in the country. Prof. Isaac Broome, of the Beaver Falls Art Tile Works, informs me that the remains of an old kiln fire-hole, saved from the ravages of time by being thoroughly vitrified, still exist a mile or two below South Amboy, N. J., supposed to be a relic of the earlier pottery ware made on this continent, and most probably built by the Dutch to make stew-pans and pots.

Among the immigrants of the seventeenth century were pot-makers, who had learned their trade in the mother-country, and Gabriel Thomas, who came from England, states in his *Description of Philadelphia*, published in 1697, that "great encouragements are given to tradesmen and others. . . . Potters have sixteen pence for an earthern pot which may be bought in England for fourpence."

Gilbert Cope, of West Chester, Pa., has discovered in his genealogical researches that one Joshua Tittery, from Newcastle-upon-Tyne, came over to Pennsylvania in the year 1683, in the employ of the "Society of Traders," as a glass-maker, and in his will he calls himself a *potter*. As early as about 1690 Philadelphia had at least one potter and one tobacco-pipe maker.

FIRST WHITE-WARE MANUFACTORY IN AMERICA.

Dr. Daniel Coxe, of London, one of the Proprietors, and afterward Governor of West New Jersey, was probably the first to make white ware in the Colonies. While he did not come to America himself, he caused a pottery to be erected at Burlington, N. J., previous to the year 1685, through his agent, John Tatham, who, with Daniel Coxe, his son, looked after his large interests here. We are indebted to Mr. John D. McCormick, of Trenton, for calling attention to the following reference to this pottery, in the inventory of property offered for sale in the Jerseys, supposed to have been written about 1688, in the Rawlinson manuscripts, in the Bodleian Library, at Oxford, England, which has been carefully transcribed from the original and forwarded to me by the obliging librarian :

" I have erected a pottery att Burlington for white and chiney ware, a greate quantity to ye value of 1200 li have been already made and vended in ye Country, neighbour Colonies and ye Islands of Barbadoes and Jamaica where they are in great request. I have two houses and kills with all necessary implements, diverse workemen, and other servants. Have expended thereon about 2000 li." [1]

In the same MS., fol. 46, are " Proposalls made by Daniell Coxe proprietary and Governor of ye provinces of East and West Jersey in America :

" The above mencioned Daniell Coxe being resolved to sell his interest in Land and Government of the Colonies of East and West Jersey. The land amounting . . . unto one million of Acres (etc).

" Itt is believed a thousand pounds per Annum cleere of all charges the said Daniell Coxe hath likewise at Burlington two houses and kill with all necessary materialls and implements with diverse servants who have made a greate progresse in a Pottery of White and China ware above 1200 li worth being already made and vended in the Country neighbour plantations and the Islands of Barbados Jamaica &c. and well managed will probably bee very

[1] MS. Rawlinson, c. 128, fol. 39 b.

Advantagious to ye undertakers D : C: haveing expended thereon to bring it to perfeccion allmost 2000 li."

It is recorded that in 1691 Dr. Coxe sold to the " West New Jersey Society " of London, consisting of forty-eight persons, his entire interests in the Province, including a dwelling-house and " pottery-house " with all the tools, for the sum of £9,000 sterling.

John Tatham bought of Dr. Coxe, in 1689, fourteen acres of land in Burlington. In 1690 he was elected Governor of East and West New Jersey, and subsequently erected in Burlington a " great and stately palace."

It is possible to gain some idea of the nature of this "white and chiney ware" by examining the statements of Dr. Plot, a contemporary, who published his *Natural History of Staffordshire* in 1686, as quoted by the late Mr. Llewellynn Jewitt, in his *Ceramic Art of Great Britain:* " The greatest pottery they have in this county is carried on at Burslem, near Newcastle-under-Lyme, where for making their different sorts of pots they have as many different sorts of clay . . . and are distinguish't by their colours and uses as followeth :—

" 1. *Bottle clay*, of a bright whitish streaked yellow colour.

" 2. *Hard fire-clay*, of a duller whitish colour, and fully intersperst with a dark yellow, which they use for their *black wares*, being mixt with the

" 3. *Red Blending clay*, which is of a dirty red colour.

" 4. *White clay*, so called it seems, though of a blewish colour, and used for making yellow-color'd ware, *because yellow is the lightest colour they make any ware of.*" [1]

[1] Page 97, vol. i., London, 1878.

In 1685 Thomas Miles made a white "stoneware" of pipe-clay procured at Shelton. A few years after this, it is said that a potter named Astbury made "crouch" and "white stone" ware in the same town, on which he used a salt glaze.[1] It is probable that the "chiney" of the Burlington pottery was in reality a cream-colored ware or a white stoneware somewhat similar to that made about the same time in England. It is not unlikely that the clay was brought from South Amboy, as Dr. Coxe owned considerable land in that vicinity. This clay has since been extensively employed in the manufacture of fine stone-ware.

Mr. Francis B. Lee, son of the Clerk of the Supreme Court of New Jersey, has recently discovered the pleadings in a case apparently relating to the old Burlington Pottery, to which my attention has been called by William Nelson, Esq., corresponding secretary of the New Jersey Historical Society, as published in the *American Potters' Journal* of April 1, 1892. This reference seems to establish the fact that this pottery was in operation at least as early as 1685. In examining a court book in and for Burlington jurisdiction, Mr. Lee found, in the records of a Court of Sessions (12 m. 20–22 days, 1685), a suit brought by James Budd against Edward Randall ("Acc' on debt"), reported as follows :

"The deed or Indenture of agreem't betweene Plain't & def't Read & proved, & also ye bond of Two Hundred pounds from ye def't to ye Plain't for p'formance, also read and proved.

[1] This was made of tobacco-pipe clay mixed with flint, and was superior to anything produced in England before.

" Mary Budd Attested sayth that shee being at London before ye Def't came away shee was told by an honest woman there who had some concerne amongst ye Potters at London that she feared ye Pott works here would come to nothing, for that the said def't Randall & ye other p'sons who were to come to manage ye same works had not skill to p'fect it.

" Wm. Winn Attested sayth that hee can finde noe Clay in the Countrey that will make white ware ; And further sayth that Edward Randall, the def't, is as good a workman as James Budd ye plaint can finde in England.

" The Jury bring in this determination (vizt.) wee can give noe fynall determination of ye matter until materialls requisite shall come from England to prove ye skill of ye def't.

" Whereupon the Bench order that the said Edward Randall recinde ye Concerne of ye said James Budd until fitt materialls be sent for from such place in England as ye said Edward Randall shall appoint."

From this it would appear that Randall, who was brought to America by James Budd to manage the Burlington works, was, for some reason, either because of lack of skill or the impossibility of procuring suitable clay, unable to fulfil his contract to manufacture white ware up to that time. Later, as Dr. Coxe states, a great quantity of the ware was successfully manufactured here.

The exact location of the old Coxe pottery is not known. It was probably situated somewhere between Burlington and Trenton, not necessarily in the former town, but somewhere in the county.

CHAPTER VI.

POTTERIES OF THE EIGHTEENTH CENTURY.

EARLY OPERATIONS IN THE CAROLINAS.

ACCORDING to tradition, china clays were sent to Europe from North Carolina more than two centuries ago. The Indians are said to have carried it from the Smoky Mountains to the coast, "under the name of Unakah," as Mr. W. A. H. Schreiber of Webster, N. C., informs me, which was "their name for Smokies (meaning white), still called Unaka in Mitchell Co. and Unakoi in Cherokee."

Previous to the middle of the last century, and before the manufacture of porcelain had been attempted in America, English potters were using china clays procured in this country. Mr. Llewellynn Jewitt, in his *Ceramic Art of Great Britain*, informs us that a patent was taken out in 1744, by Edward Heylyn, of the parish of Bow, in the county of Middlesex, merchant, and Thomas Frye, of the parish of West Ham, in the county of Essex, painter, for the manufacture of china-ware ; and in the following year they enrolled their specification, in which they state that the material used in their invention "is an earth, the produce of the Chirokee nation in America, called by the

59

natives *unaker."* In 1878 and 1879, Mr. William Henry
Goss, proprietor of the extensive porcelain works at London Road, Stoke-on-Trent, contributed to the English
Pottery and Glass Trades' Review a series of notes on Mr.
Jewitt's work. In December of the former year he wrote :
"The specification of this patent is of startling interest.
Who would have thought, until Mr. Jewitt unfolded this
document to modern light, that the first English china that
we have any knowledge of was made from American china-
clay ? Let our American cousins look out for, and treasure
up lovingly, specimens of the earliest old Bow-ware after
learning that."[1] Then follows the specification in full,
as given by Mr. Jewitt, and Mr. Goss continues : " This
'unaker,' the produce of the Chirokee nation in America,
is decomposed granitic rock, the earth or clay resulting
from the washing being the decomposed felspar of that
rock. It is curious that it should have been imported
from among the Chirokees when we had mountains of it
so near as Cornwall ; unknown, however, to any ' whom it
might concern ' until Cookworthy discovered it twenty-four
years later than the date of the above patent." William
Cookworthy was acquainted with American clays as early
as 1745, for in a letter to a friend, dated fifth month, thirti-

[1] It may be interesting to note that John Dwight, in 1671, took out a patent for the
manufacture of " porcelaine " or transparent earthen-ware, and Mr. Jewitt remarks :
" To Dwight, therefore, it will be seen by these patents, the credit of being the first
inventor and maker of porcelain in England belongs. His name is thus one entitled
to lasting honour as the pioneer of one of the best, most beautiful, most successful, and
most flourishing arts ever practised in our kingdom."

Mr. Charles Cooper, in an article, published in the *Gentleman's Magazine* of August
1892, states that John Dwight's patent for the manufacture of porcelain was dated
April 23, 1671, and informs us that the old Dwight pottery is still in operation in
Church St., Fulham.

eth, of that year, quoted by Mr. Jewitt, he writes : " I had lately with me the person who hath discovered the china-earth. He had samples of the china-ware of their making with him, which were, I think, equal to the Asiatic. 'T was found in the back of Virginia, where he was in quest of mines ; and having read Du Halde, discovered both the petunse and kaulin. 'T is the latter earth, he says, is the essential thing towards the success of the manufacture. He is gone for a cargo of it, having bought the whole country of the Indians where it rises. They can import it for £13 per ton, and by that means afford their china as cheap as common stoneware. But they intend only to go about 30 per cent. under the company."

We must not conclude from this statement that the ware which Cookworthy had seen had been made in America. It is much more probable that the pieces were some of those produced at the Bow works, within the year that had just passed, from the recently discovered American materials.

In 1765 and 1766 South Carolina clays were sent to the Worcester china works, and the Bristol works, for trial, but the results were not satisfactory.

Miss Eliza Meteyard informs us, in her *Life of Josiah Wedgwood,* that " as early as 1766, a Mr. Bartlem, a Staffordshire potter, who had been unsuccessful in his own country, emigrated to South Carolina, and commencing his trade there, induced various workmen to follow him."[1] In a letter to Sir William Meredith, Wedgwood thus expresses his alarm at this circumstance : " The bulk of

[1] See vol. ii., p. 475.

our particular manufactures are, you know, exported to foreign markets, for our home consumption is very trifling in comparison, to what is sent abroad ; & the principal of these markets are the Continent & Islands of North America. To the Continent we send an amazing quantity of white stoneware & some of the finer kinds, but for the Islands we cannot make anything to rich and costly. This trade to our Colonies we are apprehensive of losing in a few years, as they have set on foot some Pottworks there already, and have at this time an agent amongst us hiring a number of our hands for establishing new Pottworks in South Carolina ; having got one of our insolvent Master Potters there to conduct them. They have every material there, equal if not superior to our own, for carrying on that manufacture ; and as the necessaries of life, and consequently the price of labour amongst us are daily advancing, it is highly probable that more will follow them, and join their brother artists and manufacturers of every Class, who are from all quarters taking a rapid flight indeed the same way ! Whether this can be remedied is out of our sphere to know, but we cannot help apprehending such consequences from these emigrations as make us very uneasy for our trade and Posterity." [1] The apprehensions of the great potter seem to have been groundless, as the early venture to which reference is made proved abortive and " disaster and death were the results." In the same year, however, Wedgwood procured samples of the Carolina clays, from the country of the Cherokees, some 300 miles from Charleston, which,

[1] *Ibid.*, vol. i., p. 367.

proving satisfactory after trial, were for several years after used by him in larger quantities. Subsequently he imported clays from Florida, which he seems to have preferred to the former.[1]

Mines of fine kaolin are now being worked in Jackson County, N. C., which furnish clay for the best china made at Trenton, N. J., and East Liverpool, Ohio. This kaolin contains some oxide of cobalt which imparts to the ware a bluish tint, so desirable in fine porcelain bodies.

MANUFACTURE OF STONEWARE.

A stoneware factory was started in New York, at "Potter's Hill," near the "Fresh-water Pond," back of the old City Hall, in or about 1735, by John Remmey, who came from Germany. On an old map of New York City, printed in 1813, entitled, "A Plan of the City and Environs of New York as they were in the years 1742, 1743, and 1744, Drawn by D—— G—— in the 76th year of his age, who had at this time a perfect and correct recollection of every part of the same," Remmey & Crolius' pottery is marked. John Remmey died in 1762, but the business passed through three generations of Remmeys, all of the name of John, and was discontinued about 1820. Later on, Joseph Henry Remmey, a great-grandson of the founder, moved to South Amboy, N. J., with some of the machinery of the old factory, and established a pottery there. His father, John Remmey the third, owned one of

---

[1] Richard Champion, of the Bristol Porcelain works, arrived in South Carolina Dec. 6, 1784, and settled at Camden, S. C., as a planter. He did not, however, engage in the manufacture of pottery or porcelain in this country. See *Two Centuries of Ceramic Art in Bristol*, by Hugh Owen, 1873.

the largest libraries in New York in his day, and possessing literary tastes, wrote and published, in 1799, *Egypt as It Is,* and contributed numerous editorials to the newspapers of that period.   These facts have been furnished me by Mr. John F. Remmey of Brooklyn, a son of Joseph

Henry Remmey, from records in his possession.

About 1810, Henry Remmey, a brother of John Remmey the third, and grandson of the original John Remmey, went to Philadelphia and soon afterwards embarked in the stoneware business, which has been continued to the present time, the proprietor of the works now being Mr. Richard C. Remmey, one of his great-grandsons.   The Philadelphia works have grown to extensive proportions, ten

27.—*Salt-Glazed Stoneware Money-Bank by R. C. Remmy. Philadelphia Museum of Art.*

large kilns being now in use.   Here are manufactured chemical bricks of superior quality and stone and porcelain-ware of every description, for chemical purposes, some of the vessels having a capacity of two hundred to five hundred gallons.   These productions have obtained almost a world-wide reputation for hardness and durability. Mr. Remmey is now making preparations for the manufacture of porcelain bath-tubs and other large designs. Much of the clay used at these works is obtained at Woodbridge, N. J. In addition to these specialties, the factory produces an extensive line of salt-glazed household utensils, such as mugs, pitchers, spittoons, jugs, crocks, and money-banks. The decoration is such as is usually found on similar wares ;—cobalt blue designs beneath the glaze,— in addition to which a more artistic style of ornamentation is employed to some extent, consisting of incised devices touched with blue. The quality of these various products is unsurpassed and the large quantity of goods manufactured here places this factory in the front rank of such establishments in this country and abroad.

SLIP-DECORATED AND SGRAFFIATO WARE.

Perhaps there are no products of the potter's art more interesting to the antiquary and the collector than the rude " slip-decorated " pieces which were made in England and Germany during the seventeenth and eighteenth centuries. Among the most prominent of the earlier British slip-potters were Thomas and Ralph Toft, who, with others of less renown, have left some of these primitive productions, in the forms of dishes, drinking-cups, candlesticks, and miniature cradles, which are now eagerly sought by collectors, fine examples of which may be seen in the Museum of Practical Geology and the South Kensington and British Museums of London, as well as in a number of private cabinets in England.[1]   The decoration consists of childish designs, representing royal personages, lions, unicorns, birds, beasts, and flowers, executed by tracing liquid clays, or "slips," of different colors, on common red or buff pottery, through a quill attached to a hand-box, the flow of the diluted clay being controlled by means of a small air-hole in the upper part of the slip-box, which was closed or opened by the thumb of the decorator.   By this contrivance a variety of ornamental effects was produced, such as the outlining of figures, the application of dotted or trellised borders, inscriptions, and dates.

The recent discovery by the writer of slip-decorated pottery, and of *sgraffiato*, or incised red ware, among the products of old American potteries, possesses considerable interest.   This latter style of ornamentation was common with Italian potters so long ago as the fifteenth century, and in Germany and England was employed to some extent two hundred years later.   The decorative process consisted in covering the earthenware biscuit with a thin layer of lighter-colored slip, through which the designs were scratched with a style to expose the darker color below.   A coating of transparent glaze, slightly clouded with green and yellow oxides, was then applied to the surface, and, after the final firing, the ware presented the appearance of a rich red intaglio beneath a greenish or mottled-yellow ground.   During the latter half of the last century and the first half of this, many small potteries were established throughout the German settlements in

---

[1] Those who desire to go further into the subject of British slip-decorated ware are referred to *Examples of Early English Pottery, Named, Dated, and Inscribed*, by John Eliot Hodgkin, F.S.A., and Edith Hodgkin. London, 1891.

Eastern Pennsylvania, particularly in the counties of Bucks, Montgomery, Lehigh, Berks, and Schuylkill, where such ware was produced quite extensively. Its very homeliness and crude, but picturesque, ornamentation appealed strongly to the simple-minded country folk who used it in their daily avocations. The sentiments embodied in the quaint inscriptions and mottoes, which usually formed a prominent part of the embellishment of earthen plates, dishes, and jars, and the frequent presence of dates of manufacture, which were usually very exact, including the day of the month, caused such pieces to be carefully treasured and handed down from mother to daughter.

Early specimens which have recently been discovered indicate such proficiency in slip-decoration as would lead us to infer that the art was by no means new to the potters of a century and a quarter ago in this country. The old English and German craftsmen plied their trades in this new field of labor on the same principles which had governed their ancestors a hundred years or more before.

The oldest dated example of this ware which has yet come to light in the United States is a dish, fifteen inches in diameter and three inches deep, now in the Pennsylvania Museum, Philadelphia, which is embellished with floriated central devices, colored with red and green glazes, and the following inscription, carved in the white slip around the rim :

> " Not Be Ashamed I Advice thee Most
> if one Learneth thee what Thou not Knowest,
> the Ingenious is Accounted Brave,
> but the Clumsey None Desire to have, 1762."

This is evidently the work of a German potter, and was most probably made at one of the numerous old potteries in Montgomery County, Pa. (Ill. 28).

The exact origin of this interesting example is not known, though there is no doubt that it was made in

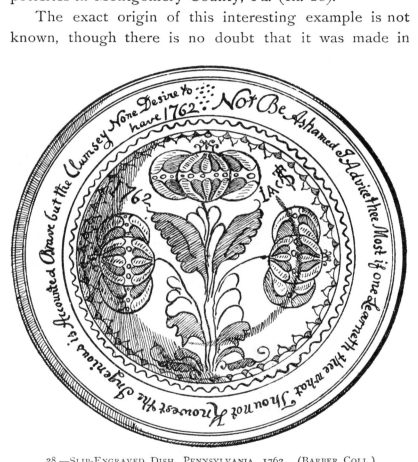

28.—Slip-Engraved Dish, Pennsylvania, 1762. (Barber Coll.)

Pennsylvania. Several potteries are known to have been in operation in Montgomery and Bucks counties at the time of the date of this piece, where such ware was made. Mr. James Terry, of New Haven, Ct., is in possession of a brown, glazed earthenware tea-caddy, five inches square. The front is covered with yellow slip, which has been cut away to show some crude designs, by bringing out the dark color beneath, and the inscription :

" Esther Smith
Her Tea Cannister Sept
    6th 1767."

There is reason to believe that this was made at the old Smith pottery in Wrights-town township, Bucks County, Pa., erected in 1763 by Joseph Smith, where such ware is known

29.—Tea-Caddy, Sgraffiato Ware. James Terry Collection.

to have been produced. The owner of the pottery had a sister Esther, who was born in 1727, but as she was married to Thomas Lacey in 1748, this piece could not have belonged to her. But Joseph Smith (born 1721) was married in 1743, and it is quite likely that he may have had a daughter Esther, named after his sister, who was probably the original owner of the cannister, shown in Engraving 29.

Mr. Isaac Eyre, of Newtown, Pa., informs me that Thomas Paxson, of Buckingham, father of ex-Chief-Justice Paxson, of the Supreme Court of Pennsylvania, once told

him of an old dish that was made at the old Smith
pottery, which contained the following legend :

> " Here is health to the man who has a *half* Joe [1]
> And has the heart to lend it,
> Let the dogs take him who has a *whole* Joe
> And has n't the heart to spend it."

Dr. Lettie A. Smith of Newtown, granddaughter of
Thomas Smith, who afterwards owned the pottery,
remembers distinctly seeing some of her grandmother's
decorated dishes, which contained four or more lines of
poetry and the name of Thomas Smith, with dates.

An earthen keg, covered with a black glaze, sixteen
inches in height, with the name J. Smith and date
1799, is also believed to have come from the same pottery. It is in the possession of Mr. J. S. Williams of
New Hope, Pa. The only examples remaining in the
Smith family are an earthen bowl and a coffee-pot decorated with raised work, now owned by Dr. Lettie A.
Smith.

Abraham or Isaac Stout, about 1775, made slip-decorated ware in Eastern Pennsylvania. A "vegetable dish,"
a foot in diameter and two and a half inches deep, with
conventional floriated pattern and the initials S. S. on
the margin, is owned by Miss Laura Swartzlander of
Yardley, Bucks Co., Pa. This was one piece of a dinner
set made by Mr. Stout for his daughter, Salome, the
great-grandmother of the present owner.

Christian Klinker, according to an old deed in possession of Mr. Wm. J. Buck of Jenkintown, Pa., was an

---

[1] A " Joe " was a gold coin in circulation many years ago.

"earthen potter maker," in 1792, near Bucksville, Bucks Co., and had resided there for at least five years previous to that date.

An interesting slip-dish in the Pennsylvania Museum, Philadelphia, remarkable for its unusual size, light weight, and perfect condition, is embellished with a conventional

30.—Large Slip-Decorated Dish, Pennsylvania German, ca. 1769. Philadelphia Museum of Art. Photograph by A. J. Wyatt, Staff Photographer.

design of tulips in white and green outlined with lavender, on an orange-colored ground. This superb specimen measures seventeen and a half inches in diameter and possesses a double band of inscriptions in low German, and the date 1769 (Ill. 30). This was made at one of the old potteries in Eastern Pennsylvania.

In the extensive ceramic collection of Mr. George H. Danner of Manheim, Pa., is a large slip-decorated earthen dish adorned with a figure of a bird, under which is a heart on which the following inscription occurs :

> "This Dish
> and Heart
> shall never
> Part, 1773."

This was made at one of the local pot-works, probably at the old Smith pottery in Bucks County.

A curious old pottery dish, dated 1789, in possession of a German family in Montgomery County, is remarkable for having three bands around the rim, each an inch wide, on which are inscriptions and ornamental devices, the central portion of the dish being decorated with a rudely executed floral design. The outer band contains a circle of words, as follows :

> "Mathalena Jungin, ihr Schüssel.
> Die Schüssel ist von Erd gemacht
> Wann sie ver bricht der Häffner lacht.
> Darum nehmt sie in Acht."

This, in English, would read :

> "Mathalena Jungin, her dish.
> The dish is made of earth
> When it breaks the potter laughs.
> Therefore take care of it."

The second or middle band contains a wreath composed of ten flowers (tulips) and leaves.

In the inner band is the following inscription :

"Blumen Mollen ist gemein
Aber den geruch zugeben vermach zur Gott allein,"—
"To sketch flowers is for me, but to give perfume belongs to God alone."

This example is one of the few pieces which contain the names of the original owners. It is said to have been made at the old Cope pottery in Frederick township, Montgomery County.

A second example inscribed with the recipient's name has recently come to light. It is a well preserved plate, similarly ornamented, with an inscription incised in the back, which may be freely translated thus: "This dish was made for Miss Hos (Hause) German Township, Berks county, June 4th 1814, so much from me, Henry Stofflet." The family tradition is that this was made by Stofflet as a wedding present for the lady whose name appears on it. Whether the prospective bride resided in Berks County, or the pottery was located there, we are unable to determine. The dish is now in possession of Mr. James Terry of New Haven, Ct.

I am indebted to Mr. H. F. Shaddinger for the discovery of a two-handled puzzle mug, nine inches high, of light-red, glazed pottery, slightly streaked with brown (Ill. 31). On one side is scratched the American eagle beneath the glaze, with the word "Leberty" above. On the reverse are inscribed the initials P × K and "May 5the, 1809." On the bottom, scratched in the clay, occurs the inscription:

"Phillip Kline
his Muge
May 5the 1809."

The maker of this piece had a brickyard and pottery for common ware in Bucks County, in the year indicated. While this is not strictly an example of slip-decoration, it is a curious piece of incised pottery, made on the same principle as the puzzle mugs which have been produced in England for two hundred years.

In searching for examples of this curious ware, I have

31.—Pennsylvania German Puzzle Mug with Sgraffiato Design, Made by Philip Kline in 1809. Philadelphia Museum of Art.

from Mr. Thomas B. Deetz, whose explorations through the old farm-houses in my behalf have resulted in the discovery of many a rare old piece, whose existence would never have been suspected had not my attention been drawn to this untrodden field by an old pie plate which I procured from him, the first example of the

kind that I had seen (see Ill. 34). His knowledge of Pennsylvania German, which is generally spoken in this section of the State, enabled him to penetrate the mysteries of ancient closets, and place at my command the hoarded treasures concealed therein.

One John Leidy, a German, made sgraffiato and slip-decorated wares a hundred years ago, near the present village of Souderton, Montgomery County, Pa. That both varieties were manufactured at about the same time is clearly shown in two elaborately ornamented dishes,

32.—Pennsylvania German Lead-Glazed Sgraffiato Dish Made in Montgomery County by John Leidy, November, 1796. Philadelphia Museum of Art. Photograph by A. J. Wyatt, Staff Photographer.

The first is adorned with floral designs carved in the yellowish slip and covered with a green mottled glaze.

33.—*Pennsylvania German, Lead-Glazed, Slip-Decorated Dish Made in Montgomery County by John Leidy, October 1797. Philadelphia Museum of Art. Photograph by A. J. Wyatt, Staff Photographer.*

The second, two inches in depth, is traced with white, green, and dark blue slips, on a bright red body, in conventional devices, with bands of white around the margin. On the inclined rim is the following couplet:

" Lieber will ich ledig leben
Als der Frau die Hosen geben,"

and the date, October, 1797 (Ill. 33). The mutinous sentiment contained in both legends evinces an inclination on the part of the ancient artist to rebel against feminine domination.

Of especial interest, from the fact that it was the first piece to call my attention to the existence of slip ware in the United States, is an incised, red pie-dish, eleven inches in diameter, ornamented with birds, branches, and the following inscription extending around the margin and overlapping below :

" Fisch und Fögel ; gehören nicht den frowen Flögel ;
Aber Fögel Fisch, gehören den Herren auf den disch,"

with the date May 16, 1826, beneath what was intended to represent the American eagle (Ill. 34). A free translation of the above would be : " Fish and birds are too good for rough fellows and should only be served to gentlemen."

We are enabled to assign this piece to a particular maker through another example which has recently come to light. This latter, now in my possession, is of the same size and form, style of decoration, and, singularly, bears the same date, May 16, 1826. On the lower half is the American eagle, clutching an olive branch in each foot, but the upper design differs from that of the former in the substitution of flowers for the two birds. The inscription around the margin is as follows :

" Wer das lieben ungesund,
   So dädens docter meiten,
   Und wans den wibern weh däd ;
   So dädens sie nicht leiten."

This may be translated thus :

" If love were unhealthy
   Then the doctor would shun it,
   And if it would pain the women
   Then they would not suffer it."

The similarity of the workmanship and the formation of the letters in the two pieces, and, above all, the corres-

34.—Sgraffiato Dish, Pennsylvania, 1826.

ponding dates, prove them to be the work of the same hand. The second piece bears on the back a name and date, which have been scratched in the clay before it was burned,—" Samuel Troxel Potter May the 16th 1826." Whether Troxel was the proprietor of the pottery or merely a workman employed there we are unable to determine, but it is certain that he made the two pieces described. These interesting specimens were probably part of a set made to fill a particular order. It is rather a remarkable coincidence that they should have been brought together again, from widely separated localities, sixty-seven years after they were manufactured.

Early in the present century John Nase produced similar ware, at a pottery one-half mile west of the hamlet of Tyler's Port, Montgomery County, Pa., about four miles distant from Souderton, having, it is said, succeeded his father in the business. A dish in my possession bears the name Johannes Neesz (the father of John), and the date 1812, with the reverent words :

> " Lieber Vatter im Himmel reich,
>   Was du mir gibst das es ich gleich."

35.—Slip Pitcher and Sugar-Bowl. Made by John Nase about 1830. Barber Collection.

I have procured from some of his descendants a number of examples of the work of John Nase, who manufactured both slip and incised ware in plates, mugs, vegetable dishes, and other useful forms. One of these is a small pie-plate with sgraffiato decoration,—a leaping stag and spray of conventional flowers, Pennsylvania German inscription, and date, 1814. He also made pottery toys, such as small tubs and bird-shaped whistles. That he was a skilful potter is amply shown in some of his finer work. An elaborate sugar-bowl and small creamer with twisted handle, which I have recently acquired from a reliable source, are decorated with dotted figures and festoons of yellow slip, and covered with a heavy, rich, dark-brown glaze which sparkles with an auriferous sheen akin to

36.—*Pennsylvania German, Lead-Glazed, Slip-Decorated Dish Made in Montgomery County by John Nase in 1847. Philadelphia Museum of Art. Photograph by A. J. Wyatt, Staff Photographer.*

goldstone. The bowl is mounted with a lid that is built up into a crown-shaped ornament by the coiling of thin ropes of clay into spirals and scrolls. In form the piece bears a remarkable resemblance to some of the early English posset-pots (Ill. 35).

A characteristic piece of slip-decoration from the Nase pottery is shown in Illustration 36. Black and white slips have been traced on the red body to form the figure of a bird surrounded with foliage, and the words :

"Ich koch was ich kan
Est mein sau net so est mein man,"—

"I cook what I can
Is my pig neat, so is my man."

37.—DULL-FINISHED SGRAFFIATO DISH.   MADE BY JOHN NASE ABOUT 1847.

A peculiarity of some of the work of John Nase is the absence of glazing on some of the sgraffiato ware. These pieces have the appearance of being covered with a thin glossy wash or varnish, an effect produced by smearing the inside of the saggers in which they were fired with glaze, which in the kiln would vaporize and form a slight deposit on the ware, technically known as "*smear*" glaze. A large pie-dish of this character has scratched upon it the figure of a mounted soldier, in Continental uniform, with trumpet and sabre (Ill. 37).

38.—Pennsylvania German, Sgraffiato Plate Made in Montgomery County by Frederick Hildenbrand, ca. 1830. Philadelphia Museum of Art. Photograph by A. J. Wyatt, Staff Photographer.

In some instances the trumpet has been replaced by a tobacco-pipe in the right hand of the rider, as in a highly glazed specimen in the Pennsylvania Museum, Philadelphia, which bears the date 1847. A large pistol

is sometimes substituted for the sabre. It has been suggested that the mounted figure was intended to represent
General Washington, but the inscriptions which are found
on such pieces bear no allusion to the central design.

Frederick Hildenbrand was a contemporary of John
Nase, and had a pottery two miles west of Tyler's Port.

39.—Sgraffiato Plate. Made by Jacob Sholl, Montgomery County,
Pa., 1831.

Examples of his work are scarce, but one which has been
carefully preserved by a daughter serves to show the
character and quality of his productions. This is a dull-
finished plate, eight and a half inches in diameter, ornamented with the figure of a lion, *passant*, picked through
a coating of white slip. On the back the name of the

workman, Johanes Leman, is scratched in the paste. Leman is said to have worked at several of the potteries in the vicinity at different times (see Ill. 38).

Another pottery was in operation about a mile south of Tyler's Port, which was owned by one Jacob Sholl. He made incised ware of a good quality and considerable artistic merit. Some of his plaques were embellished with floral designs, with and without inscriptions, a number of them being dated 1831. An interesting plate from this pottery is shown in illustration 39. It is unglazed, save where patches of green have been applied to petals, and bears the above date. A large pie-dish from the Sholl pottery (Barber collection) contains the incised device of a large eagle which covers the entire surface. In each talon it grasps a spray of flowers, and in its beak it holds a scroll with the English inscription, "Liberty in the year 1832." The plumage is represented by numerous small curved incisions, revealing the red body beneath.

A pair of covered jars, in the possession of one of Sholl's descendants, are objects of considerable beauty and reveal the touch of an artist. Bold floral designs are engraved in the yellow slip which covers the surface, and the leaves and petals are tipped with green and blue pigments under the rich glazing. On the bottom of each a conventionalized flower is stamped in the paste (see chapter on Marks). These are the only examples of such ware which have come to my notice that bear factory marks. Michael Fillman was a potter at Sholl's establishment, and is said to have executed some of the best work produced there.

40.—*Pennsylvania German, Lead-Glazed, Sgraffiato Jar & Cover Made in Mont-gomery County by Jacob Scholl, ca. 1830. Philadelphia Museum of Art. Photograph by A. J. Wyatt, Staff Photographer.*

From the old pottery of Benjamin Berge, which was also situated in Montgomery County, the author has a pie-dish, thirteen inches in diameter, containing the figure of a bird, apparently a pigeon, standing on a branch, in the attitude of plucking its breast. Entirely around the border extends a curved spray of coarse flowers. This effective piece is decorated with yellow slip, but the design is not raised, as in the other examples figured, but beaten

or pressed into the red body, as is done at the present
day in the common red kitchen earthen-ware, presenting
a perfectly smooth surface (Ill. 41).

41.—*Pennsylvania German, Lead-Glazed, Slip-Decorated Pie Dish Made by Benjamin Berge in Montgomery County, ca. 1830. Philadelphia Museum of Art.*

Many of the inscriptions which occur on the old slip-
decorated wares of Pennsylvania were intended for ornament rather than the perpetuation of valuable precepts,
while others were designed solely to amuse; hence we
find among them some whose sentiments are more forci-
ble than elegant. They were executed generally by
illiterate German workmen, which fact will account for
the introduction of misspelled words, which are often diffi-

cult of translation, even to those familiar with the Pennsylvania German dialect.

42.—Pennsylvania German Sgraffiato Pottery Flower-Vase (12" high) Made in Bucks County by Charles Headman in 1849. Philadelphia Museum of Art.

A coarse, red pottery, with rude floral slip designs in low relief, the raised parts covered with yellow, brown, and green glazes, was made by Michael and Andrew Headman, near Rich Hill, Bucks County, Pa., more than half a century ago.

The earlier potters of this section, bringing their art with them from the fatherland, employed tolerably correct German in these inscriptions, but their descendants in time drifted into the Pennsylvania German. There were English potters, however, among them, though pieces with English legends are scarce. The old potteries where inscribed ware was produced have entirely disappeared, and I have seen no pieces which were made later than the middle of the present century.

TERRA-COTTA.

The terra-cotta works now operated by Messrs. A. H. Hews & Co., at North Cambridge, Mass., were started in Weston, Mass., previous to 1765, by Abraham Hews, great-grandfather of the present senior member of the firm. The ware manufactured at first consisted of household utensils, such as bean-pots, pudding and milk pans, jugs, etc., and the entry of transactions for one year was confined to a single page of the day-book. These products were usually sold in exchange for such commodities as molasses, New England rum, and other staple merchandise which formed the basis of barter in those days.

The clay used at Weston for some years was brought from Watertown, and at a more recent date from Cambridge, Mass.

During the first century of this pottery's existence, the firm name was changed several times, first to Abraham

Hews & Son, then to Abraham Hews & Sons, and later to Abraham Hews' Sons, three brothers of Abraham Hews second. In 1865 the present proprietor was admitted to partnership in the business, and five years later the establishment was moved to its present location, at which time the firm consisted of Messrs. A. H. & Horatio Hews. The latter soon after retired and the business was continued in the name of the former. Previous to the fire, which destroyed a portion of the works and all of the machinery, on December 1, 1891, it was claimed that this factory manufactured more hand and machine-made flower pots than any other establishment in the world. Large numbers of umbrella stands, *jardinières*, cuspidors, lamp-stands, garden vases, and other fancy earthenware were made from natural clays, a specialty in art pottery being reproductions of antique shapes, after Grecian, Roman, Etruscan, Phœnician, and Cypriote models, including creditable imitations of the productions of the Widow Ipsen of Copenhagen. In the plain biscuit state, for decorators,

43.—Terra-Cotta Jardinière and Pedestal. A. H. Hews & Co.

such ware is known as Albert and Albertine, the latter differing from the former in the application of floral designs in high relief. Copies of old Peruvian vases have also been attempted, which included some of the double "whistling-jars" so well known to collectors of Incarial vessels. The most artistic and characteristic variety of terra-cotta made here, however, are the garden vases and pedestals of a rich, dark color which may be seen in the shop windows of almost any of our city florists. These are made of natural clays, without artificial coloring, and ornamented with classic designs in relief. The works have been rebuilt and are now running again, with improved facilities for supplying the ever growing demand for goods of this character, which the intelligent efforts and conscientious business methods of more than a century and a quarter have so abundantly merited.

As early as 1760, a pottery and glassworks had been established at Germantown, now a suburb of Quincy, Mass., through the exertions of Joseph C. Palmer and Richard Cranch, two progressive land owners, who were instrumental in establishing manufacturing enterprises of various kinds at that point. The late Mr. E. P. Cranch, of Cincinnati, Ohio, a grandson of the latter, left among his personal effects some fragments of pottery and glass which had been picked up by his father on the site of the old works. One of the pieces of pottery is three quarters of an inch in thickness, coarse in texture, and heavily glazed. Other examples are thinner, almost vitreous, and slightly iridescent, and were apparently never glazed, or but thinly. There seem to be no evidences of any sort of decoration.

FIRST CHINA WORKS IN PHILADELPHIA.

Not until 1769 was there any serious attempt made to manufacture fine china on this side of the Atlantic. In Watson's *Annals of Philadelphia*, we find the brief statement that "the desire to encourage domestic fabrics gave rise, in 1771, to the erection of a flint-glass manufactory near Lancaster, by which they hoped to save £30,000 to the province. A china factory, too, was also erected on Prime Street, near the present Navy Yard, intended to make china at a saving of £15,000."[1] In a foot-note the author adds : " This long row of wooden houses afterwards became famous as a sailors' brothel and riot-house on a large scale. The former frail ware proved an abortive scheme." The glassworks to which Mr. Watson refers were established at Manheim, Lancaster County, Pa., by Baron William Henry Stiegel, who came from Manheim in Germany. Examples of colored glass goblets and other pieces may be seen in the extensive collection of Mr. George H. Danner of that town. Mr. Charles Henry Hart, of Philadelphia, made the interesting discovery, a few years ago, of some old advertisements in the newspapers of the last century which throw considerable light on the early American china works, and he has kindly placed at my disposal the results of his researches. The first of these announcements, which appeared in the latter part of the year 1769, is as follows ;

" NEW CHINA-WARE.—Notwithstanding the various difficulties and disadvantages, which usually attend the introduction of any important manufacture into a new country,

[1] *Vide*, vol. ii., p. 272.

the Proprietors of the China Works, now erecting in Southwark, have the pleasure to acquaint the public, they have proved to a certainty, that the clays of America are productive of as good Porcelain, as any heretofore manufactured at the famous factory in Bow, near London, and imported into the colonies and plantations, which they will engage to sell upon very reasonable terms ; and as they purpose going largely into this manufacture as soon as the works are completed, they request those persons who choose to favor them with commands, to be as early as possible, laying it down as a fixed principle, to take all orders in rotation, and execute the earliest first ; dealers will meet with the usual encouragement, and may be assured, that no goods under Thirty Pounds' worth, will be sold to private persons out of the factory, at a lower advance than from their shops. All workmen skilled in the different branches of throwing, turning, modelling, moulding, pressing, and painting, upon application to the Proprietors, may depend on encouragement suitable to their abilities ; and such parents, as are inclined to bind their children apprentices to either of these branches, must be early in their application, as only a few of the first offering will be accepted, without a premium ; none will be received under twelve years of age, or upwards of fifteen. All orders from the country, or other provinces, inclosed in letters, post paid, and directed to the CHINA PROPRIETORS in Philadelphia, will be faithfully executed, and the Ware warranted equal to any, in goodness and cheapness, hitherto manufactured in, or imported from England."

This card, which was printed first on December 29, 1769, fixes the date of the beginning of this enterprise, as it clearly states that the works were then in course of erection. Subsequently the proprietors advertised for bones, offering twenty shillings per thousand "for any quantity of horses or beeves shank-bones, whole or broken, fifteen shillings for hogs, and ten shillings for calves and sheep (a proportionable price for knuckle bones), delivered at the china factory in Southwark," concluding with the announcement that the capital works of the factory were then completed and in full operation. The projectors of this enterprise were Gousse Bonnin, who had most probably learned his trade at Bow, and George Anthony Morris, of Philadelphia. In January, 1771, they applied to the Assembly for pecuniary assistance, in the form of a provincial loan, the petition as laid upon the table in the Assembly room, being given in full by Colonel Frank M. Etting, in his History of Independence Hall, which reads as follows :

"THE ADDRESS OF THE PROPRIETORS OF THE CHINA MANUFACTORY.

" Worthy Sirs :—We, the Subscribers, actuated as strongly by the sincerest Attachment to the interest of the Public as to our private Emolument, have at our sole Risque and Expense introduced into this Province a Manufacture of Porcelain or China Earthen Ware, a Commodity, which by Beauty and Excellence, hath forced its way into every refined Part of the Globe, and created various imitative Attempts, in its Progress through the different

Kingdoms and Principalities of Europe, under the Sanction and Encouragement of their several Potentates. Great Britain which hath not been the least backward, in Royal Testimonials of Favour to the first Adventurers, in so capital an Undertaking, cannot yet boast of any great Superiority in Workmanship, surpassing Denmark, France and the Austrian Netherlands, she yields the Palm to Saxony, which in her Turn gives place to the East Indies. America, in this general Struggle, hath hitherto been unthought of, and it is our peculiar Happiness to have been primarily instrumental in bringing her forward ; but how far she shall proceed, in a great Measure, depends on the influence of your generous Support. We have expended great Sums in bringing from London Workmen of acknowledged Abilities, have established them here, erected spacious Buildings, Mills, Kilns and various Requisites ; and brought the work, we flatter ourselves, into no contemptible Train of Perfection. A sample of it we respectfully submit to the Inspection of your Honourable House, praying it may be viewed with a favourable Eye having Reference to the Disadvantages under which we engaged ; if happy enough to merit your approbation we would not wish to aspire at the Presumption of dictating the Measure of your Encouragement, but with all Humility hint at the Manner. You, Gentlemen, who are appointed to a dignified Pre-eminence by the free Votes of your Countrymen, as well for your known Attachment to their truest Welfare, as superior Knowledge, must be sensible, that capital Works are not to be carried on by inconsiderable Aids or Advancements : Hence it is, we beg leave to point out the Propriety of a Provincial Loan, at the Discretion of your Honourable House, independent of Interest, for a certain Term of Years. Under such Indulgence, on our Part we shall not be deficient in the Display of a Lively Gratitude, and the Promotion of the Colony's service, by the introducing of an additional Number of Experienced Workmen the Extension of our Buildings, and Improvement of the Manufacture, endeavoring to render it equal in Quality to such as is usually imported, and vending it at a cheaper Rate. We have the Honour, etc., etc."

Whether they were successful in procuring the loan does not appear, but later in the same year they advertised for "zaffer or zaffera," without which they could not make blue ware.

A curious old lottery ticket, in the possession of Mr. Ferdinand J. Dreer, of Philadelphia, issued in 1771, evidently has reference to this factory, and shows the straits to which the proprietors were driven to raise funds for the enterprise. The ticket reads as follows :

NEW CASTLE LOTTERY

FOR THE ENCOURAGEMENT OF THE AMERICAN CHINA MANUFACTURE.

1771.   No. 2257.

This Ticket entitles the Bearer to such Prize as may be drawn against its Number, free from any Deduction.

D.

TOBIAS RUDOLPH.

In April, 1772, the following appeared in the Philadelphia papers :

"WANTED.

"By the Proprietors of the China Manufactory in Southwark, Several apprentices to the painting branch, a proper person being engaged to instruct them : The advantage resulting to poor people by embracing such an opportunity of bringing up their children creditably, are too obvious to be overlooked.

"WANTED ALSO, several apprentices to the other branches, of equal utility and benefit to children. None will be received under indentures for less than seven years, and will be found during that term in every necessary befitting apprentices."

Shortly afterward they advertised for "fifty wagon loads of white flint stone." The attempt to make porcelain at this time, however, proved a failure in a financial point, and in the latter year the proprietors made a public appeal for charity in behalf of the workmen who had been brought to a foreign country and were left without means of support. After running about two years, the factory was permanently closed, the real estate was sold, and Bonnin returned to England.

Little is known of the ware made here. The fact that zaffre was used shows that blue decorated ware was made. The employment of bones in large quantities indicated that if porcelain was made here, it was similar to the English bone china. No mention is made in any of the ad-

vertisements of kaolin, and we may therefore conclude
that hard porcelain was not attempted. The Bow works
at that period were making little but blue and white china,
as was the case with all of the early English factories,
which employed almost exclusively lapis lazuli and zaffre
to color beneath the glaze. It is curious, however, to note
what Messrs. Bonnin and Morris assert in their petition
in relation to the wares produced in Great Britain, because the fame of Josiah Wedgwood's Basaltes or Egyptian Black Ware, first made in 1766, and the earlier
productions of the Etruria works, which began operations
in June of 1769, should have reached America previous to
1771. For several years before the latter date Chelsea
had been turning out some fine porcelain exquisitely
moulded and decorated in several colors. At other factories throughout England artistic china was also made to
a limited extent with polychrome decoration. Previous
to the year 1770 the Bow factory had commenced to use
gold and colors over the glaze, but this fact may not have
been known to the American potters. Whether any of
the ware produced here was ornamented above the glaze
in colors is not known, because we have not been able to
positively identify any pieces of this character, although
several examples, embellished with baskets of roses in
natural colors and other floral decorations, are claimed to
have been made at the Southwark factory. In the light
of all the evidence which we possess, we can only be certain that cream-colored ware was made here, both in plain
white and decorated in blue. An example of the latter is
a small white ware fruit-basket in the cabinet of the

Franklin Institute in Philadelphia, six inches in diameter and of excellent workmanship. The sides are of basket or openwork pattern, studded with flower-shaped orna-

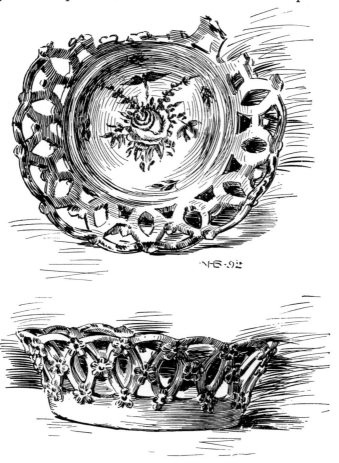

44.—White Ware Fruit-Basket, Blue Decoration. Made in Philadelphia about 1770. Pennsylvania Museum of Art.

ments in relief. The decoration is blue, under the glaze, consisting of a floral design in the bottom and zaffre blue rosettes around the sides. Underneath occurs a small P in blue, which may have been the factory mark (Philadelphia), or the initial of the decorator. There is little reason to doubt the authenticity of this piece, which was "made about the time of the Revolution," and deposited in the Institute by Dr. James Mease, author of *A Picture of Philadelphia* (1811), who was an authority on historical matters and generally reliable in his statements. We know of no other white ware factory in this country which was in operation at that time.[1]

"The broken China fruit basket which I have the pleasure to present to the Franklin Institute, was part of a dinner set, and the first attempt at the manufacture of China in the United States, the history of which is as follows :

"Mr. Gousey Bonnin of Antigua, came to Philadelphia before the American War, and his father having been a correspondent of my father's, they became intimate. What led him to the speculation, I never heard, but in an unfortunate hour, he resolved to undertake the manufacture of China the clay for which he procured from *White-Clay-Creek* in the State of Delaware, a few miles from the City of Wilmington, and with the aid of five hundred pounds loaned him by my father he erected a long frame building in Prime St. southward, which I believe now leads from the navy yard west.

"The workmen were doubtless procured from England, and China or Ware of quality of the broken Specimen

---

[1] Since the above was written, the example described has been placed in the Pennsylvania Museum, together with the original letter of presentation by Dr. Mease to the Franklin Institute in 1841, which has recently come to light. This letter, given here in full, absolutely identifies this piece and gives us further facts relating to the old Southwark factory.

was made, but to what extent I cannot say : However the news was soon conveyed to England that the manufacture had commenced, when speedily arrived cargoes of the English or Dutch Ware sufficient to supply the demand of the Colony or Colonies. Unable to withstand the competition with the manufacturers in Europe, Mr. Bonnin ceased his labours.

" The dinner set of his China was all that my father got for his £500.

" The quality of it was about equal to the Delft ware of Holland of which much of the American table sets was composed, and which was first imported into England previously to being sent to this Country, the direct trade being prohibited.

" JAMES MEASE.

"February 22, 1841."

It does not seem probable that porcelain was ever made here. All white ware was known, at that time, as " china." The wording of some of the advertisements, however, would seem to indicate that the proprietors had the manufacture of a finer ware in contemplation before the disastrous termination of the enterprise. At least no examples of true porcelain made at this factory have, as yet, come to light.

The year 1769 seemed to have marked the establishment of several important ceramic manufactories in the United States. While the Philadelphia china works were in course of erection, a similar project was under consideration in Boston, as appears by an advertisement in the *Boston Evening Post* (weekly), of May 15, 1769, a transcript of which has been kindly furnished by the librarian of the Boston Athenæum, which reads as follows:

" WANTED :

" Samples of different Clays and fine white Sand. Any Person or Persons that will send about 3lb. of Clay and a Pint of fine white Sand to Leigh's Intelligence Office in Merchants Row, *Boston*, (if its the Sort wanted) the Proprietors will have advantageous Proposals made to them to supply a Quantity. *Boston, May 12, 1769.*"

A subsequent advertisement in the same paper, under date of October 16, 1769, shows that the enterprise was then in full operation :

" Wanted immediately at the new Factory in New-Boston, four Boys for Apprentices to learn the Art of making Tortoise-shell, Cream and Green colour Plates, Dishes, Coffee & Tea Pots, Cups and Saucers, and all other Articles in the Potter's Business, equal to any imported from England. Any Persons inclining to bind out such Lads to the aforesaid Business, is desired to apply immediately at the said Factory or at Leigh's Intelligence-Office. *Boston, Octo. 16, 1769.*"

In *Holt's New York Journal* of 1774 and 1775 an advertisement appeared describing the ware made in that city at that early day. It is given here in full :

" EARTHEN WARE.

" Now manufacturing, and to be sold at the well known House called Katechemet's Mead-House, about mid way between the New City-Hall and the Tea-Water Pump, on the left hand side of the road as you go out of the city ; where city and country store-keepers may be supplied with any quantity of said Ware, at reasonable rates. The Ware is far superior to the generality, and equal to the best of any imported from Philadelphia, or elsewhere, and consists of butter, water, pickle and oyster pots, porringers, milk pans of several sizes, jugs of several sizes, quart and pint mugs, quart, pint, and half pint bowls, of various colours ; small cups of different shapes, striped and coloured dishes of divers colours, pudding pans and wash basons, sauce pans, and a variety of other sorts of ware, too tedious to particularize, by the manufacturer, late from Philadelphia,

" JONATHAN DURELL.

" N. B.—The purchaser of twenty shillings, or upwards, may depend on having it delivered to any part of this city, without charge."

From the above it would appear that even before the Revolution the wares made in Philadelphia had acquired a reputation abroad for excellence. It seems that Jonathan Durell had been previously a manufacturer in Philadelphia. In his new field of labor he produced "*striped and coloured dishes of divers colours,*" which he claimed to be "equal to the best of any imported from Philadelphia." What was the nature of this ware ? Most probably the red and black pottery, variegated with green and yellow oxides, which was so commonly made at that period.

Mrs. S. L. Oberholtzer of Norristown informs me that her ancestors, Thomas, John, and Paxson Vickers, successively carried on the manufacture of earthenware in Chester County, Pa., in West Whiteland township, for an uninterrupted period of seventy years previous to 1823, and from that date until 1865, in Uwchlan township. In addition to the ordinary household pottery, they made elaborate vases for flowers, animal and ornamental figures. Mrs. Oberholtzer has in her possession an interesting series of objects from t h i s pottery, consisting of pie-dish moulds, rollers, pounders, and other tools used in the work, the oldest dated example being a mould on which occur the initials J. V., and the date 1806.

45.—POTTERY " MONEY-BANK," NORWICH, CT.
JAMES TERRY COLLECTION.

The buildings of this old pottery have long since disappeared.

Before the beginning of the present century several stoneware and earthenware potteries were in operation in Connecticut. At " Bean Hill," near Norwich, good ware was made and specimens of pottery in the form of " money-safes " for children, one bearing the date 1794, and another 1812, the latter owned by Mr. James Terry, of New Haven (Ill. 45), are still in existence. A cider-bottle, in the shape of a hollow ring, made to carry on the arm of a mower in the field, is also extant.

In 1791, John Curtis was making a good quality of pottery in Philadelphia, from clay obtained where the brewery now stands, at Tenth and Filbert streets, and his name is found in the city directories as late as 1811, in the same business.

One of the earliest potteries established in Vermont was that of John and William Norton, two brothers, who came from Connecticut and commenced making red earthenware at Bennington, in 1793. Seven years later they took up the manufacture of plain stoneware, which has been continued down to the present time. The business is at present carried on by Messrs. C. W. Thatcher and E. L. Norton, the former being the first person not a Norton who has ever had an interest in the establishment. The junior member of the firm is a great-grandson of John Norton, one of the founders.

It is probable that other potteries in America followed the example of the Burlington pottery in the manufacture of white ware previous to the opening of the previous century. Mr. John D. McCormick, proprietor of the *American Potters' Journal*, Trenton, N. J., states that " the *New Jersey Journal*, printed at Elizabethtown, in its issue of January 25, 1792, contains the following: 'The Pennsylvania Society for the Encouragement of Manufactures and the Useful Arts,' in their list of premiums for that year offer the following : The conditions are—

" ' 1.—To such person as shall exhibit the best specimen of Earthenware or Pottery, approaching nearest to Queensware, or the Nottingham or Delf ware, of the marketable value of fifty dollars—a plate of the value of fifty dollars, or an equivalent in money.

" ' 2.—To such person as shall exhibit the best specimen of Stoneware, or that kind of Earthenware which is glazed with salt, of the value of fifty dollars, a plate of fifty dollars' value, or that sum in specie.'

" The exhibitors were required to have the ware manufactured in New Jersey or Pennsylvania. Here we have abundant proof that there was ware manufactured here closely resembling Queensware in quality, and that its manufacture was encouraged by the society whose advertisement we have just quoted." As we have already seen, salt-glazed stoneware had been made by at least one pottery, in New York, which started in 1735.

A stoneware pottery was in existence at Norwalk, Connecticut, as early as 1780. Mr. James Lycett, who is at present operating the establishment which is said to be a continuation of the original concern in that place, belongs to a family of potters who have been identified with the trade in Stoke-upon-Trent for a hundred years. It is claimed that his grandfather built the kilns for the Spode works when the first porcelain was made there in the year 1800. His father and uncle came to this country in 1849, and for some time worked at the United States Pottery in Bennington, Vt., where the uncle died. The senior Lycett then went to Norwalk, where he worked in the pottery of Mr. Asa Smith, afterwards the A. E. Smith's Sons Pottery Co., and subsequently the Norwalk Pottery Company, now owned by Mr. Lycett.

At Old Bridge (now Herbertsville), N. J., stoneware was made at Van Wickle's pottery, from South Amboy clays, in the first decade of the present century, and similar ware was manufactured at Roundabout (now Sayreville) on the Raritan, about 1802.

CHAPTER VII.

OPERATIONS DURING THE FIRST QUARTER OF THE PRESENT CENTURY.

ANDREW MILLER had a pottery at 37 and 39 Sugar Alley, Philadelphia, previous to 1791, where he continued to make common earthenware for many years. He was succeeded by Abraham and Andrew Miller, Jr., who, from 1810 to 1816, operated a pottery at the corner of Seventh and Zane streets. Shortly afterwards Abraham Miller became sole proprietor, and at the Exhibition of the Franklin Institute, held in October, 1824 (the year in which the Institute was founded), he displayed some " red and black glazed tea-pots, coffee-pots, and other articles of the same description. Also a sample of platinated or lustre pitchers, with a specimen of porcelain and white ware, all of which," according to the report of the judges, " exhibited a growing improvement in the manufacture, both in the quality and form of the articles. It is but a few years since we were under the necessity of importing a considerable proportion of this description of ware for home consumption, but since our potters have attained the art of making it equal, if not superior, to the imported, and as cheap, they have entirely excluded the foreign ware from the American market."

In the Report of the Exhibition of the Franklin Institute, held in October, 1835, it is recorded that "a novel and interesting exhibition was furnished from the pottery of Mr. Abraham Miller, of Philadelphia, consisting of a variety of specimens of black and red earthenware, in the various stages of its manufacture, from the crude material to the finished ware," and at the Exhibition of 1842 he made a display of finer earthenware, such as plates, vases, and ornamental flower-pots. Soon after he commenced the manufacture of charcoal furnaces in great numbers, the larger patterns being provided with a cylinder attachment for roasting coffee, and open grates of fire-brick.

About 1840 Mr. Miller moved his factory to James Street near Broad, as appears in the following card, which has been furnished by Mr. J. H. Buck:

ABRAHAM MILLER

HAS REMOVED HIS MANUFACTORY

From Zane Street to James, near Broad Street,

SPRING GARDEN,

Where his Works are now in full operation, conducted by his late Foreman, Mr. C. J. BOULTER.

His Warehouse continues in Zane Street,

Next door West of its former place, where he has constantly for Sale, by

WHOLESALE OR RETAIL,

A large Assortment of PORTABLE FURNACES, STOVE CYLINDERS, FIRE BRICKS and SLABS, TEA-POTS and EARTHENWARE, PIPE CASES, DENTISTS' FURNACES, MUFFLES, SLIDES, &c. &c.—KAOLIN and CLAYS, crude or prepared; SILEX and SPAR, crude or levigated to an impalpable powder, and free from impurities.

Sales made only at the Warehouse, Zane Street.

SILEX, or FELSPAR *ground*, or any article in his line *made* to order, as speedily as practicable.

☞All Orders are to be left at the Warehouse, only, where they will be promptly attended to.

Philad'a. December 22d, 1840.

Elliott, Printer, 51, Chestnut St

Abraham Miller was one of the most progressive American potters of his day and a man of more than ordinary intelligence and ability, and at one time represented his district in the State Senate, where he was the courageous advocate of numerous reform measures. He was one of the most prominent members of the Franklin Institute for many years, and was frequently selected as one of the judges for the awarding of premiums at the annual exhibitions.

It will thus be seen that Mr. Miller was probably the first in this country to make the lustred or silvered ware which had become celebrated in England. He was also one of the first on this side of the Atlantic to experiment in making porcelain, in which he was remarkably successful, but for some reason he never produced it for the market. His standard or staple productions were red, yellow, Rockingham, and a limited quantity of white ware. He was well versed in the constitution and peculiarities of clays, and at one time made, for his own gratification, some figures with lace-work drapery, which he produced by employing real lace, which he carefully covered with slip of the proper quality and consistency, and which, after being burned away in the kiln, left the clay form as perfect in texture as the original. He made a Tam O'Shanter mug in Rockingham which was very popular at one time, large numbers of them being produced about 1840. Mr. Miller procured much of the machinery and many of the moulds of the Tucker and Hemphill factory when the latter was closed in 1838. He died about 1858 and the business was continued by his foreman,

MR. CHARLES J. BOULTER,

who was at one time connected with the Tucker and Hemphill China Manufactory in Philadelphia, where he remained until the works were closed. Subsequently he became connected with Mr. Abraham Miller at Zane and Seventh streets in the capacity of foreman, and when this pottery was moved to James Street near Broad, in 1840, he became superintendent of the new establishment. After Mr. Miller's death Mr. Boulter carried on the business for many years, manufacturing watch-makers' supplies, dentists', assayers', and cupellers' portable furnaces, muffles, slides, tiles, and fire-bricks. He subsequently moved the works to 1617–1627 North Street, and when he died, on March 2, 1872, the business passed into the hands of his daughters, two of whom, Misses E. A. and A. L. Boulter, still carry it on.

A "china" manufactory existed in Philadelphia in 1800, but very little is known regarding it. A friend has recently shown me a letter, dated August 14, 1800, written by a merchant of that city to his wife, who was then visiting in New Jersey, in which occurs the following interesting bit of news : "On account of a man being murdered at the *China Factory* on Monday evening last, a block maker by trade, a number of the same profession, with Rope makers and Carpenters, assembled and on Tuesday evening began to pull down the buildings ; they continued at their work till yesterday mid-day,—it was pulled down by Ropes in spite of all the Squires and Constables that could be collected—say every house, only leaving the Chimneys standing." The writer, an ancestor of the present owner of the letter, was in business at that time near Fourth and Chestnut streets, and we are led to infer that the factory was somewhere in that neighborhood. All white ware at that time was known as *china*, and the term was evidently applied to queensware,—hardly to porcelain.

Messrs. Binney and Ronaldson made yellow and red tea-sets in South Street, Philadelphia, in 1808.

A queensware pottery in Philadelphia, in 1808, was known as the Columbian Pottery, of which Alexander Trotter was proprietor, and examples of his work were exhibited at Peale's Museum in that year. At the great Republican dinner of July 4, 1808, an "elegant jug and goblets from the new queensware manufactory of Trotter & Co." formed part of the table service. Governor Simon Snyder, in his message to the Pennsylvania Legislature, in December, 1809, referred to this factory when he stated that "we have lately established in Philadelphia a queensware pottery on an extensive scale."

The Columbian Pottery was situated on South Street, between Twelfth and Thirteenth, in 1810. The ware produced there was claimed to be equal in quality and workmanship to the best made in Staffordshire. Mr. Trotter retired from business about 1813.

Captain John Mullowny was a brickmaker on Locust Street, near Schuylkill, Philadelphia, in 1808 and 1809. A year later he moved to No. 228 Pine Street, the Washington Pottery, where he made bricks and earthenware. Little is known of this manufactory save what is contained in the following advertisement, which appeared

in the *Aurora,—General Advertiser*, published in Philadelphia, in May, 1810 :

" WASHINGTON WARE,

Manufactured in Philadelphia at the

WASHINGTON POTTERY :

Red, yellow, and black coffee-pots,
Tea-pots, pitchers, etc., etc.
and for sale,

Wholesale and retail at the ware-house in High,
between Schuylkill 6th and 7th streets.

———

Any device, cypher, or pattern put on China or other ware at the
shortest notice, by leaving orders at the ware-house as above.

Journeymen Potters, and a few *Boys*, may find constant employment,
by applying at No. 228, Pine St. or the Ware House above."

From this it will be seen that the warehouse was on
Market Street, near Seventeenth, in 1810, while the works
were on Pine Street. In 1813 the latter seem to have
been moved to the Market Street warehouse, and Captain
Mullowny became director, in which capacity he served
for three years or more.

In the early part of this century many of Philadelphia's
prominent potters learned their trade at the old Mullowny
pottery.

Israel Seymour made stoneware in Troy, N. Y., from
about 1809 to 1865.

Paul Cushman had a stoneware factory at Albany,
N. Y., in the first decade of this century, and some examples of his salt-glazed ware are now in the possession
of Mr. S. L. Frey, of Palatine Bridge, N. Y., one of which
bears the inscription, impressed on the surface of the jar,

and twice repeated around the body, " Paul Cushman Stone Ware Factory 1809 Half a Mile West of Albany Gaol." Another, in the form of a jar, fourteen inches in height, is marked with the maker's name ; while a third, possessing two ear-shaped handles, is decorated with incised vine-work, in addition to the name (Ill. 46).

The *Central New York Pottery*, of Utica, N. Y., was built by a Mr. Nash about the year 1819. In 1828, Noah White came into posses-
sion, and in 1840 the firm name became Noah White & Sons, the new partners being Nicholas A. and William White. About 1853, the last named member withdrew, and the style became Noah White, Son & Co., William N., a son of Nicholas, being admitted. In 1865, on the death of the head of the house, the name was altered to N. A. White & Son, and at the

46.—ALBANY STONEWARE. COLLECTION OF MR. S. L. FREY. MADE ABOUT 1809.

decease of the latter, in 1876, the business passed into the hands of the survivor. In 1880, the firm name was again changed to N. A. White & Son, when Charles N. White, the present manager of the works, was admitted. In 1886, Mr. N. A. White died, at the age of sixty-eight, having been on the property for sixty years.

The original business was the manufacture of coarse

stoneware, such as butter crocks, jugs, and jars. In 1852, the manufacture of fire-brick was added, and still continues. At present the works make a specialty of " Flemish " stoneware goods of a high grade. The decorations are artistic and attractive, the colors used being blue, brown, and green. Beer-mugs, tankard-jugs, " growlers," wine-jugs, flower-vases, punch-bowls, match-stands, and spit-toons, in many handsome designs and sizes, form but a portion of the products of these works. The metal-

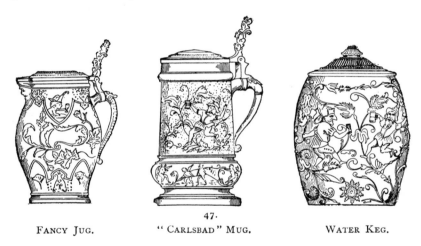

47.

FANCY JUG.   " CARLSBAD " MUG.   WATER KEG.

covered mugs and tankards made here compare favorably with the best imported manufactures of the same class both in form and ornamentation. Special designs and decorations, with suitable inscriptions in English and German, are made to order. The pieces are marked on the bottom with a number corresponding to the price-list number, which gives capacity and size. It is gratifying to Americans to know that goods of such superior excellence and artistic merit can be made at home and at prices which insure successful competition with foreign wares.

Daniel Freytag was making at No. 192 South Fifth Street, Philadelphia, in 1811, a finer quality of china-ware than had yet been produced in the United States. It was made of various colors, and was embellished with gold and silver ; and in 1817 David G. Seixas manufactured an imitation of the Liverpool white crockery from native American clays with great success, continuing the business until 1822.

Porcelain was made in New York City early in the century, probably by Dr. Mead. How long this factory was in operation is not known, but it is believed that a fine grade of ware was made there from American materials. A vase fifteen inches in height, of soft body and exceedingly white glaze, is preserved in the Pennsylvania Museum. This was "finished in New York in 1816," and is supposed to have been made at that factory. The handles are modelled in the semblance of female figures (Ill. 48). It is entirely devoid of gilding or coloring, and is made in two parts, held together by a screw and nut, after the French manner.

48.—PORCELAIN VASE, NEW YORK, 1816.

THE HAIG POTTERY, PHILADELPHIA.

In 1812 Thomas Haig, who came from Scotland, where he had learned his trade as a queensware potter, established a pottery in the Northern Liberties, Philadelphia, where he commenced the manufacture of red and black ware. At the second annual exhibition of the Franklin Institute, Philadelphia, in 1825, Mr. Haig exhibited some specimens of red and black earthenware, "which, if they had been sent in time, might have entitled him to the silver medal." This exhibit consisted of teapots, coffee-pots, pitchers, strainers, cake-moulds and pans, "from clay taken in the city. These articles are considered of very superior quality, and are in the opinion of the judges better than goods of the same kind, brought from England. The body of the ware is perfectly burned and deprived of all absorbent qualities. The glaze is good and free from cracks, and the workmanship is neat." Judging from examples in my own possession, which were made at that pottery about that time or a few years later, this flattering description of the ware does not seem to have been undeserved. Indeed the quality of the glazing and neatness of the workmanship are superior to similar wares made at the present time by other potteries.

At the third annual exhibition, in 1826, the Franklin Institute awarded Thomas Haig a "Bronzed Medal" for the best red earthenware sent in.

In 1833, after the death of the founder, his two sons, James and Thomas, carried on the business, and in 1858 were making stoneware, chemical ware, crucibles, etc., in addition to earthenware, and were using steam for grinding the clay. At the death of the former, Thomas Haig assumed complete control, and died recently, in his eighty-third year. The manufacture of stoneware was discontinued some years ago, but fire-brick, tile, Rockingham, and yellow wares are still made. A few years ago relief plaques and vases were produced, a number of female artists being employed in their decoration, but this branch was soon discontinued for want of sufficient patronage.

At the present time this pottery is also producing terra-cotta flower-pots, fancy earthenware pitchers, glazed hanging baskets, and vases after antique designs, which latter are furnished in biscuit to decorators. One of the potters employed here, Mr. John S. Jennings, has produced some very ingenious miniature pieces in the form of vases, molasses jugs, mugs, and pitchers, which are said to be the smallest specimens ever made in the regular manner on the potter's wheel, some of them being scarcely as large as a pea. Another of Mr. Haig's workmen makes a specialty of "puzzle mugs," on the principle of those made at Brampton, England, in the last century, which are almost identical in form to some produced by John Wedgwood as early as 1691, of which an interesting example may be seen in the Museum of Practical Geology, London.

A stoneware pottery was started at Elizabeth, N. J., somewhere about 1816. At a later date it was operated by a Mr. Pruden who made yellow and Rockingham wares. We have seen some large, heavy water pitchers, decorated with patriotic symbols in relief, which were produced about the time of the Centennial Exposition. The factory is now owned by Messrs. L. B. Beerbower & Co., who make ironstone china, cream-colored and print-decorated goods in druggists' ware, toilet, table, and culinary sets.

The pottery now managed by the widow of Henry Gast, Lancaster, Pa., dates back to about 1825. Common red and yellow wares were made there, and at one time a limited amount of white ware. Fancy figures, fountains, and statuettes were also produced to some extent in red clay. Latterly this pottery has produced a considerable number of cinerary urns for crematories. At one time white clay tobacco pipes were made, and a few fancy glazed umbrella and cane handles. Floor tiles of yellow clay, octagonal and rhomboidal, were also made to some extent some fifteen years ago. These were heavy, unglazed tiles, six or eight inches across, and an inch in thickness.

THE JERSEY CITY POTTERY.

The Jersey Porcelain and Earthenware Company was incorporated in " the town of Jersey, County of Bergen," on December 10, 1825, under an act of the New Jersey Legislature, in which George Dummer, Timothy Dewey, Henry Post, Jr., William W. Shirley, and Robert Abbatt, Jr., were named as incorporators. In the following year the products of the factory were awarded a silver medal at the exhibition of the Franklin Institute, Philadelphia, as being the " best china from American materials." In the Trumbull-Prime collection is a small porcelain bowl, with heavy gold band, which was made at this pottery, of good body and excellent glaze. The manufacture of porcelain, however, does not seem to have been continued there for more than about three years.[1]

The works were purchased by Messrs. D. & J. Henderson about 1829, and a year later they exhibited "flint stoneware" of a superior quality at the Franklin Institute. Mr. A. G. Richmond, of Canajoharie, N. Y., possesses a

49.—THE OLD POTTERY, JERSEY CITY, N. J.

mottled Toby jug made at that period and marked "D & J. Henderson, Jersey City," in a circle, impressed in the paste (Ill. 50). In 1833, David Henderson organized *The American Pottery Manufacturing Company*, "for the purpose of manufacturing the various kinds of pottery, at

[1] In a pamphlet on *The Mineralogy of Chester County, Pa., Delaware, and Maryland*, published by George W. Carpenter in 1828, it is stated that "the manufactory of porcelain at Jersey City has been discontinued, and that at Philadelphia is stated to be the only one in the United States."

the works already erected." By an act of Assembly passed January 18th in that year, Messrs. David Henderson, John V. B. Varick, Robert Gilchrist, John Cassedy, and J. Dickinson Miller, of Jersey City, and Edward Cook, George Tingle, and John Steele, of New York, were appointed commissioners to receive subscriptions to the stock, which was to be limited to $150,000. We know little about the ware produced here during the next seven years, excepting the fact that a buff or cream-colored body, of excellent quality, was used extensively. For the first time in America the English method of transfer printing in decoration was adopted by these works. During the exciting Presidential campaign of 1840, or shortly after the election, a large eight-sided water-pitcher of cream-colored ware was produced, bearing on each of the four front panels black underglaze prints, consisting of an engraving of a log cabin at the top, over the legend "The Ohio Farmer," a portrait bust of W. H. Harrison in the centre, and the American eagle below. This piece was marked on the

50.—TOBY ALE JUG.   MADE BY D. & J. HENDERSON.   COLLECTION OF A. G. RICHMOND.

bottom, in black, under the glaze, with a flag bearing the inscription, "AM. POTTERY MANUF^G. CO. JERSEY CITY" (see chapter on Marks).   At this time Daniel Greatbach, who came from a family of noted English potters, and is said to have been at one time a modeller for the Ridgways of Cauldon Place, England, was employed at this factory, and designed a large number of ornate pieces, some of which were produced until the factory was closed.

An earthen water-pitcher, embellished with hunting-scenes in relief, and handle in form of a deer-hound, continued to be a popular design for nearly half a century (see Ill. 51).

In 1842, an exhibit of goods produced by this company was made at the Franklin Institute, con-sisting of embossed ware, jugs, tea-ware, etc., which took a silver medal.   A

51.—HUNTING PITCHER. DESIGNED BY DAN-IEL GREATBACH, JERSEY CITY POTTERY.

glazed white-ware spittoon, evidently one of this series, is still preserved in the cabinet of the Institute, which is decorated with raised, conventional designs in white, on a dark-blue ground, the upper surface being fluted and in solid blue.   A cream-colored pottery pan or nappie, of fine body and glaze, in the same collection, with impressed mark, AMERICAN POTTY CO. JERSEY CITY, is another ex-ample of the excellent ware produced at that time.

The name of the establishment was changed to *The Jersey City Pottery* about forty years ago. Many of the best potters of the old school in the United States learned their trade at this factory. In 1848 large quantities of druggists' jars were being made. After several alterations in the firm name, Messrs. Rouse and Turner became proprietors. The former, Mr. John Owen Rouse, came from the Derby Works, England, nearly forty years ago. Mr. Nathaniel Turner was born and reared among the Staffordshire potteries at Tunstall, and since his death, in 1884, the business has been carried on by Mr. Rouse alone. The products of the factory for some years have been ornamental forms in white biscuit and glazed ivory white for decorators, and porous cups for telegraphic purposes, of which some 5,000 have been produced weekly. Of the plain shapes in ivory white ware, one of the most graceful is the "Worcester" vase, so-called because it is a repro-

52.—"Worcester" Vase, Jersey City Pottery. Decorated by Mr. Edward Lycett.

duction of an old pattern produced at the Worcester Works in England. It is said that George Washington was

presented with a vase of this shape by Mr. Samuel Vaughan of London, in conjunction with a pair of vases of different design, which have been identified as Worcester pieces. An example of this form, from the Jersey City Pottery, is shown on p. 122. It measures two feet in height and was decorated by Mr. Edward Lycett. On a turquoise blue, mottled ground are artistically painted flowers, poppies on one side, and on the other hollyhocks in natural colors. A graceful wreath of convolvulus ornaments the cover. The handles are gilded, and bands of gold encircle top and bottom.

53.— "KING" VASE, JERSEY CITY POTTERY. DECORATED BY MR. W. LYCETT.

Another effective form was called the "King" vase. The example here figured was decorated by Mr. W. Lycett, now of Atlanta, Georgia. The subject on the side shown in the engraving

is " The Tired Dancing Girl." The painting is applied to
the ivory tint of the ware, the borders and handles being
of dead gold, heightened with black. On the reverse side
is a floral group. This piece measures sixteen and a half
inches in height.

When Mr. Rouse first became connected with the
works he found a large quantity of the old stock of undecorated porcelain in the warerooms, which has since
been sold. A large number of engraved copper plates on
hand at that time, since stolen or lost, showed to what extent transfer printing had formerly been practised. Hundreds of the old moulds were, until recently, stored in the
loft of the old building, among which were four different
varieties and sizes of Toby jugs, a pitcher with rope and
anchor decoration in relief, and another with raised designs
of tulips, a figure of Christ, an Apostle jug with raised
representations of apostles in panels, hunting pictures,
etc., some, if not all, being the work of Greatbach. We
have seen examples of the largest Toby pitcher made here
(about 1840), nearly a foot in height, with excellent brown
glaze outside and lined with white. Pitchers and other
pieces were also decorated with medallion portraits of
prominent men, modelled in relief, a likeness of Daniel
O'Connell being among the best.

In the summer of 1892 the old pottery property passed
into other hands, and the old buildings, which had stood in
almost their original condition for more than sixty-five
years, were torn down to make way for a new manufacturing establishment. Both wings of the original structure
were standing, in a good state of preservation until November of that year, when the work of demolition commenced,

and at the same time wagon loads of the old moulds, which had cost thousands of dollars, the accumulation of over half a century, were hauled away and ruthlessly dumped on the meadows. Thus has disappeared one of the oldest ceramic landmarks, dear to the memory of many an old potter still living, as the cradle of the pottery industry in the United States. All of the moulds of vessels were destroyed, but from this wreck a small series of ornamental designs, believed to have been, for the most part, made by Greatbach during the earlier years of the pottery's existence, were rescued by Mr. Rouse and, at the solicitation of the writer, placed in the collection of the Pennsylvania Museum of Art. These consist of finely modelled leaves, animals in hunting scenes, floral designs, and other decorative details.

In 1878 Messrs. Rouse and Turner presented to the Metropolitan Museum of Art, New York, a pottery barrel, with relief ornaments, made about 1830, at this pottery, by David Henderson. A many-sided pottery pitcher, surmounted with Toby head, is owned by Rev. F. E. Snow, of Guilford, Conn., on which is the mark, "AMERICAN POTTERY CO., JERSEY CITY, N. J." impressed in a circle.

Mr. John O. Rouse still continues the manufacture of porous cups within two blocks of the site of the old pottery.

CHAPTER VIII.

THE AMERICAN CHINA MANUFACTORY.

A
S we have already seen, several partially successful attempts had been made toward the manufacture of porcelain by progressive potters in the United States previous to the year 1825, but to Mr. William Ellis Tucker, of Philadelphia, belongs the honor of being the first to supply the home market with a purely American product of this character. The story of his remarkable life-work and the history of the factory which he established, the first important one of its kind on this side of the Atlantic, cannot fail to prove of especial interest to the ceramic student. Commencing his investigations with no previous knowledge of the composition of the ware, nor of the processes of its fabrication, he set resolutely to work to discover its hidden mysteries, and, wholly unaided by the practical experience of others, he succeeded in a few years in perfecting from new and untried materials, a porcelain equal in all respects to the best which England had produced after eighty years of continual experiment. His body was neither that of the French potters nor the true bone of the English, but partook of the characteristics of both, the proportion of phosphate of lime, as shown by analysis, being about eight per cent., a very much

smaller percentage than in the English bone body. While, therefore, the Tucker china cannot be classed as a soft paste, its specific gravity and thoroughly vitreous character would seem to fairly entitle it to be called a hard porcelain, which it more nearly resembles. Indeed, fire-tests made by Prof. Isaac Broome, to whom I submitted specimens, show that the Tucker porcelain will stand a higher degree of heat than the Sèvres ware.

Strange as it may appear, but little has been published relative to this early venture, although sixty years ago Philadelphians justly prided themselves on their " China Factory," and were in the habit of taking strangers to visit it, as one of the principal points of interest in the city. The following account of this enterprise includes most of the material which I prepared for *Lippincott's Magazine* of December, 1892, and a number of the illustrations used here have been furnished through the courtesy of the editor of that journal.

During the years 1816 to 1822, Benjamin Tucker, a member of the religious Society of Friends, had a china shop on the south side of Market (then called High) Street, at No. 324, between Ninth and Tenth streets, Philadelphia, near where the new Post-Office building now stands.[1] Within this period he built a small kiln in the rear of his property for the use of his son, William Ellis Tucker, who was thus enabled to employ much of his time in painting on the imported white china and firing it in

[1] Some time previous to 1825, Benjamin Tucker, the father, retired from the china business and established a select academy at the southwest corner of Fifth and Mulberry streets, where for several years he was known as a prominent educator. He had been a teacher from 1799 to 1814, as the Philadelphia directories show.

the kiln.   These attempts at decoration were at first crude and unsatisfactory, but they served to arouse an interest in the subject, which soon led him to commence experimenting with different clays which he procured in the vicinity of the city.   These investigations finally resulted in the production of a fair quality of opaque queensware.   He then turned his attention to kaolin and feldspar, and, after repeated failures, he at length succeeded in discovering the proper proportions of these ingredients, with bone-dust and flint, necessary for the manufacture of a high grade of porcelain.   The body thus obtained was translucent and of considerable hardness, density, and toughness, and capable of withstanding extreme changes of temperature.   The glaze was perfectly adapted to the body and of excellent composition.

About the year 1825, Mr. Tucker first seriously attempted the manufacture of the ware as a business venture. The old water-works at the northwest corner of Schuylkill-Front (Twenty-third) and Chestnut streets were obtained from the city, in which the necessary kilns, etc., were erected.[1]   On October 23, 1826, he purchased four acres of land, on which a feldspar quarry was situated, from Alexander Dixon, of Newcastle County, Delaware.

Mr. Thomas Tucker, a younger brother, who was at a later date, as we shall see, associated with him in the business, prepared an historical sketch of this factory, which was read before the Historical Society of Pennsylvania, on June 8, 1868.   The following quotations from this paper

[1] Mr. Charles Henry Hart informs me that a water-color, by Captain Watson, of the Royal Navy, entitled, "View from the Porcelain Factory near the Schuylkill Permanent Bridge," was exhibited at the Academy of Fine Arts, Philadelphia, in 1829.

will show some of the difficulties encountered in the manufacture of porcelain at that period :

" He burned kiln after kiln with very poor success.
The glazing would crack, and the body would blister ; and,
besides, we discovered that we had a man who placed the
ware in the kiln who was employed by some interested
parties in England to impede our success.

54.—The Old Water-Works, Philadelphia, Used as a China Manufactory
in 1825.

" Most of the handles were found in the bottom of the
seggars after the kiln was burned. We could not account
for it, until a deaf-and-dumb man in our employment
detected him running his knife around each handle as he
placed them in the kiln.

" At another time, every piece of china had to be
broken before it could be taken out of the seggar. We
always washed the round O's, the article in which the

china was placed in the kiln, with silex; but this man had washed them with feldspar, which of course melted, and fastened every article to the bottom. But William discharged him, and we got over that difficulty."

While the body and glaze of Tucker's earlier pieces were good, the workmanship and decoration were inferior.

A premium was offered by the Franklin Institute, at its Fourth Annual Exhibition, held in Philadelphia on October 18, 1827, "for the best specimen of *porcelain,* to be made in Pennsylvania, either plain white, or gilt,"

55.—TUCKER CREAMER.
SEPIA DECORATION.

and the following is taken from the report of the Committee on awards: "This is a manufacture of great importance to the country, as most of the capital expended is for labour; the materials being taken from our soil, in great abundance and purity. The highest credit is due to Mr. Wm. E. Tucker for the degree of perfection to which he has brought this valuable and difficult art. The samples (No. 174) of this ware were made by him. The body of the ware appeared to be strong, and sufficiently well fired, the glaze generally very good, the gilding executed in a neat and workmanlike manner. Some of the cups and other articles bear a fair comparison with those imported," and for this exhibit a silver medal was awarded.

In 1828 Mr. Thomas Tucker commenced to learn the different branches of the business. At the exhibition of the Franklin Institute in this year, Mr. Tucker received a second silver medal for the exhibit of one hundred pieces of best porcelain made in the United States, gilt, painted, and plain. The Judges compared it favorably with the best French china, and pronounced it superior in whiteness and gilding. During the same year, Mr. Thomas Hulme, of Philadelphia, invested some money in the business and was admitted to partnership, as appears by the mark found on a number of pieces made in that year, being printed in red, beneath the glaze,—"Tucker & Hulme, China Manufacturers, Philadelphia, 1828." These examples show a marked improvement in decoration over anything that had emanated from this factory before. The rough brown daubs intended for embellishment, but execrable to a degree, gave place during this period to artistic groupings of flowers and fruits, painted in natural colors. This partnership, however, does not seem to have continued for more than a year or so. Whether the withdrawal of funds from the business by Mr. Hulme proved an embarrassment to the senior partner does not appear, but it is known that Mr. Tucker soon afterward experienced the necessity of government support, and applied to Congress for aid. He placed himself in communication with some of the public men at the national capital, among others Andrew Jackson, as the following letter will show :

"WASHINGTON, April 3d, 1830.

"SIR,—I have had the honor to receive your letter of the 3d of March, and since, the porcelain which it offered to my acceptance. I was not apprised before of the perfection to which your skill and perseverance had brought this branch of American manufacture. It seems to be not inferior to the finest specimens of French porcelain. But whether the facilities for its manufacture bring its cost so nearly to an equality with that of the French, as to enable the moderate protection of which you speak to place it beyond the reach of competition in the markets of the world, is a question which I am not prepared to answer. If congress could be made acquainted with the experiments on the subject, and they should confirm your favorable anticipation, there would be scarcely a doubt of its willingness to secure the important results of the manufacture. I do not see, however, any mode by which this can be effected on any other principle than that of protection. You would probably have a right to a patent for the discovery, but this right would have to be determined in the usual way. Congress have refused to make a donation to the heirs of Robert Fulton for the national benefits resulting from his discovery, upon the principle that the Constitution does not provide any other reward for the authors of useful discoveries than that which is contained in the article in relation to Patents. The same objection would of course defeat your application for $20,000, as a remuneration for this discovery, or as a reward for its free communication to the world.

"It will give me much pleasure to promote the objects you have in view, so far as they are within my constitutional sphere. There is no subject more interesting to me than that which concerns the domestic economy of our country, and I tender you my sincere thanks for an example of its success so creditable to yourself.

"With great respect believe me
"Yr. Obt. Svt

"ANDREW JACKSON.

"Mr. WM. ELLIS TUCKER,
"Philadelphia."

While his application to Congress proved futile, he continued the manufacture, and in 1831 received from the American Institute of New York a silver medal for an exhibit of his wares in that year.

On the 22d of August, 1832, William Ellis Tucker died, but previous to that date Judge Joseph Hemphill,[1] of Philadelphia, had been admitted as a partner in the business. The latter had recently returned from a trip to Europe, where he had become deeply interested in the manufacture of porcelain. Messrs. Tucker and Hemphill purchased the property at the southwest corner of Schuylkill-Sixth (Seventeenth) and Chestnut streets, where they erected a large factory, storehouse, and three kilns, and greatly increased the producing capacity of the works. In 1832, scarcely two months before Mr. Tucker's death, they made another appeal to Congress for the passage of a tariff bill which would afford them protection from foreign competition. In reply to a letter written to

56.—"GRECIAN" PITCHER.

Henry Clay at that time, the following, bearing on this subject, was received :

[1] Judge Hemphill was born in Delaware Co., Pa., on January 7, 1770, and was appointed President Judge of the District Court in Philadelphia, by Gov. Snyder, in 1811, serving in that capacity for several years. He afterwards represented that city in Congress for three terms. He died on May 29, 1842.

I have not been able to ascertain that William Ellis Tucker, the china manufacturer, was related to William E. Tucker, who was at one time a prominent landscape and historical engraver in Philadelphia. The latter, while a contemporary of the former, lived until 1857, and was never interested in the porcelain industry. The similarity of names has naturally led to the erroneous impression that the potter and the engraver were one and the same, especially as the earliest productions of the Philadelphia China Factory were often decorated with landscapes and historical views.

"WASHINGTON, 23d June, 1832.

"GENTLEMEN :—I received your favor of the 21st inst. on the subject of your manufacture of Porcelain. I had been previously aware of its existence, and had seen some beautiful specimens of its production.

"When the Tariff bill shall be taken up in the Senate, I will take care that its attention shall be drawn to it. Such is the state of parties here, however, the friends of protection combating against the Treasury

57.—PORTRAIT OF JUDGE JOSEPH HEMPHILL.

bill, sustained by the whole weight of the Administration, that it is extremely difficult to anticipate results or any part of the Tariff.

"With great respect,

"I am your ob. serv.,

"Messrs. TUCKER & HEMPHILL,   "H. CLAY.

"Porcelain Manufacturers,

"Philadelphia."

A card in my possession, which has been kindly sent to me by Mr. James H. Buck, of Philadelphia, was issued from the new factory at Seventeenth and Chestnut streets about that time, a fac-simile of which is here given. It is interesting on account of the information it contains.

AMERICAN CHINA MANUFACTORY,
S. W. Corner of Schuylkill Sixth & Chesnut Sts.,
OR AT THE DEPOSITORY,
~~No. 206 Chesnut Street, above Eighth Street.~~

Where is constantly kept on hand, a superior assortment of CHINA, comprising DINNER SETS, TEA SETS, VASES, MANTEL ORNAMENTS, PITCHERS, FRUIT BASKETS, &c., &c., either plain or ornamented, and of the latest patterns, which may be purchased for Cash, at reduced prices.

ALSO ARE OFFERED FOR SALE,

FIRE-BRICK & TILE,

Of a superior quality, manufactured in part from the materials of which the China is composed.—These have been proved, by competent judges, to be equal to the best Stourbridge Brick.

After the death of the founder, Mr. Thomas Tucker continued to superintend the business, which was carried on in the name of Joseph Hemphill, who associated with him his son, the late Mr. Robert Coleman Hemphill, of West Chester, Pa.

In the settlement of Mr. Tucker's estate, the value of three kilns and slip pan, at the new factory, was estimated by Mr. Brinton Corlies, the appraiser, at $1,100, "the iron work not included."

Soon after the business passed into the hands of Judge Hemphill artists and artisans were brought over from France, England, and Germany, and a more pretentious style of decoration was introduced. The French methods of ornamentation came much into vogue about this time. The ware was sold very extensively to the well-to-do people in Pennsylvania and New Jersey, and nearly every family of prominence or wealth had table services or pieces made to order and decorated with initials, monograms, medallions, or amorial bearings, usually enclosed in wreaths of flowers or gold tracery. Compact bands of exquisitely painted flowers, in which the rose, tulip, and forget-me-not were generally prominent, encircled many of the finer pieces. Some of the vases and pitchers and many of the table pieces were close

copies of Sèvres forms, and some of the ware sold at the present time for French work by bric-a-brac dealers, was made in Philadelphia between 1833 and 1838. Excellent portraits of prominent men were painted on some of the larger pieces, an example of the latter being still preserved in a pitcher

58.—Hard-Paste Porcelain Pitcher Made by Tucker & Hemphill ca. 1833. Given by John T. Morris to the Philadelphia Museum of Art.

owned by Hon. William Wayne, of Paoli, Pa., which is embellished on one side with a view of the historic monument at Paoli, and on the other with a colored likeness of Major-General Anthony Wayne, copied from an oil portrait by Charles Wilson Peale. This interesting piece is one of a pair made for Colonel Isaac Wayne, son of General "Mad Anthony," and is marked on the bottom, in red, "Manufactured by Jos.

Hemphill, Philad." A similar example, in the Pennsylvania Museum, is a pitcher containing a tinted portrait of General Washington, which, according to Mr. Charles Henry Hart, an authority on Washington portraits, is evidently a copy of one of William Birch's enamels after Stuart's first picture, known as the Vaughan portrait, now in the possession of Mrs. Joseph Harrison, of Philadelphia. Mr. Ferdinand J. Dreer, of the same city, also owns a porcelain vase on which is a painting of Napoleon at the burning of Moscow, which he purchased at the factory in 1833.

In this year Judge Hemphill received honorable mention at the Exhibition of the Franklin Institute for his exhibit of "various samples of American porcelain, in the moulding and glazing of which great improvement has been made since the last exhibition ; the body of the article is considered equal, if not superior to that of the imported." He also received a diploma and silver medal from the American Institute of New York in the same year.

59.—VASE, NAPOLEON AT THE BURNING OF MOSCOW. MR. FERDINAND J. DREER.

The porcelain works continued with varying success for several years. By an Act of Assembly dated April 15, 1835,[1] an American Porcelain Company was incor-

[1] An Act to Incorporate an American Porcelain Company, passed April 15, 1835. Thomas P. Cope, Alexander Read, William P. Bryan, Thomas Tucker, Rockland

porated, consisting of Eastern gentlemen, to whom Judge
Hemphill sold his interest.   Whether this company ever
operated the works does not fully appear, but it would
seem doubtful, as Judge Hemphill made an exhibit of
wares again at the Franklin Institute in 1836.   It is said
that the company, being unfortunate in other enterprises,
were not able to give the porcelain manufacture proper
attention.

On October 1, 1837, after the retirement of Judge
Hemphill, the factory was leased for a term of six months
by Mr. Thomas Tucker, who purchased all of the unburned
ware then on hand, with the other materials and fixtures, as
appears in an article of agreement signed by John Rynex,
at Boston, who seems to have acquired the property, or
acted in the capacity of agent.   The new proprietor continued the manufacture of fine porcelain for about a year,
until he had filled a store, which he had taken on Chestnut street, above Seventh, with the ware.   He then
discontinued the making of porcelain, and engaged in the
business of importing china from Europe.   In the latter

Thompson, Robert Coleman Hemphill, and William M. Muzzey were appointed Commissioners.
    "Sec. 5.   The said company in the name and style of the American Porcelain
Company . . . shall have the further right . . . to rent or purchase, in
fee simple, the existing factory and house adjoining, at the corner of Schuylkill
Sixth and Chestnut streets, in the city of Philadelphia, with such other ground
as may be deemed necessary, also to purchase and hold, as aforesaid, quarries of
feldspar, beds of kaolin and clay and to procure every material used in the manufacturing of Porcelain, either plain, white or decorated with paintings and gilding,
and all the machinery, apparatus, tools and utensils required for the above purpose,
and to employ all such workmen, tradesmen, painters, gilders and other artists of every
description that may be necessary to carry on the establishment, either by sending
to Europe or otherwise :   And further, in order to enable the company to commence
immediate sales, they shall have the right to purchase the American Porcelain on hand
at the above factory, whether finished or in an unfinished state."—(*Pamphlet Laws of
Pennsylvania*, 1835, p. 338.)

part of 1841 he sold out his entire stock at his store, 100 Chestnut St., through Mr. C. C. Mackey, auctioneer. Mr. Tucker afterwards engaged in the cotton business, and died in Philadelphia in July, 1890.

It thus appears that the manufacture of Tucker and Hemphill porcelain was discontinued in the year 1838, after extending over a period of about thirteen years.

Kaolin for the earlier Tucker factory was obtained from the land of Israel Hoopes, in New Garden township, Chester County, Pa., now occupied by Graham Spencer. Feldspar was quarried from a large deposit on property owned by Alexander Dixon, near Christiana Hundred, Newcastle County, Delaware, about six miles from Wilmington, placed in barrels, hauled to the latter place, and loaded on vessels for shipment to Philadelphia. Blue clay, or fire-clay, was brought from John Flood's farm, four miles from Perth Amboy, N. J., which property came into possession of the heirs of W. E. Tucker at his death.

Mrs. Moses Johnson, of Berlin, Md., a great niece of Alexander Dixon, owns some of the earlier pieces made by Mr. Tucker, which were sent to her grandmother, as samples of the ware, about 1825 ; and Wilton Agnew, of Kennet Square, Pa., a nephew of Mr. Dixon, has in his possession two saucers, the remains of a set which was made for his mother about the same time, of spar taken from the Dixon quarry. These examples are all embellished with sepia landscapes.

Joseph S. Quarll, of Toughkenamon, Pa., is the possessor of two handsome pitchers, with floral paintings, made from kaolin which he helped to haul from New Garden to Wilmington in 1828, for the Tucker and Hulme factory. These are marked on the bottom, in red, "Tucker & Hulme, China Manufacturers, Philadelphia, 1828," and Esther H. West, of Avondale, near by, has a third piece, similarly signed and dated.

The feldspar quarries of Tucker and Hemphill were situated, in 1832, on Jacob Way's farm, directly opposite the Alexander Dixon quarries in Delaware, and in 1837, Judge Hemphill procured kaolin from the land of John Pennington, West Grove, Pa.

The first productions of the W. E. Tucker period are now scarce. The only attempts at ornamentation were crude and inartistic. Simple landscapes, butterflies and the like were painted roughly, always over the glaze, in sepia or brown monochrome. The former were all of the same general character,—a house, with lake in the foreground and mountains in the distance, produced by a few sweeps of the brush,—but no two exactly alike in details. The decoration was always done by hand; the printing or transfer process does not seem to have been employed at any time in the history of the works. A sugar-bowl and coffee-pot, with large butterflies rudely painted in brown, are the property of Joseph S. Quarll, and are characteristic examples of this period. Occasionally historic buildings were represented, as in a small plate in the possession of Mrs. Annie C. Tyndale, of Media, Pa., who received it from Mr. Horace J. Smith, of Philadelphia. This contains a painting of William Penn's cottage in monochrome.

During the Tucker and Hulme period, as has already been shown, there was a decided improvement in decoration. In addition to the pieces already mentioned, Mrs. Francis D. Wetherill, of Philadelphia, owns two pairs of pitchers made in 1828, one being marked in gold with the initials of her grandfather, Mr. John Price Wetherill, and the other pair with those of her great-uncle, Mr. Samuel P. Wetherill, the latter being dated. These were all made at the same time and are ornamented on both sides with bunches of tulips, roses, etc., in natural colors.

60.—SMALL COVERED FLOWER-VASE, SEPIA LANDSCAPE. MRS. R. C. HEMPHILL.

In my own possession are a teacup and saucer of fine, smooth paste and graceful form, embellished with gold fern work, and a small pitcher decorated in colors. In the Pennsylvania Museum at Fairmount Park, Philadelphia, may also be seen another specimen, presented by Mr. Charles Henry Hart, which is somewhat thicker and heavier than the others described above, and decorated only with gold bands and the letters C. B. This piece was made for Mr. Charles Burd and is marked on the bottom, in red, beneath the glaze, "Tucker & Hulme, Philadelphia, 1828."

A complete tea service belonging to Mrs. William McIlvaine, of Reading, Pa., procured from the factory in 1834 or '35, is decorated with sepia landscapes and gold bands, and conclusively shows that the monochrome style was still employed to some extent after Judge Hemphill took control.

We have no means of identifying the ware produced during the Tucker and Hemphill era, because the partnership was of such brief duration and none of the pieces appear to have been marked. Of the Hemphill period, however, numerous exam-

61.—*Hard-Paste Porcelain Pitcher Made by Tucker & Hemphill ca. 1835. Given by John T. Morris to the Philadelphia Museum of Art.*

ples are in existence. Perhaps some of the finest are owned by Mrs. Robert Coleman Hemphill, of West Chester, Pa., a daughter-in-law of Judge Hemphill, which were made expressly for the family by the best workmen in the factory. A small flower-vase, painted in colors, shows the best work produced. A cylindrical flower-pot, with wreath of flowers encircling the circumference ; a toilet-set, decorated in the same elaborate manner and heavily gilded ; a large water-pitcher,

62.—HEMPHILL VASE.   COLLECTION OF HON. JAMES T. MITCHELL.

the lower half with raised ornamentation in white, consisting of horses and dogs, the upper portion decorated with a band of artistically painted flowers and gold tracery, are a few of the pieces which remain of a large collection. The relief design on the latter bears a

remarkable resemblance to that which occurs on an old English parian pitcher in the Trumbull-Prime collection at Princeton. The *chef-d'œuvre* of the series, however, is a cylindrical night lamp, of thin, transparent porcelain, exquisitely decorated with a continuous rural scene in bright colors, extending around the centre (see Ill. 70).

Hon. James T. Mitchell, of the Supreme Court of Pennsylvania, is the owner of a flaring vase, six inches high, on which

63.—HEMPHILL VASE, WITH PAINTING OF A SHIPWRECK.

is painted a group of fruits and flowers and on the opposite side, in gold, "E. Tyndale, 1833," having been made for his mother at the Hemphill factory and presented to her in that year.

A pair of amphora-shaped vases in the possession of Mrs. Amanda Spiegel, of Philadelphia, which were presented to her father-in-law, Mr. Isaac Spiegel, when in the employ of Judge Hemphill, are copies of an old Sèvres form and measure about a foot in height, being in two parts. They are of a good semi-transparent body, decorated with much goldwork and marine views depicting shipwrecks. The painting is excellently executed, evidently by a French artist (Ill. 63).

Mr. William S. Negus, of Bound Brook, N. J., has a

64.—HEMPHILL PORCELAIN TABLE-WARE. COLLECTION OF MR. W. S. NEGUS.

table service which was made by Judge Hemphill about 1834. It is remarkable for its bands of pink roses and heavy goldwork, the interior of the cups being solidly gilded half-way to the bottom.

A christening-bowl, " Presented to the First Presbyterian Church, West Chester, Chester County (Pa.), February 22, 1834, by Joseph Hemphill of Philadelphia," is a fine example of the ware made at that time. It measures nine and one half inches across and is decorated with heavy gold bands at the top and bottom, solidly gilded handles, and gold wreath with blue forget-me-nots, in which is inclosed the above inscription, also in gold.

In the family of the late Mr. Thomas Tucker, of Philadelphia, some of the best pieces of the later productions of this factory are preserved. These include two pairs of cologne bottles (see Ill. 69), of different size and design, made after Chinese patterns, elaborately ornamented with goldwork applied to relief designs, and the date 1837; a vase with painting of the factory at

65.—CHRISTENING-BOWL. MRS. THOMAS W. MARSHALL.

Seventeenth and Chestnut streets, and a pitcher painted with flowers and birds, after nature, the mate of which is owned by Mrs. General Hector Tyndale of the same city. Perhaps one of the finest examples ever made by Mr. Tucker is the large vase, owned by his widow, which is over two feet in height and embellished with a wreath of richly painted flowers and gold and salmon-colored bands. The plinth is solidly gilded, as are the handles, which are in the form of eagles' heads, with wings meeting above.

66.—*Hard-Paste Porcelain Vase made (1832-1838) by Tucker & Hemphill and Showing Their Factory (see drawing below). Facing page 147: A page from the Thomas Tucker Polychrome Book, 1832-1838. Both given in memory of Thomas Tucker by Eliza Amand Tucker to the Philadelphia Museum of Art.*

One of the most characteristic patterns produced by the old Philadelphia China Factory was the classical pitcher with circular body, arched handle, and corrugated band at base. This form has become the most familiar

№ 34

to the public because it was a favorite with the manufacturers and seems to have been peculiar to this factory.   It was known as the "vase-shaped" pattern.   Another rather common form was the cylindrical vase with flaring mouth, a reproduction of an old French form.   It is not generally known that the Tucker and Hemphill productions included an almost endless variety of ornamental as well as utilitarian forms, hence some of the rarest pieces are not recognized by collectors, but are thought to be French.   Some idea may be obtained of the variety of forms when it is known that the original pattern

67.—Large Porcelain Vase, Over-glaze Decoration in Gold and Colors.   Owned by Mrs. Thomas Tucker.

books (which at the suggestion of the writer have been presented to the Pennsylvania Museum by Mrs. Thomas Tucker) show, during the last six years of the factory's history, over 140 different standard designs in table pieces and vases alone. Many other pieces, such as spirit lamps with teapots, flower jars, miniature and picture frames, smelling vials, inkstands, mantel ornaments, etc., were made to some extent, and examples of these are still occasionally met with. Small porcelain bottles with stoppers were made in three forms,—cordate,[1] shell-shaped, and eared, and daintily decorated in colors, for holding smelling salts and cologne.

68.—" VASE-SHAPED " PITCHER, OVER-GLAZE DECORATION IN COLORS AND GOLD. PENNSYLVANIA MUSEUM.

Other forms of pitchers made at these works were called the " Star," " Grecian," " Fletcher," and " Walker" shapes. Some of the most characteristic decorations, in addition to those already described, were landscapes in black, or in brown and green, tiny pink roses scattered over the entire surface, and large bold roses in natural colors. On table ware, festoons of gold and minute bands of gold flowers ; small blue, green, and brown " corn flowers " ; purple and green vines ; green periwinkles with brown stems ; pink, blue, and green

[1] The plaster mould for the heart-shaped scent bottle was until recently in the Franklin Institute. It is now in the collection of the Pennsylvania Museum, Philadelphia.

sprays; wreaths and bunches of flowers in which the
rose, tulip, forget-me-not, morning-glory, ragged-robin,
honey-suckle,—all in delicate colors,
and fern leaves and moss rose-buds
in gold. Scalloped cups and saucers,
with broad vertical bands of alter-
nate pink and brown, were also
made, and handles of sauce boats
and other utensils were often moulded
in the forms of serpents' and lizards'
heads.

The following price list of articles
made at Seventeenth and Chestnut
streets, between 1832 and 1838, copied
from the records of the factory, will
show what the public paid in those
days for undecorated pieces of the
ware :

69.—Cologne Bottle,
Raised Decorations,
Gold Tracery. Mrs.
Thomas Tucker.

Pitchers	$1.00	each.
Teapots	1.06¼	"
"	1.25	"
"	1.00	"
Sugars	75	"
"	62½	"
Coffee-pots	2.00	"
Creams	37½	"
Gravy boats	50	"
Shell dishes	1.00	"
Custard stands	3.00	"
Square comforts	1.00	"
Round dishes	75	"
Fruit baskets	2.00	"
Stands for same	75	"

High comporteers........................ 2.50 each.
Cake stands.............................. 1.00 "
Salads, octagon.......................... 2.00 "
Tumblers................................. 3.00 doz.
Large plates............................. 4.50 "
Cup plates............................... 1.50 "
Plates................................... 2.50 "
   "   .... 4.00 "
Muffins.................................. 2.00 "
Dishes................................... 2.00 each.
   "   .... 1.75 "
Saucers.................................. 1.50 doz.
   "   .... 2.00 "
Cake saucers............................. 0.25 each.
Terrenes................................. 3.50 "
Cups..................................... 1.50 doz.

The pattern books of the china factory contain drawings of pieces not enumerated in the foregoing list, on
which the selling prices were marked.   From these books,
which have been kindly placed at my disposal, I take the
following :

Cylindrical spirit lamps, with teapots........$1.60 each.
Vase shaped "   "   "   "   .... 2.50 "
Large pedestal vases (undecorated, of course) 1.50 "
French vase (amphora-shaped)............ 1.50 "
Butter coolers.......................... 1.00 "
Funnels................................. 2.00 "
Pitchers (Fletcher's shape).............. 1.50 "
   "   (Walker shape) third size......... 37½ "
   "   (Grecian shape)................. 75 "
   "   (Vase shape).................. 1.00 "
   "   (Star shape).................. 1.00 "
Round jugs, small....................... 50 "

Some of the wages paid at the factory to artists, in
1832, for decorating pieces were as follows :

Landscapes (in brown)...................	4 cts each.
Phœnix	2 " "
Bands (gold)...........................	8 " doz.
Best groups (colored)...................	18¾ " each.
Common groups........................	12½ " "
Fruit baskets..............	18¾ " "
Mantels,[1] richly ornamented...............	25 " "
Cyphers, from one to four................	2 " "

Prices for burnishing, same date :

$10 Pitchers...........................	15 cts.
Vases, full gilt.........................	15 cts.

The wages paid for making, turning, finishing, etc., were as follows :

Mantel ornaments, large size.............	8 cts. each.
" " second size...........	6 " "
Large size coffee-pots...................	20 " "
Oyster dishes, large size.................	25 " "
Slop bowls.............................	4 " "
Moulded cups......	1 " "
" saucers......................	1 " "
Extra large size dinner plates.............	3 " "
" " " breakfast plates...........	2 " "
Tea plates.............................	1 ct. "
Cup plates.............................	1 ct. "

For Moulding :

Teapots...............................	12¼ cts.
Pitchers (two quarts)...................	12¼ "
Gravy boats	12¼ "
Fruit baskets	20 "

John Basten, from England, was foreman of the factory for many years. Mr. George Morgan, who is still living and now in the employ of the S. S. White Dental

[1] Mantel ornaments.

Manufacturing Company, Philadelphia, when a boy turned a wheel for one of the throwers in the old China Manufactory. His elder brother, Joseph Morgan, was a moulder in the works during the entire period of the factory's existence. Andrew Craig Walker, recently deceased, was one of the best hands employed in moulding the finer pitchers and many pieces are still preserved with his mark, a " W," scratched under the glaze. Isaac

Spiegel and Jacob Baker tended the kilns and superintended the preparation of the clays, and it is said that the former made many valuable suggestions to the proprietors of the works in regard to improvements in the construction of the kilns. Other workmen in the factory were William Hand, an Englishman, widely known among the craft on account of his diminutive stature, Thomas B. Harned, Charles Frederick and one

70.—NIGHT-LAMP DECORATED WITH RURAL SCENE IN COLORS. MRS. R. C. HEMPHILL.

Vivian, a Frenchman. Charles J. Boulter was also connected for some time with the establishment and William Chamberlain, a Philadelphian, was employed as one of the decorators. It is difficult, at this late day, to procure information relative to many of those connected with the establishment, as nearly all have passed away. The private marks of some of the moulders and turners are given in our chapter on American Marks and Monograms, but other initials are frequently met with on pieces of the Tucker and Hemphill ware, which cannot now be identified.

It is impossible to set down any rules by which this ware can always be known. There are certain peculiarities of form and decoration which are easily recognized and some pieces may be identified by the private marks upon them. Many, however, which are not marked, can with difficulty be distinguished from French productions, even by the connoisseur.

Just why this venture should not have proved more of a financial success, we are unable to understand at this remote period, though it can readily be seen that the high cost of foreign skilled labor and the expensive gilding which was used so lavishly were, doubtless, important factors in the heavy losses which the promoters of the undertaking sustained. The pieces yet in existence are generally carefully preserved as heirlooms in the families of those who procured them from the manufacturers, and the few examples which, from time to time, find their way into the market are eagerly purchased by collectors, both on account of their comparative rarity and because they possess qualities which have not been surpassed by the best of imported or domestic productions.

CHAPTER IX.

THE POTTERY INDUSTRY FROM 1825 TO 1858.

A STONEWARE pottery was established in Baltimore, Md., in 1827 by Mr. Perine, who was afterwards joined by his son, Mr. T. P. Perine. At the death of the senior partner, the latter became sole proprietor. The style is at present M. Perine & Sons. They manufacture stoneware in the usual lines of useful articles, Rockingham, hand- and machine-made flower-pots, terra-cotta drain pipe and fire-clay chimney pipe. They make a specialty of fancy flower-pots and stands and hanging-baskets, in unique designs. They received the Centennial medal for superiority of goods exhibited in 1876. The trade of this house is mainly wholesale and extends throughout the Southern as well as the Northern States.

In 1831 Messrs Horner & Shirley were engaged in the manufacture of flint stoneware in New Brunswick, N. J., in which year they exhibited some of their productions at the Franklin Institute, Philadelphia.

As early as 1832, or thereabout, plain fire-brick and tile were made by the American China Factory in Philadelphia, then operated by Messrs. Tucker & Hemphill. They advertised these products as being " of a superior quality, manufactured in part from the materials of which the china is composed. These have been proved, by competent judges, to be fully equal to the best Stourbridge brick," which have been celebrated for their excellence for nearly a century and a half. The fire-clays of the Stourbridge district have been used for upward of three hundred years by British manufacturers.

Isaac Spiegel, a workman at the old Philadelphia China Factory of Messrs. Tucker & Hemphill, started in business for himself in Kensington, Philadelphia, about the year 1837. He made Rockingham, black and red ware of good quality, some in ornamental shapes, such as miniature barrels, card-baskets, and Rockingham figures. Some of the machinery was moved to his pottery from the Hemphill factory on the closing of the latter, and he secured many of the moulds which had been used for making ornamental porcelain pieces. In 1855 Mr. Spiegel retired from active business, and was succeeded by his son, Isaac, who carried on the works until 1879. He made fire-brick and tiles in 1858, and later produced mantel ornaments in Rockingham, such as figures of lions and dogs. In 1880 John Spiegel, a brother of the latter, resumed the business, and a few years after made Barbotine ware, biscuit decorated with floral designs moulded separately and attached to the surface of vases. He also made vases and plaques in biscuit for decorators, but discontinued this branch some years ago. At present he is engaged in burning magnesia for the drug trade.

THE OHIO VALLEY.

Mr. John Hancock came to America from England in 1828 and commenced the erection of a pottery at South Amboy, N. J.   In the following year he sent over for his wife and son Frederick, who brought with them two turners, one from Minton's named Bernard Houston, and one thrower, Charles Harrison.   On the arrival of these workmen Mr. Hancock had his pottery finished and commenced at once the manufacture of yellow ware.   Mr. John Hancock was a potter of large and varied experience, having served an apprenticeship at Etruria with Josiah Wedgwood.   According to his son, Mr. Frederick Hancock, who is still living in Bennington, Vt., at an advanced age, he was at one time manager for Mr. James Clews at Cobridge, England, and made the colors used in decorating the wares at that factory.   In 1821 he left Clews and went with Mr. Lewis Weston Dillwyn, at the Cambrian Potteries, Swansea, Wales.

In 1840, Mr. Hancock, with his son, went to Louisville, Ky., and started a stoneware pottery there.   In 1841 the elder Hancock went to East Liverpool, Ohio, and engaged in the manufacture of yellow and Rockingham wares, in the building called the Mansion House, in company with Messrs. James Salt and Frederick Mear.   Mr. Hancock died in East Liverpool in 1842.

Mr. Frederick Hancock, who was born in 1817, came to the United States from Hanley, Staffordshire, in the fall of 1829, and learned the stoneware trade with Mr. Israel Seymour of Troy, N. Y.   In 1839 he went to Bennington, Vt., and worked in the stoneware pottery of

Messrs. Norton & Fenton for a short time.   In 1840, as
we have seen, he accompanied his father to Louisville.
In the following year he returned to Bennington, where,
in the spring of 1851, he worked in the United States
Pottery.   He next went to Worcester, Mass., in 1858,
and established another pottery which he operated
until 1877, when he sold his interest and returned to
Bennington.

The Lewis Pottery Company was incorporated in
Louisville, Ky., in the year 1829, for the purpose of making queensware and china, the incorporators being Robert
Ormsby, James McG. Cuddy, Jacob Lewis, Edmund T.
Bainbridge, and John J. Jacob.   Messrs. Vodrey & Frost,
who had been in business in Pittsburgh, Pa., for about
two years, were induced by these parties to move their
plant to Louisville in that year, and began the manufacture of a fair grade of cream-colored ware.   Mr. Frost
retired in two or three years, and the business was continued by Messrs. Vodrey and Lewis until about 1836,
when the firm was dissolved.   The dissolution was oc-
casioned by the advent of a prominent English potter,
Mr. James Clews, who, being a man of fine presence and
a fluent talker, so impressed some of the capitalists of
Louisville that he succeeded in forming a company with
an ample capital for building and operating a new pottery
at Troy, Indiana.

POTTERY AT TROY, INDIANA.

Mr. James Clews operated the extensive potteries at
Cobridge, England, from about 1820 to 1829, which had

been worked since 1808 by Messrs. Bucknall & Stevenson, and afterwards by Mr. A. Stevenson. He was also proprietor of other works lying between Cobridge and Burslem, and manufactured extensively white-ware table services for the American market. Many of his now highly prized pieces were decorated with dark-blue transfer prints of American views, examples still being common in the cabinets of American collectors. Among the most familiar of these are views on the Hudson River, the Erie Canal, the "States" plate, of which I have seen nine varieties, and services embellished with a representation of the "Landing of Gen. Lafayette at Castle Garden, New York, 16 August, 1824." Perhaps no English potter was better known on this side of the Atlantic through his wares than Mr. Clews. The deep, rich coloring of his under-glaze printing was not surpassed by any other manufacturer of that day, and the mark, "Clews Warranted Staffordshire," impressed in a circle around a crown, made his name a household word throughout the States.

It is not generally known that Mr. James Clews, after the closing of his English works in 1829, came to America and took charge of a similar manufactory in the United States, yet such was the case, and this fact will add greater interest to his productions, which, having preceded him to this country, we still preserve. The town of Troy, Indiana, was selected for the location of the new works, on account of its favorable situation on the Ohio River, which furnished excellent transportation to the larger cities of the South, East, and West, and because of its proximity to the necessary materials for manufacturing, which had been recently discovered, of excellent quality and in great abundance. The Indiana Pottery Co. was incorporated by special act of the Legislature of January 7, 1837, the incorporators being Reuben Bates, James Clews, Samuel Casseday, William Bell, James Anderson, Jr., Edmund T. Bainbridge, Perly Chamberlin, William Garvin, John B. Bland, Jacob Lewis, and Willis Ranney. The capital stock was $100,-000, with privilege to increase to $200,000, and the act recited that the same parties had previously been transacting business as the " Lewis Pottery Co." From the *History of Warrick, Spencer, and Perry Counties* (Ind.) we extract the following relating to this enterprise : " It was thought that the finer ware made so extensively in England could be made from the Troy clay. Reuben Bates gave as his portion of the investment a tract of about 160 acres of land, on much of which was the clay. The other members of the company furnished means to build the necessary houses and buy the necessary apparatus. Supposed experienced potters in considerable numbers were induced to come from England, as this was thought necessary to insure success to the new enterprise. . . . The pottery started up with flattering prospects, but in a short time . . . . the impossibility of making white ware from the clay was demonstrated, and after a year of anxiety and effort on the part of the company, business was suspended and the property was either transferred to, or placed in charge of, Samuel Casseday, of Louisville, who after that, from time to time, leased it to the leading workmen who had come from England, or others."

It is a matter of surprise that under Mr. Clews' management the products of the Troy works should not have proved of a higher order, since his earlier cream-colored ware and stone china, made in England, were of a superior quality. His failure in this respect can only be explained by the incompetency of his workmen and the unsuitableness of the clays which were used. The attempt to make white ware resulted only in the production of an inferior grade of pottery of a dark cream color, fragments of which have been sent to me by Mr. Benjamin Hinchco of Troy, who unearthed them in digging around the premises. The manufacture of this was soon discontinued, and yellow and Rockingham wares were substituted. I have searched in vain for pieces of print-decorated ware made by Mr. Clews in America from plates used by him in England, since it would seem reasonable to suppose that he would bring some of the old engravings, which had originally been made for the American market, with him to his new field of labor. The only style of decoration which I have been able to find on any of his American-made wares is a rudely painted border in blue, under the glaze, such as was common on the cheaper grades of white ware made at that time. Messrs. William Brownfield & Sons, who now carry on the Cobridge works in England, inform me that none of the old plates are now in existence.

After considerable money had been sunk in the Troy venture, the business was discontinued, and Mr. Clews returned to England, where he died, in 1856, at the age of about seventy. He was a remarkably sagacious and enterprising manufacturer in his day, and at one time amassed considerable wealth, much of which he subsequently lost.   His son, Mr. Henry Clews, of New York City, is well known in financial circles.

In the spring of 1839, the company induced Mr. Jabez Vodrey to move to Troy and take charge of the pottery.   With what hands he could procure in Louisville, he put the pottery in operation in March of that year, and continued to run it with varying success until 1846, when, from lack of skilled labor and capital, he was forced to abandon it, and in 1847 moved to East Liverpool, Ohio.

In 1851, John Sanders and Samuel Wilson leased the Troy works from Mr. Casseday, who was then the recognized owner of the property, and continued the manufacture of yellow and Rockingham goods until 1854, when the buildings were burned down ; but another pottery was soon afterwards erected on the same site.   Mr. Sanders continued the business until 1863, when he died. Mr. Benjamin Hinchco then leased the property and operated the works until they were torn down, about twenty years ago.

William Ridgway, of Hanley, England, was another eminent potter who commenced operations in this country after having manufactured extensively for the American trade for' many years in England.   He was associated there with his brother John, under the firm name of J. & W. Ridgway, and many of the old blue pieces now so eagerly sought for by collectors, with American views, were made at the Hanley potteries.   Of these, the series entitled " Beauties of America," which included views of the Philadelphia Library, Staughton's Church, Philadelphia, Capitol at Washington, and City Hall New York, were the most familiar. William Ridgway afterwards left his brother and became interested in no less than six important potteries in England. He continued to hold the American trade by making extensively china with light blue and black prints of American scenery. Of the latter I have before me some river scenes, such as views on the Hudson, the Delaware Water Gap, the Bridge at Harper's Ferry, the Columbia Bridge on the Susquehanna (Pa.), and others. Few collectors who are familiar with the Ridgway china are aware that the younger brother, William, contemplated the removal of his manufactory to this country. He pushed his plans so far as to commence the erection of a pottery on a large scale in Kentucky, which for some reason was never completed. The ruins of the partially built walls are still to be seen near the mouth of the Big Sandy River, near the West Virginia line.

A family of German potters, whose name was Boch, commenced the manufacture of porcelain hardware trimmings on Long Island, N. Y., about 1850, which industry has since flourished.to such a remarkable degree at Greenpoint. They started, at various times, several potteries and were sometime connected with the " Empire " and " Union Porcelain Works," and two different factories at Flushing. William Boch & Brother exhibited at the Crystal Palace Exhibition of New York, in 1853, stair rods and plates of decorated porcelain, plain and gilded porcelain trimmings for doors, shutters, drawers, etc. Noah Boch, a grandson, is now connected with the knob department of the Greenwood Pottery, at Trenton, N. J.

Charles Cartlidge had a china factory at Greenpoint previous to the middle of the present century. He had been a potter in England, and was agent for the Ridgways, an English house, before he commenced potting himself in the United States. Messrs. Charles Cartlidge & Co. exhibited at the New York Crystal Palace bone porcelain tea sets, pitchers, bowls, and fancy ware, also door knobs, door plates, etc. A large curtain knob, of bone porcelain, decorated with gold, has been sent to me by Mr. W. J. Stickney, of Salem, Mass., who procured it from the stock of an old crockery shop in that town which forty years ago was a depository for American wares. It is reasonably certain that this example was made at one of these establishments on Long Island, in all probability the Cartlidge works. The body is of excellent quality, the glazing good, and the gilding evidently the work of an experienced decorator. The disk measures four inches in diameter and the stem is three and a half inches in length. Mr. Cartlidge became a prominent man in the community in which he resided and founded a church there, in which, it is said, he sometimes preached. At his death his brother William, who had been associated with him, went to East Liverpool, Ohio, where he died some years ago.

Mr. Cartlidge employed good artists to model and decorate his wares. Much of his porcelain was painted in colors and gold over the glaze. I have seen door plates and table pieces of excellent paste with artistically grouped floral designs after nature. Among the best decorators connected with the establishment were Mr. Frank Lockett and Mr. Elijah Tatler.

In addition to hardware porcelain and table pieces, Mr. Cartlidge produced some very excellent jewelry cameos and portrait busts in biscuit porcelain. Of the latter, heads of Chief-Justice Marshall, Archbishop Hughes, Daniel Webster, and Zachary Taylor were among the best, and a diminutive bust of Henry Clay, made for a cane handle, is a beautiful piece of modeling and a striking likeness. In the possession of Mrs. Annie C. Tyndale, a daughter of Mr. Cartlidge, are some finely executed brooch medallions, consisting of miniature family portraits, ideal heads and grotesque faces in relief, and a rhyton or drinking cup in the form of a wolf's head. Work of this high order of merit, however, was not in sufficient demand in the United States at that day to insure financial success and much money was lost in the enterprise. The factory was closed in 1856 and Mr. Cartlidge died in 1860.

Mr. J. L. Jensen, who was at one time connected with the Union Porcelain Works, took the Greene Street factory, called the "Empire Pottery," which had been built some time previously by the Bochs, and commenced the manufacture of porcelain hardware fittings, electrical supplies, jugs, cuspidors, etc., and is still successfully operating it.

The East Morrisania China Works of D. Robitzek, on 150th Street, near Third Avenue, New York City, formerly made porcelain door knobs and hardware trimmings. The present products are white granite, cream-colored, and decorated wares.

In 1843, at the exhibition of the Franklin Institute, Philadelphia, two porcelain baskets, made by Messrs. Bagaly & Ford, were shown by General H. Tyndale. The judges pronounced them "a well finished article for American manufacture."

THE UNITED STATES POTTERY, BENNINGTON, VT.

Messrs. Christopher Weber Fenton, Henry D. Hall, and Julius Norton commenced making yellow, white, and Rockingham wares at Bennington, Vt., about the year 1846, in the north wing of the old stoneware shop (which had been erected in 1793 by the Norton family), operated by Messrs. Norton and Fenton. The new firm brought from England one John Harrison, who did their first modelling. Mr. Hall did not remain long in the company and after he and Mr. Norton withdrew, the style was changed to Lyman & Fenton, by the admission to the firm of Mr. Alanson Potter Lyman, a prominent practising attorney of Bennington, and shortly after to Lyman, Fenton, & Park. Rockingham, yellow, and white wares continued to be made and some creditable work in parian was turned out.

In 1849 Mr. Anson Peeler, a master carpenter, was engaged to erect suitable buildings for the company. The new quarters were finished in this year and the factory became known as the United States Pottery. Mr. Fenton took out a patent about the same time for the coloring of glazes for pottery. The manufacture of "Patent Flint Enameled Ware" (which was a fine quality of Rockingham, somewhat analogous to our modern so-called majolica) was added, white granite ware was made extensively, and soft-paste porcelain was produced in a small way. Artists were procured from abroad to decorate the ware, among whom was Mr. Theophile Fry, a skillful painter, who is believed to have come from Belgium or France. Mr. Daniel Greatbach, who belonged to a family of prominent English artists, went from the Jersey City Pottery and modelled some of their best pieces. The trade-mark adopted and used to a limited extent on parian pieces was a raised scroll or ribbon with the letters U. S. P. impressed, and a number indicating the pattern. This ware was decorated with raised figures in white, sometimes on a blue ground. Pieces were also frequently made after English designs. An example of this style is a graceful parian pitcher belonging to the writer, which is embellished with raised foliage and human figures on a "pitted" dark-blue ground. This is an enlarged reproduction of a syrup jug from the Dale Hall Works, England. Pieces with similar decoration are owned by Mr. G. B. Sibley, of Bennington. Mr. L. W. Clark, of the New England Pottery Co., who, when a young man, was connected with the United States Pottery, while his father, Mr. Decius W. Clark, was superintendent of the works, informs me that the "pitting" on the grounds of such pieces is done in the model with a single pointed tool, only one indentation being made at a stroke. The pit marks are made close together, covering the parts to be colored, which presents the appearance of a thimble surface. A mould made from the pitted model, of course, carries the reverse impressions, or points. The rough or pointed surface of the interior of the mould is covered with a blue slip by means of a camel's-hair brush. Then the mould is set up and white slip poured in, as is usual in casting. The white slip attracts the blue and takes it

71.—BENNINGTON PARIAN. BLUE PITTED GROUND.

from the slip-painted sides of the mould. A group of Bennington blue and white parian is here figured, consisting of pitchers, a vase, and cane handle (Ill. 71). The blue ground varies in different pieces from a light to a dark shade, the raised decorations being pure white. The uncolored parians were generally of a grayish white color and more refined and marble-like in tone than those with blue ground.   A group is shown in Illustration 72.

Parian pitchers were usually glazed inside, while many, particularly the blue and white, were finished outside with a "smear" glaze, produced by coating the interior of the seggar, in which they were burned, with glaze, which, under the fire, vaporizes and imparts to the ware a glossy surface.   Small parian and porcelain statuettes, designed

72.—WHITE PARIAN.   U. S. POTTERY.

for mantel ornaments, were also made to some extent. Toilet-sets, pitchers, door plates, escutcheons, and other pieces, in white granite and porcelain, were often decorated with gold and colored designs, and with the names of customers or recipients.   The group of white granite ware shown (Ill. 73) consists of a cow-creamer with gold decoration, swan mantel ornament with base edged with blue under the glaze, and water-pitcher with dark blue

under-glaze and heavy gold decorations. The latter bears
the date February 28, 1858, and was one of the last
pieces made at this factory. The large ornamental figure
represents a girl at prayer. Mr. Charles R. Sanford of
Bennington Centre was at one time connected with the
U. S. Pottery, and he has preserved a number of interesting pieces made there, including two dogs of parian,
several pitchers, and a Rockingham figure of a deer.

73.—WHITE GRANITE WARE.   U. S. POTTERY.

In 1851, or the year following, Mr. Fenton had a
large monumental piece made, ten feet in height (see
Illustration 74), in four sections, the lower, or base, being
composed of several varieties of clay, mixed together to
produce the appearance of unpolished, variegated marble.
This represented the "lava ware" made at that time.
The second section was made of pottery, covered with

colored glaze, and represented the "Flint Enameled Ware." Above this was a life-sized parian bust of Mr. Fenton, surrounded by eight Rockingham columns, and the whole was surmounted by a parian figure of a woman, represented in the act of presenting the Bible to an infant. This work is said to have been designed by Mr. Fenton, but modelled by Greatbach, and was placed on exhibition at the New York Crystal Palace in 1853. It now stands on the porch of Mr. Fenton's former residence in Bennington, a monument to his enterprise and genius. I am informed by Mr. L. W. Clark that several duplicates of this monument were made, as it was at first the intention of Mr. Fenton to utilize them as stoves, but the idea was afterwards abandoned.

By quoting from Horace Greeley's *Art and Industry at the Crystal Palace, New York*, we are enabled to gain an excellent idea of the various wares produced at the Bennington factory at that time. He says: "Around this monument are displayed table and scale standards, Corinthian capitals, figures, vases, urns, toilet-sets, and a great variety of other specimens in porcelain, plain and inlaid. The pitchers in porcelain are deserving of notice, as a branch of natural industry; though not decorated beyond a gilt molding, and, therefore, not attractive as china, yet they possess the first elements of good ware— that is, an uniform body without any waving, and of well-mixed and fine materials. . . . The superiority of the Flint Enamel Ware over the English consists in the addition of silica combined with kaolin, or clay from Vermont, which, when in properly adjusted proportions, produces

74.—ROCKINGHAM MONUMENT. MADE AT BENNINGTON, VT., 1851.

an article possessing great strength, and is perfectly fireproof.   Telegraph insulators in white flint are on exhibition ; this material being one of the best electric non-conductors that can be found.   Various forms of insulators are in the collection.   This ware has been employed on the telegraphs in the vicinity of Boston.   Among these specimens is a patented form, recommended by Mr. Batchelder, which has a shoulder with a re-entering angle of forty-five degrees ; this angle causes the wind and rain to pass downward, and prevents the inside of the insulator from being wet.   This enamel ware comprises a variety of assorted articles, candlesticks, pitchers, spittoons, picture-frames, tea-pots, etc.   This ware has become a favorite article in New England and possesses much merit as cottage furniture.   The lava ware is a combination of clays from Vermont, New Jersey, Carolina, etc. ; composed of silica and feldspar, intermixed with the oxydes of iron, manganese and cobalt.   It is the strongest ware made from pottery materials ; the glaze upon this lava ware and upon the flint ware is chiefly flint and feldspar, and has, therefore, to be subjected to such an intense heat to fuse it, as would destroy the glaze upon common crockery.   The colors upon the flint ware are produced by different metallic oxydes applied on the glaze, which latter serves as a medium to float them about upon the surface, while in a state of fusion, thus producing the variegated tints.

"The Parian ware of this Company is remarkably fine, especially in the form of pitchers.   They are light in material, of graceful outline, and of two tints—one fawn-colored, from the presence of a little oxyde of iron, and the other white, from its absence. To us the former appears the more pleasing to the eye. These are made of the flint from Vermont and Massachusetts, the feldspar from New Hampshire, and the china clays from Vermont and South Carolina. This Company has the credit of first producing Parian ware on this continent."

Some of the specimens of the above described exhibit are figured in Silliman and Goodrich's *New York Exhibition of 1853*, published by George P. Putnam. Here may be seen illustrations of examples of flint enamelled and parian pitchers and a water-cooler made by the United States Pottery Company. Another design peculiar to the Bennington factory was a large water-pitcher intended to represent a waterfall, with rocks in front and water overflowing the mouth and falling in volumes down the sides, in relief.

In 1853 the works were enlarged and six kilns of improved construction were erected. The main building of the new plant was one hundred and sixty feet long ; water power was used for grinding and preparing the materials, and one hundred hands were employed in the various branches of the business. At this time the selling headquarters of the establishment were in Boston. Mr. G. B. Sibley and Dr. S. R. Wilcox, of Bennington, both of whom learned the " presser's " trade at the United States Pottery, have kindly placed at my disposal a choice series of pieces made there, a number of which are represented in these illustrations. Examples of flint enamelled ware, with mottled or variegated glaze, include a picture frame, lion, hot-water bottle in form of a book, candlestick, and goblet vase. The stamp used occasionally on this ware was " Lyman, Fenton & Co., Fenton's Enamel, Patented 1849, Bennington," arranged in a large ellipse. A curious old Toby jug, of flint enamelled ware, with handle in form of a human leg and foot, has been deposited in the collection of the Pennsylvania Museum of Art by Miss Hannah A. Zell.

75.—Flint Enamelled Ware, Bennington Factory.

In the Trumbull-Prime collection, now on exhibition at Princeton College, may be seen a number of Bennington pieces, including two lions in flint enamelled glaze, a reclining cow, book flask, and pair of candlesticks in Rockingham, and a flattened parian vase, of old French or German form, with blue pitted ground, and white modelled bunches of grapes in high relief and handles formed of series of grape leaves.

" Scrodled " ware was made to some extent at the United States Pottery, being what Mr. Greeley calls

" lava ware," as shown in the Fenton monument.   This
was produced by combining different colored bodies,
mixed with layers of white clay by partial "wedging."
A bowl and pitcher of this ware, with impressed mark,
" United States Pottery Co., Bennington, Vt.," in an
ellipse, is owned by Rev. F. E. Snow, of Guilford, Conn.

Captain Enoch Wood, of South Norwalk, Conn.,
who was connected with the Lyman and Fenton works in
1850, states that John Lee and Enoch Barber at that time
were mould-makers, and that Enoch and Thomas Moore,
William and Charles Leek, John Coughclough, Stephen
Pies, and Joseph Lawton worked there.   Enoch Barber
afterwards was a mould-maker at Kaolin, South Carolina.
Most of these are now dead.

The Bennington factory was closed in 1858, and in
the following year Mr. Fenton moved to Peoria, Ill.,
where, in connection with his former superintendent, Mr.
Decius W. Clark, he established a pottery for the manufacture of Rockingham, yellow, and white wares.   Mr.
Fenton was born in Dorset, Vermont, and learned his
trade there at a common red-ware pottery.   After a career
of over thirty years as one of the foremost practical
potters in the United States, he died at Joliet, Ill., on
November 7, 1865, at the age of fifty-nine.   The United
States Pottery buildings were torn down in 1870.   Mr.
Lyman died on May 2, 1883, in his seventy-seventh
year.

I have recently seen two white parian pitchers bearing the mark " Fenton's Works ; Bennington, Vermont."
We have no knowledge that Mr. Fenton was at any time

sole proprietor of the works which afterward became the United States Pottery, though he may have been alone for a short time previous to his partnership with Mr. Lyman. It is possible that this stamp was used by him in some of his previous operations, and that inadvertently, or for some special purpose, it was placed on a few of the pieces made during his connection with the United States Pottery. One of the pitchers so stamped is owned by Mr. G. B. Sibley, and the other is now in the collection of the Pennsylvania Museum of Art. They are the first two shown in Illustration 72.

BEACH'S POTTERY, PHILADELPHIA.

Previous to the middle of the present century, Mr. R. Bagnall Beach established a pottery in the upper part

76.—O'CONNELL PITCHER.

of Philadelphia, in the neighborhood of the forks of Germantown Road and Second Street. He came from the Wedgwood Works, Etruria. In 1846 he was awarded third premium for earthenware at the Exhibition of the Franklin Institute, the judges pronouncing his ware "a good article, —well finished." He used a number of excellent pitcher moulds, one of which was said to be a correct likeness of Daniel O'Connell, the Irish patriot, who died in 1847. According to Mr. Joseph Bailey, formerly connected with the Beach Pottery, but now with the Rookwood Pottery, Cincinnati, this portrait piece came originally from the Doulton Works, London, about 1848, and Mr. Beach made them in several sizes in yellow and Rockingham. After Beach retired from business, about 1851, Thomas Haig, of Philadelphia, procured some of his moulds, among them that of the O'Connell pitcher, which is still in use (Illustration 76).

A patent for the inlaying of pearls, gems, etc., on china and baked earthenware, was taken out by Ralph B. Beach, of Kensington, Pa., evidently the same person, in 1851, but with what result we are unable to state.

OTHER POTTERIES.

Mr. William Wolfe carried on a pottery in Sullivan County, near Blountville C. H., Tenn., from 1848 to 1856, where glazed earthenware was made. In 1875 he operated a pottery in Wise County, Va., at East Big Stone Gap, where he continued to manufacture a fine quality of hard brown pottery, or stoneware, until the year 1881. The ware produced was mostly plain, but included a few jugs, vases, etc., of ornamental form, with incised decoration, entirely devoid of coloring. Specimens of the latter are now rare, though I am informed that one or two pieces are preserved in the Exposition building at Big Stone Gap, and a few other examples are owned by persons in that vicinity.

George Walker, who was associated with William Billingsley, his father-in-law, in some of the most important ceramic enterprises at Worcester, Nantgarw, Swansea, and Coalport, came to America with his family about 1835, after the death of his partner, and about 1850 established a pottery at West Troy, N. Y., which was named " The Temperance Hill Pottery." Although in Great Britain he had been identified with the higher art movements in the porcelain factories of the above-mentioned places, and is said to have first introduced the *reverberating enamel kiln* at the Worcester works, he seems to have been content to engage in the manufacture of Rockingham ware, in a small way, on this side of the Atlantic. His principal products were tea-pots, pitchers, and toys, which he continued to make for a number of years. He died in poverty some ten or twelve years ago, at an advanced age.

The stoneware pottery now operated by Messrs. Shepley & Smith, at West Troy, was established in 1831 by Mr. Sanford S. Perry. After passing through several changes, the business has grown to considerable proportions, the staple products now being stone, ale, beer, and ink bottles, snuff jars, and the usual lines of Rockingham ware.

Mr. Moro Phillips started a stoneware pottery on the James River, Virginia, about six miles below Wilson's Landing, in 1850, on a property which he had recently acquired, on which were large deposits of suitable clay. In 1853 the works were moved to Philadelphia, at the northwest corner of Chestnut and Thirty-first streets.

Here the business was superintended by Mr. George L. Horn, who is still living in Philadelphia. Chemical stoneware was manufactured for a number of years, Wolf's jars being a specialty. The demand for this class of goods was limited in those days, and Mr. Phillips introduced the manufacture of household stoneware. He had in his employ a German, named Hermann Eger, who decorated the ware in blue underglaze designs. He had been working previously in the Gloucester China Works, and died as recently as the summer of 1891.

In or about 1862 the works were moved to Erie and Trenton avenues, where they continued, under the management of Mr. Horn, until about 1867, when they were taken to Camden, N. J., where they are still operated by the heirs, for furnishing apparatus used in the extensive business interests of the estate.

Mr. James Carr, who came to the United States in 1844, worked for the American Pottery Company of Jersey City until 1852, when he went to South Amboy and took the Swan Hill Pottery in partnership with Mr. Thomas Locker, which had been established in 1849 for the manufacture of yellow and Rockingham wares. In October, 1853, he started a pottery in New York City under the firm name of Morrison & Carr, where table services in opaque china, white granite, and majolica were made. Mr. Carr directed his efforts toward the attainment of higher standards, and his experiments resulted in the production of some artistic pieces of bone china and parian, excellent both in design and execution. For a period of about two years he continued the manufacture of majolica, and made a large variety of ornamental designs in pitchers, vases, sardine and match-boxes, comports and centre pieces, in addition to the standard forms of useful ware. In parian he executed some good portrait busts of eminent men, and a number of fancy figures and groups. In 1888, owing to the close competition of out-of-town manufacturers, the New York City Pottery was closed and the buildings torn down. He has recently built on the premises in West Thirteenth Street, several large stores, the rentals from which, he claims, yield him better returns than potting.

The trade marks used by this factory are as follows : 1. Arms of Great Britain, monogram J. C. in centre, and "Stone China" beneath. 2. Heraldic shields of the United States and Great Britain joined. 3. Parallelogram with "Stone Porcelain, J. C." in centre. 4. Clasped hands, with "J. C." on either side, and "N. Y. C. P." below.

Mr. Carr is one of the fathers of the pottery industry in this country. He experimented extensively with clays, fuels, and materials, and had in his employ, at different times, the best modellers and decorators that could be procured.

In 1853 Messrs. Young, Roche, Toland & Co., and also Messrs. Wintter & Co. of New Jersey, were exhibitors of terra-cotta wares at the Crystal Palace Exhibition, New York City. In 1858 Lorenze Staudacher was making terra-cotta chimney tops, garden and hanging vases, and brackets for churches and private dwellings, in Philadelphia.

NORWALK, CONN.

Dr. Isaac H. Hall, of the Metropolitan Museum of Art, New York, informs me that he can remember two potteries in Norwalk, Conn., where, forty years ago, pottery knobs, hardware trimmings, and variegated glazed coat buttons were made.

At South Norwalk, Mr. L. D. Wheeler was making "mineral knobs" for doors, furniture, and shutters in 1853. These were composed of red, white, and black clays, mixed together, burned, and covered with ordinary Rockingham glaze. Several years previous to that date he had, in connection with Dr. Asa Hill, made pottery buttons, which were of a similar body and glaze. This was one of the establishments which Dr. Hall remembers. Captain Enoch Wood, who was a potter at the United States Pottery at Bennington, Vt., went to Norwalk in that year and commenced working for Mr. Wheeler, afterwards his father-in-law, and three years later, in connection with Mr. Wheeler's son, purchased the business and carried it on until 1865, when the factory was destroyed by fire. Enoch Wood, the great potter of Burslem, Staffordshire, was a cousin of Captain Wood's grandfather, and Josiah Wedgwood was related to the family. Thomas Wood, of Wood & Challinor, Tunstall, John Wood, of Stoke-upon-Trent, a china painter at Copeland's, and Hugh Wood, a noted engraver, were brothers of Captain Wood's father.

The buttons referred to were made of plastic clay and not by the "dust" or powdered clay process which was patented by Mr. Richard Prosser in England, in

1840. At first they were made in plastic moulds and afterwards were pressed in dies. Some had four perforations for the thread and others were furnished with metal shanks, examples of the latter style having been sent to me by Captain Wood. They are of two qualities, a coarse red body covered with a light brown glaze, and a fine white body with an excellent mottled glaze. The manufacture of buttons was discontinued previous to 1853.

DECORATING WORKS OF HAUGHWOUT AND DAILY.

Messrs. Haughwout & Daily had a decorating establishment in New York City forty years ago, at 561 and 563 Broadway, and employed about fifty hands in painting French china for the American market. They exhibited at the Crystal Palace Exhibition in that city, in 1853, a fine collection of decorated ware, including pitchers with salmon-colored ground and lotus leaves ; a vase with painted portrait of William Woram, a former partner in the business, presented to him by the employés ; handsome toilet sets, elaborately painted with designs differing in each piece ; dessert services ; a centre piece ; coffee cups, and plates richly decorated with landscapes, figures, flowers, etc.; a specimen plate of a dinner service manufactured for the President of the United States, with the American eagle and blue band in Alhambra style, and a service with crimson ground and gilt decoration in varied designs. As the ware so decorated was imported, it is not now possible to identify pieces bearing the work of this firm, unless obtained through persons who procured them direct from the decorators at that time and can vouch for their authenticity. The decoration of European pieces was frequently copied, but they did also some creditable original work.

This firm did an extensive business, in ante-bellum days, with Cuba and the Southern States. It was not uncommon for a wealthy planter to order a large service of decorated ware, with massive gilding, often in duplicate to provide against breakages.

The partnership was afterwards dissolved. Mr. Daily with a new partner opened a decorating shop on Broadway, taking with them some of the painters of the original firm. The latter subsequently started decorating works on Greene Street, where Mr. Edward Lycett joined him. Mr. Haughwout's successor removed to Great Jones Street, where he continued the business for some time.

WORKS AT GLOUCESTER, N. J.

The American Porcelain Manufacturing Company of Gloucester, N. J., was incorporated in 1854, the corporators being John C. Drake, Abraham Bechtel, George B. Keller, Peter Weikel, and Martin H. Bechtel, of Philadelphia, Pa. ; William Reiss, Sr., Gloucester, N. J. ; Matthew Miller, Jr., George Setley, and George Bockins, of Camden, N. J. It is said that experiments were previously carried on in Philadelphia and Wilmington, Del. The venture seems to have been a financial and commercial failure. Mr. Philip Hallworth, who worked at the Gloucester factory, informs me that the ware would often come from the kiln melted into a conglomerate mass, and much was destroyed in this manner and considerable money lost. A single marked example of this ware is the only one I have seen. It is a cream pitcher, remarkably translucent and quite thin, roughly moulded with raised designs intended to represent roses and other flowers. This bears the mark A. P. M. Co. impressed on the bottom (Illustration 77).

77.—PORCELAIN PITCHER, RAISED DECORATION. AM. POR. MFG. CO., GLOUCESTER, N. J.

The Gloucester China Company, incorporated in 1857, was a continuation of the former. Jacob Sheetz, Abel Lukens, and John H. Shultz, of Philadelphia; Peleg B. Savery, of Camden Co., N. J., and Abraham Browning, of Camden, were created a body politic and corporate for manufacturing and selling " porcelain, china, chemicals, drugs, and other articles of which clay, sand, and other earthy substances, form the basis or principal ingredients." A Mr. McIntire was appointed manager of the works and Mr. Scharf superintended the manufacture of the products. Mr. Edwin T. Freedley, in his *History of Philadelphia and Its Manufactures*, published in 1858, states that the company produced ware " possessing the qualities of being not only semi-transparent but very strong. The articles are such as are required in every household and the product compares favorably with the European." In reality the quality of the porcelain was good, but the workmanship and glazing were inferior.   No attempt at decoration was made, all pieces being sold in the white, except such ornamentation in relief as was derived from moulds.   Although large quantities of china were made at the time, the company having practically a monopoly of the trade in Western New Jersey and Eastern Pennsylvania, few pieces can now be found that can be absolutely identified.   A piece from the same mould as the one last figured, but unmarked, now in the Pennsylvania Museum, was procured from Mr. Hallworth, who has assured me that it was made at the Gloucester works about 1858.   Much trouble was experienced in glazing and firing, the first ware placed upon the market being blistered and rough.   Mr. Hallworth also informs me that experiments were made at one time to produce yellow and Rockingham wares, but after some three kilns had been drawn without success, the attempt was abandoned.   In 1858 the company had an office at No. 17 North Sixth St., Philadelphia.   It is said that large quantities of imperfect ware were dumped on the river bank at Gloucester, the broken crockery being deposited in such quantities as to gain for the spot the name of the "China Wharf."   Some of the workmen employed were William Hand, Philip Hallworth, Messrs. Horseman, Lock, Lawton, and Gerard.   No other marks seem to have been used excepting the private marks of the workmen, the letter C being on the bottom of the pitcher figured.   The factory was closed about 1860, after which, it is stated, some of the operatives started other factories in various parts of New Jersey.

Messrs. Jones, White, & McCurdy were manufacturing artificial porcelain teeth, in 1858, at No. 528 Arch St., Philadelphia. They were then turning out one and a quarter millions a year, which were claimed to be of a better grade than those produced in Europe. The original seat of manufacture of porcelain teeth in the United States was in Philadelphia.

A porcelain factory was in operation on Germantown Road, Philadelphia, in 1858.

THE SOUTHERN PORCELAIN MANUFACTURING CO.

For more than half a century deposits of fine porcelain clay have been known to exist in the hills about half way between the city of Augusta, Georgia, and the village of Aiken, S. C., in what is now Aiken County. In 1856 Mr. William H. Farrar, one of the stockholders in the United States Pottery Co., of Bennington, Vt., went to South Carolina and established works at a small settlement called Kaolin, close to the clay banks, after first having interested a number of wealthy citizens of Augusta, six miles distant, in a scheme for producing fine white ware and porcelain. A stock company was formed, of which the Lamars, then prominent planters, and afterwards distinguished in national affairs, and Alexander H. Stevens, Esq., who, a few years later, became Vice-President of the Southern Confederacy, were members. Attracted by the extensive beds of fine kaolin in that vicinity, Mr. Farrar thought he saw an opportunity of making a fortune by erecting works close to the sources of supply. For many years the inhabitants of the surrounding district had been using this clay for whitewashing their fences and buildings, but beyond such use it was not thought to be of any particular value. Mr. Farrar took with him from Vermont brick masons, who constructed the most approved kilns of that day, and Mr. Anson Peeler, a master carpenter, who had previously built the United States Pottery at Bennington. Potters were also procured from Vermont and other places. The works were operated the first year under the management of a newly imported English potter who, however, did not prove satisfactory. His experiments were unsuccessful and much ware was destroyed in firing. Under his administration considerable money was lost to the stockholders. During the second year, Mr. Josiah Jones, a skillful designer and competent potter, who had previously modelled for Charles Cartlidge at Greenpoint, assumed the management, and succeeded in producing some very fair porcelain and good white granite and cream-colored wares. The business did not prove a commercial or financial success, however, chiefly because Mr. Jones was limited to the use of the local clays, as Mr. Farrar, not a practical potter himself, could not divest himself of the erroneous idea that first-class ware could be made from the South Carolina clays exclusively. He allowed his manager, Mr. Jones, so little of other requisite clays that failure was inevitable. In 1857, Mr. Farrar arranged with Mr. Decius W. Clark, of the Bennington works, to take the South Carolina potteries in hand, which change took effect late in that year. In February following, Mr. L. W. Clark, now of the New England Pottery Co., went south to relieve his father, who then returned to Vermont, and the son at once assumed charge of the preparation of bodies and glazes, the other branches of the business continuing under the general supervision of Mr. Farrar. During 1858, the works were fairly successful in the production of white granite and cream-colored wares, but at the close of that year Mr. Clark sold his combinations to the company, the transfer being made in the office of Alexander H. Stevens, and shortly after returned north.

The Kaolin factory continued, in a reasonably successful way, making table, toilet, and a general line of white ware, until after the war commenced, when, under the name of the Southern Porcelain Manufacturing Company, it is said to have gone into the extensive manufacture of porcelain and pottery telegraph insulators for the Confederate Government. Earthenware water-pipes were also made, to some extent, for the general Southern trade, until the works were destroyed by fire in 1863 or '64. In 1860 the manufacture of the finer grades of ware was discontinued.

Examples of the products of these works are now exceedingly scarce, but through the courtesy of Dr. G. E. Manigault of Charleston, S. C., I am enabled to

78.—PORCELAIN PITCHER, MADE BY THE SOUTHERN PORCELAIN COMPANY ABOUT 1861. OWNED BY MRS. EDWARD WILLIS.

give the illustration of a white porcelain pitcher made here, which is decorated with relief representations of stalks of Indian corn (Ill. 78). The piece is ten and a half inches in height with excellent glaze, free from crazing. It belongs to Mrs. Edward Willis of Charleston, to whom it was presented while visiting the factory in 1861. Mrs. John S. Porcher, of Eutawville, S. C., daughter of Bishop Davis and great-granddaughter of Richard Champion, the eminent potter, who came from England in the last century and settled at Camden, S. C., is the owner of a small parian syrup-jug, which was purchased at these works in 1859. One of the insulators, of brown stoneware, made here, has been sent to me by Col. Thos. J. Davies. It is a rather clumsy affair, marked with an impressed shield containing the inscription, "S. P. Company, Kaolin, S. C." This mark is said to have also been used to

79.—PARIAN JUG. SOUTHERN PORCELAIN CO., KAOLIN, S. C. MRS. J. STONEY PORCHER.

some extent on porcelain pieces (see chapter on Marks).

The enterprise was destined to failure from the beginning. Good potters could not be induced to remain in the woods at a distance from any large town or city. The best workmen became dissatisfied with their surroundings, and returned north. Transportation of wares to the railroad, one and a half miles distant, was found to be expensive, and much difficulty was experienced in getting the product to market. In locating the works the projector lost sight of the fact that clay is a small item in the total freight expenses of a pottery. It is said that much money was lost in the venture, the amount being placed as high as $150,000. Some of the ware, however, was of excellent quality. Rockingham pitchers and spittoons of ornate form were made in the earlier days, and cream-pots, pitchers, etc., in white ware and porcelain, with raised leaves and imitation of wicker or basket work, were made to some extent at a later date. The pitchers of this character were quite popular, and were produced in great numbers.

The Kaolin factory was probably the only one in the South, during the Civil War, which produced white or porcelain ware. Some china was imported by the Confederate Government from England, however, decorated to order, such as the table service used on board the warship *Alabama*, which was embellished with a central design consisting of two crossed cannon behind an anchor, above the initials C. S. N. (Confederate States Navy). Around this device is a circle of cable, outside of which is a wreath, formed on one side of a spray of leaves and flowers of the tobacco plant, and on the other of the cotton plant, with leaves, flowers, and cotton bolls. Below the design is the motto of the *Alabama*, "Aide Toi et Dieu t'Aidera." Each piece is bordered with a blue band. This service was made by the firm of E. F. Bodley & Co., of Burslem, England. The body of the ware was "Ironstone China." Mrs. Annie Trumbull Slosson, in *The China Hunters Club*, states that there were three sets of this china, each of a different color, one of which was printed in a gray tint, for use at the officers' table. Examples of this service are owned by Mrs. King of Atlanta, Georgia, one of which is decorated in a blue-gray tint, and others in green, with the same finish of blue lines.

At the close of the war, in 1865, a new porcelain company was organized, with Mr. R. B. Bullock, afterwards Governor of Georgia, president. He prosecuted the business with great vigor, but this second attempt proved abortive, and after twelve years of varying success, the pottery was sold to Messrs. McNamee & Co., of New York. The old kilns and buildings have long since disappeared, but the clay is still being mined and shipped in its crude state to the north and west, where it is used extensively by the paper trade. There are at present four mines in active operation here, that of Messrs. McNamee & Co., and another, worked by Col. Thomas J. Davies, being the most important. The clay is of the finest quality, much too fine, it is claimed, for use alone in the manufacture of pottery, but admirably adapted to the manufacture of wall papers. In 1891 about 20,000 casks of clay were shipped from these mines.

CHAPTER X.

EAST LIVERPOOL, OHIO.

THE history of East Liverpool is, in a great measure, the history of the pottery industry in the United States. Mr. James Bennett, the first to engage in the pottery business there, came from Newhall, near Woodville, a pottery district in Derbyshire, England, in the year 1834, and found employment at the Jersey City Pottery, which, at that time, was one of the foremost establishments of the kind in the United States, where he remained until about 1837, when he went to Troy, Indiana, at which point some Louisville (Ky.), gentlemen had recently established works for the manufacture of white ware, under the name of the Indiana Pottery Co. After remaining there for about a year, Mr. Bennett was forced to leave, on account of ill-health, and proceeded up the Ohio River with the double purpose of improving his health and selecting a more suitable location for the establishment of a pottery. At East Liverpool he found clay of the proper quality for yellow ware, and here, in 1839, he built a small pottery, with the assistance of Mr. Anthony Kearns, who furnished the necessary means. This was the pioneer pottery in that section, which has

80.—The Old Bennett Pottery, East Liverpool, O.

The Baltimore Engraving Co.

since become one of the greatest centres of the pottery industry in the United States. After paying Mr. Kearns a portion of the profits for the use of the plant for a short time, Mr. Bennett leased the works for a period of five years. In April of 1841 he sent to England for his brothers, Daniel, Edwin, and William, all practical potters, who shortly after started for America, reaching East Liverpool in September of that year, when the four entered into a co-partnership under the style of Bennett & Brothers. In connection with yellow ware they immediately commenced the manufacture of Rockingham ware, the first to be made in the United States, and some of their patterns which were originated at that time, notably the octagon-shaped spittoons, are still in demand, after fifty years of uninterrupted popularity.

For the next three years the business increased steadily, the products of the factory being sold to the wholesale crockery merchants of Cincinnati, Louisville, St. Louis, Cleveland, and other western cities. The lack of proper facilities for shipping goods, however, induced the firm to look around for a more favorable location, and accordingly in 1844 they decided to move their plant to Birmingham, now a part of Pittsburg, Pa., where, at that period, better coal and cheaper transportation to the eastern as well as the western trade centres could be procured. In this year they erected a larger plant at that point and the business was resumed with greatly increased facilities. Samples of their Rockingham and yellow wares were exhibited at the American Institute, New York, and the Franklin Institute, Philadelphia, from both of which they

13

received medals for superiority of manufacture. At the exhibition of the latter, held in 1846, their display of earthenware took the first premium, a silver medal, and was pronounced by the judges to be superior to the English. An eight-sided glazed "tortoise-shell" pitcher, with Druid's head beneath the lip, one of the pieces then exhibited is still preserved in the cabinet of the Institute. In this year Mr. Edwin Bennett withdrew from the firm, after having selected Baltimore, Md., as the field for his future operations, and here he erected a small pottery, the first to be established south of what was known as the Mason and Dixon line, for making the finer grades of ware. About two years after, he admitted his brother William to partnership, and the firm became E. & W. Bennett, and so continued until the spring of 1856, at which time the latter retired from active business on account of failing health. During this period silver and gold medals were awarded the firm by the Maryland Institute for "superiority of Queensware," the exhibits consisting of yellow and Rockingham, sage and blue-colored hard-body wares, such as coffee-pots, pitchers, water-urns, vases, etc. Since 1856 Mr. Edwin Bennett has carried on the business alone. In 1869 he enlarged the factory and more than doubled the output, and the manufacture of white ware was commenced. Shortly afterwards a decorating department was added. Mr. Bennett originated and first made the "Rebekah" teapot in 1851, in Rockingham ware, and has continued its manufacture to this day, the demand for it being regular and constant. So popular has this pattern become that nearly all the other potteries in the United States have copied it. On opposite sides of the vessel is a figure of a maiden in

relief, with water jar, resting or standing by a well, and beneath are the words " Rebekah at the Well." The design is familiar to nearly every one, and may be seen in any crockery store. A few years ago Mr. Bennett devoted some attention to the pro-

81.—SAGE-GREEN MARINE PITCHER.
E. & W. BENNETT, 1853.

duction of parian and Belleek wares. A small quantity of the egg-shell china was made in 1886, of excellent quality, in tea sets, but as its manufacture would have interfered with the general business of the works, it was discontinued.

In 1887 Mr. Bennett produced some parian plaques which were modelled by Mr. James Priestman, an artist of ability in that line.

In 1890 Mr. Bennett changed his business into a corporation, under the style of the Edwin Bennett Pottery Co. With Mr. Henry Brunt as manager they commenced the manufacture of high-grade dinner, tea, and toilet ware in American porcelain. Their shapes are characterized by correct designs and refined decorations. Especially worthy of mention are their underglaze decorations

in old blue and gold. Another specialty is the manufacture of *jardinières* in colored glazes. These they make
in a variety of forms, with ornamentation in relief. A
deep ultramarine blue and an olive-green are particularly
fine, while the modelling shows decided originality and
merit.

The trade-mark is a globe, showing
the western hemisphere, with a sword
driven through the United States.
The guard of the sword carries the initials of the company, while underneath
is their motto.

Mr. Edwin Bennett was born in the year 1818, and
has been identified with the pottery industry from his

82.—RECENT PRODUCTIONS OF THE EDWIN BENNETT POTTERY CO.

youth, and in this country for upwards of half a century.
In 1890 and 1891 he was the honored president of the
United States Potters' Association.

Mr. Bennett's display of historical wares at the Chicago
Fair was the only one of the kind in the American section.

This included pieces produced in the earlier years of the pottery's existence such as a large Rockingham vase with cover and dolphin handles and raised grapevine decoration, made by him in 1853 ; a majolica bust of Washington, by E. & W. Bennett, 1850; a pair of mottled majolica

83.—MR. EDWIN BENNETT.

vases, two feet in height, with raised grapevine designs and lizard handles, produced by him in 1856 ; enormous octagonal majolica pitcher, with blue, brown, and olive mottled glazes, 1853 ; coffee-pots, and other pieces in blue, green, and olive bodies.

One of the most striking pieces of his more recent

work is a large majolica *jardinière*, three feet in height, consisting of a trefoil basin supported by three griffins. This was designed and modelled by Mr. Herbert W. Beattie of Quincy, Mass., and is produced in robin's-egg blue, lemon, and other colors.

After Bennett & Brothers left East Liverpool, in 1844, for Pittsburgh, the old Bennett Pottery was rented for several years by Samuel, Jesse, Thomas, and John Croxall, the latter being the only one now living, who is the senior member of the present firm of John W. Croxall & Sons, who are still making the same class of goods originally made by the Bennetts,—Rockingham and yellow wares. The old buildings were afterwards washed away by the encroachment of the river.

Mr. Benjamin Harker, Sr., established a pottery in East Liverpool in 1840 for the production of similar wares. This was in operation for a number of years when the business came into possession of George S. Harker, son of Benjamin, and carried on under the name of George S. Harker & Co. until his death, many years ago, after which his widow and two sons, William W. and Henry N., continued it under the same style until 1890, in which year it was incorporated as The Harker Pottery Company. In 1879 the manufacture of Rockingham and yellow wares was discontinued, and white granite ware is now made exclusively, the plant having been greatly enlarged in recent years. Many of the proprietors of other establishments in East Liverpool and elsewhere learned their trade at this factory. Mr. James Taylor, who died a few years ago at Trenton, N. J., was at one time a partner in the concern, and was afterwards largely instrumental in expanding the industry in the latter city.

Mr. John Goodwin, who worked in the pottery of James Edwards, Dale Hall, Burslem, England, came to America in 1842, and immediately after his arrival went into the employ of James Bennett & Bros. In 1844, Mr. Goodwin embarked in the business on his own account, and with one small kiln began to make yellow and Rockingham goods, with eminent success. In 1853, owing to ill health, he sold the business to Messrs. Samuel and William Baggott, and lived in retirement until 1863, when he erected the Novelty Pottery Works, now operated by the McNicol Pottery Company, who have added the manufacture of C. C. ware. In 1870, Mr. Goodwin went to Trenton and purchased an interest in the Trenton Pottery Company, when the style was changed to Taylor, Goodwin, & Co., manufacturers of iron-stone china, C. C. and sanitary and plumbers' earthenware. Desiring to be again with his old friends in Ohio, however, Mr. Goodwin sold out his interest in 1872, and, returning to East Liverpool, purchased the Broadway Pottery from Messrs. T. Rigby & Co., and immediately began to improve the works with a view to adding white ware to the products. The realization of these plans was, however, delayed by Mr. Goodwin's death in 1875, but in the following year the business was resumed by his three sons, and the new firm, under the name of Goodwin Brothers, has since enlarged the works, and continues to manufacture pearl-white, cream-colored, and decorated wares of an excellent quality.

Messrs. Salt & Mear went to East Liverpool and commenced making yellow and Rockingham wares, in the building called the Mansion House, in 1841.

Messrs. Woodward & Vodrey began business in the spring of 1848, and were burned out in March, 1849. They then associated with them John S. and James Blakely and Richard Booth, under the firm name of Woodward, Blakely, & Co., and rebuilt the works during the summer of 1849. The experienced potter of the company was Jabez Vodrey, who, in company with a Mr. Frost, came to this country in 1827 and built and operated a pottery at Pittsburgh, Pa. The firm of Woodward, Blakely, & Co. continued to enlarge their works until they had one of the largest potteries in East Liverpool, their products being yellow and Rockingham ware of the finest quality. Their plant occupied the ground upon which three potteries now stand,—those of Wm. Brunt, Son, & Co., George Morley & Son, and Vodrey & Brother. The year 1857, however, carried the firm of Woodward, Blakely, & Co. down in the financial panic which stranded so many mercantile houses.

THE KNOWLES, TAYLOR, & KNOWLES CO.

In 1854, the works now owned by The Knowles, Taylor, & Knowles Company were established. The business was started in a small way by Isaac W. Knowles and Isaac A. Harvey, who made yellow ware in a single kiln, which was used alternately for bisque and glost-ware. A few years later Rockingham ware was added to their products.

In 1870, Mr. Knowles, who had purchased the interest
of his former partner, was joined by Messrs. John N.
Taylor and Homer S. Knowles, and in 1872 they commenced the manufacture of ironstone china or white
granite ware. Since then they have rapidly enlarged
their works to enable them to fill the orders which came
to them from every State in the Union. At the present
time their plant includes thirty-five kilns used in the manufacture of white granite ware and china and for decorating,
and covers ten acres of ground. Their vitreous-translu-

84.—Thin China Tête-à-Tête Set. K., T., & K. Co.

cent hotel china is made in large quantities for the trade
and is of a superior quality. About seven hundred hands
are employed.

In 1888 Messrs. Joseph G. Lee and Willis A. Knowles
were admitted to the firm, and in January of 1891 a stock
company was formed and incorporated under the title of
The Knowles, Taylor, & Knowles Company, with a paid-
up capital of one million dollars. Previous to the disastrous fire of November 18, 1889, which burned their china
works to the ground, a considerable quantity of Belleek

china was made, but since the rebuilding of the works that branch has been discontinued. Little was attempted in the production of art ware, however, until a recent date, because the marvellous growth of the business and ever-increasing demand for staple products taxed the producing capacity of the factory to the utmost. They are now turning out some good things in fine bone china of a more ornamental character, and indications point to an early revival of a high order of decorative work. Among their recent achievements are a number of excellent designs in extra thin china, which is beautifully translucent and of dazzling whiteness. This is sold both plain and decorated. At present they are producing quite a number of elaborate

85.—Decorated Thin China Chocolate Pot. K., T., & K. Co.

and expensive decorations, and have twelve decorating kilns.

The mark used on vitreous hotel china and thin art ware consists of the initials of the company above the word "china," thus : $\frac{K., T. \& K.}{CHINA}$, and that used on their white granite ware is an eagle enclosed in a five-rayed badge, as here shown.

The Knowles, Taylor, & Knowles Co. have produced some highly artistic pieces for exhibition at the Chicago Exposition. Especially worthy of notice are two vases. One of these is a nine-inch piece, made of the peculiarly translucent bone china body with soft, velvety glaze, which is designated by the manufacturers "Lotus" ware. The entire exterior surface is covered with an underglaze mazarine

blue of a rich tone. On one side is a figure of Cupid chasing a bird and on the other Cupid driving a pair of butterflies. While the subjects are not new, the treatment is original, the figures being executed in white Limoges enamel built up *over* the glaze instead of *under* it, as in the *pâte-sur-pâte* method. The effect is particularly pleasing. The neck of the vase is decorated in raised coin-gold after the Renaissance style, while the handles are solidly gilded and chased.

86.—SMALL VASE, RELIEF DECORATION.
EXHIBITED AT CHICAGO FAIR.

The second piece referred to is a large vase, which stands thirty and three quarters inches high, mounted on a pedestal twelve inches in height. Owing to the large size of the vase the body employed is that of the regular hotel china made by this firm. The ground color is a

87.—LARGE VASE, BLUE GROUND, GOLD DECORATION. CHICAGO FAIR.

rich mazarine blue applied under the glaze. Flowers in relief coin-gold of various tints are applied to the surface, representing petunias, and on the side of the piece is an excellently painted pair of golden partridges. The neck of the vase and the pedestal are embellished with solid, raised gold borders in the Renaissance style.

Particularly noteworthy in their Chicago exhibit were some exquisite pieces of "Lotus" ware, decorated in dainty colors, and several vases with jewelled decoration and open-work effects.

Col. John N. Taylor, the president of the company, was born June 23, 1842, near Port Homer, Jefferson County, Ohio.

88.—COL. JOHN N. TAYLOR.

In 1849 he came, with his parents, to East Liverpool, Ohio, where he has since resided. In 1861 he enlisted in the Union army as a member of Battery " B," known as " Cooper's Battery," First Pennsylvania Light Artillery, and afterward became Second Lieutenant of Company

"I," 143d Regiment, O. V. I. He was appointed post-master at East Liverpool in 1864. In 1868 he connected himself with the pottery business, and, as we have seen, in 1870 became a member of the firm of Knowles, Taylor, & Knowles. On the incorporation of The Knowles, Taylor, & Knowles Company, he became its first president, and has since continued to occupy that position. He is also vice-president of The Knowles, Taylor, & Anderson Co., a corporation with a paid-in capital of a half million dollars, organized for the manufacture of sewer pipe and other clay products at a large plant in the East End, a suburb of East Liverpool. Stilts, pins, saggers, and other potters' supplies are also made by this company at the works known as The Potters' Supply Co.

Col. Taylor's life has been a busy one, and to his personal efforts are due, to a large degree, the bringing of the establishments with which he has been identified to their present high place in the business world. He was appointed chairman of the Committee on World's Columbian Exposition, appointed by the U. S. Potters' Association.

Col. Taylor has long been a warm personal friend of Gov. William McKinley, dating back to the time and before the "Little Major" entered the halls of Congress, and upon his elevation to the gubernatorial chair in Ohio the Governor appointed him a member of his staff, with the rank of colonel.

OTHER EAST LIVERPOOL WORKS.

Henry Speeler, a German, was one day wandering along the river bank near the Harker Pottery, when he became engaged in conversation with a laborer who was employed there. The former applied for and was given employment, and proved to be an excellent thrower. Later he sold ware through the country, and after accumulating some money, associated himself, about 1858, with William Bloor and James Taylor, the latter having been at one time a partner of George S. Harker, under the firm name of Harker & Taylor. This partnership, however, was after a time dissolved, and Mr. Speeler then built the original part of what is now known as the International Pottery in Trenton, N. J.

The works of Messrs. C. C. Thompson & Co. were established in 1868 by C. C. Thompson and J. T. Herbert. Two years later the dry-goods firm of Josiah Thompson & Co. purchased the interest of the latter, and the firm became C. C. Thompson & Co., composed of Josiah Thompson, the father, C. C. Thompson, J. C. Thompson, and B. C. Simms. After the death of Mr. Josiah Thompson, in November, 1889, the firm was incorporated, and is known now as the C. C. Thompson Pottery Company, and the establishment is among the largest producers of yellow and Rockingham wares in this country. In 1884 the plant was increased and the manufacture of

C. C. ware commenced. In 1890 a decorating department was added, which is now an important factor in the business. The trade-mark used on the semi-granite wares of this factory is here given.

Among the first attempts to produce artistic commercial ware in East Liverpool were some underglaze stoneware cups and saucers made at the works of Mr. Homer Laughlin (formerly Laughlin Brothers), and decorated by Mr. Edward Lycett in 1879. Some toilet sets exhibited by Mr. Laughlin at the World's Columbian Exposition have been much admired. They are decorated with raised designs in dull gold and dark coloring on tinted grounds, and are of novel and graceful forms.

The Dresden Pottery Works of the Potters' Co-operative Company were established in 1876, of which Mr. H. A. McNicol is president. They produce ironstone china and decorated wares in table and toilet services. The decorations are particularly praiseworthy.

Messrs. Cartwright Brothers manufacture, at their Industrial Pottery Works, C. C. goods, plain and decorated, and specialties in ivory decorated ware.

The Standard Pottery Company are manufacturers of ironstone china and decorated wares in the usual lines.

Messrs. Wallace & Chetwynd commenced business about 1882 and are now making a high grade of opaque china, American stone china and decorated goods. Mr. Joseph Chetwynd learned the business in his father's pottery in England, and was for several years employed as manager and modeller by Messrs. Cockson & Chetwynd of Staffordshire.

Messrs. Rowe & Mountford have for a number of years been engaged in the manufacture of stilts, pins, and spurs, and in 1891 added a china department, and are now producing vitreous translucent hotel ware.

The American Pottery Works of Messrs. Sebring Brothers & Co. were established in 1887. They make

14

white granite and decorated wares for the jobbing trade in dinner and tea services.

Among the other important establishments in East Liverpool are the Riverside Knob Manufacturing Co. of Henry Brunt & Son ; Burford Brothers ; Burgess & Co., makers of bone china, staple, and fancy goods ; J. W. Croxall & Sons, successors to Croxall & Cartwright ; the Eagle Pottery Works of S. & W. Baggott ; Great Western Pottery Works of John Wyllie & Son, established in 1868 ; Globe Pottery Co. ; Novelty Pottery Works of McNicol, Burton & Co. ; R. Thomas & Sons, hard vitreous porcelain electric goods ; the American Stilt Works, and E. M. O'Connor, maker of saggers and fire-brick.

East Liverpool is distinctively a pottery city and nearly half of its inhabitants are interested in some manner in the pottery industry. At the present time it has twenty-nine potteries, nine decorating works, two stilt and triangle manufactories, one sagger factory, and three establishments for the manufacture of door-knobs. It enjoys the distinction of being the oldest important centre of the pottery industry in the United States and of producing the men who established many of the most successful potteries in every section of the country.

CHAPTER XI.

TRENTON, N. J.

THE pottery industry, which has reached such a marvellous growth in Trenton as to gain for that city the title of the " Staffordshire of America," had its actual beginning there in 1852, when Messrs. Taylor and Speeler commenced the manufacture of yellow and Rockingham wares. At the present time the establishments engaged in Trenton in the production of all grades of ware, from common pottery to majolica, and from white granite to the finest porcelain, both plain and decorated, number thirty-seven, having the capacity of producing in value about five million dollars' worth of wares per annum. The central location, superior railway, canal, and river transportation facilities, and close contiguity to the clay deposits of New Jersey, have all contributed to the concentration and enormous development of the manufacture at this point. Interesting as is the subject to the ceramic student, we must of necessity confine ourselves to a review of the history of the most important and representative of these establishments.

We can but briefly allude to the difficulties encountered by the early potters in seeking the various clays necessary

for the production of white wares, as well as the feldspar
and flint required in the manufacture of these goods.   It
must be remembered that no mines, except of the common
New Jersey fire-clays, had been developed at that time.
Many thousand miles were travelled by the first potters of
Trenton in search of suitable kaolin.   The first deposit
was found near Hockessin, Delaware, and was known as
the Graham mine.   This afterwards changed hands and
several other mines were developed in that section, the
most notable being that operated by Israel Lacy. Another
deposit was discovered a few years later at Brandywine
Summit, Delaware County, Pa., and worked by the National
Kaolin Company.   This clay was probably the best used
in the early years of the industry and is still largely in
demand.   The first flint used in Trenton for the production of white ware was picked up in Pennsylvania and in
different places near Trenton, wherever a piece could be
found on the surface.   Later, the vast quarries of Harford
County, Maryland, on the Susquehanna, were discovered,
and the bulk of this material has come from that section.
The first feldspar mines operated were in Connecticut,
near Hartford.   A number of mines have since been developed in that State, in Maine, Pennsylvania, and Maryland, and kaolin deposits of fine quality are at present in
course of development in North and South Carolina,
Florida, and various other sections of the country.   When
it is realized that the clay and mineral mines of England
have been worked for perhaps three hundred years, while
in this country the raw materials have not been developed
in a systematic way until within the past forty years or so,

we can more fully appreciate the obstacles which our potters have surmounted in bringing the industry to its present condition. Until a comparatively recent period each pottery manufactured the same class of wares, white granite and C. C. or cream color, and in a very limited way decorated toilet ware. Of late there has been a great diversification and specialization of the business, so that now a number of manufactories produce sanitary and plumbers' earthenware exclusively ; others make nothing but vitrified china, while some confine their productions to semi-porcelain and white granite, and a few have embarked in the manufacture of the finer grades of porcelain. To all of these establishments extensive decorating departments have been added.

The Glasgow Pottery was established in 1863 by Mr. John Moses, who has ever since been prominently identified with the pottery business in Trenton. He was born in County Tyrone, Ireland, in 1832, and came to the United States at the age of twenty. He first served an apprenticeship at the dry-goods business in Philadelphia, where he acquired a practical business training. In the year first mentioned above, he rented a pottery with two small kilns that had been used for making yellow and Rockingham wares, and immediately commenced the manufacture of cream-colored ware, shortly afterward extending the business to the production of white granite or ironstone china. At the time he introduced decorations on table and toilet sets there was only one man in Trenton who understood this branch of the art, who did all the decorating for the ten potteries then in operation. The first ornamentation attempted was the application of plain color bands, then gold lines, and by a gradual development the more elaborate decorations were finally introduced. The capacity of the factory was increased as the growth of the business required, and in a short time Mr. Moses was successfully making wares fully equal to any made by the practical

89.—MR. JOHN MOSES.

English potters who were his competitors in Trenton. His present productions are dinner, tea, toilet, and decorated wares of every description. The name of the Glasgow Pottery is widely known throughout this country in connection with the John Hancock cups and saucers used at the Centennial Tea Parties, which were made extensively just previous to the Exhibition of 1876. Mr. Moses is also a large producer of white granite and cream-colored wares, thin hotel and steamboat china of excellent grades, and has always taken an active part in upholding the protective tariff on American crockery before the Ways and Means Committee of Congress.

THE ETRURIA POTTERY.

The Ott & Brewer Company, of Trenton, N. J., now operate the factory which was built by Messrs. Bloor, Ott, & Booth, in 1863. Mr. John Hart Brewer, president of the company, entered the firm in 1865, and, being an artist himself of considerable ability, soon made his influence felt in the improvement of methods and elevation of standards. Until 1876 the chief products of this factory consisted of white granite and cream-colored ware.

The first attempts in the manufacture of "Belleek" egg-shell china were made by Mr. Brewer in 1882, in conjunction with Mr. William Bromley, Jr., but these early trials were not entirely satisfactory. Encouraged by partial success, however, Mr. Brewer induced Bromley to send for his father, William Bromley, and his brother, John Bromley, who, with two or three other hands, came over in the following year from the Belleek factory in Ireland. Mr. William H. Goss, of Stoke-on-Trent, invented this body some thirty years ago, at which time the elder Bromley was acting as his manager. Messrs. David McBirney and Robert Williams Armstrong were then attempting to make first-class ceramic goods at their recently established manufactory in the village of Belleek,

county of Fermanagh, Ireland.   Mr. Armstrong induced
Bromley to take a number of Mr. Goss' best workmen to
Ireland and introduce the egg-shell porcelain there.   The
ware produced at that factory has since become world-
famous, being characterized by extreme lightness of body
and a beautiful, lustrous glaze.

90.—Belleek Vase, Jewelled Decoration.   91.—Belleek Vase.
Ott & Brewer Company.

The ware now manufactured by the Ott & Brewer Company at the Etruria Pottery is made entirely from American
materials, and is a vast improvement over the body and
glaze first introduced by the Bromleys ten years ago.
The rich iridescence of the nacreous glaze is fully equal
to that of the Irish Belleek which is produced from salts
of bismuth colored with metallic oxides; in delicacy of
coloring and lightness of weight the Trenton ware is even

superior. A dozen cups and saucers, making twenty-four distinct pieces of the ordinary size, almost as thin as paper, weigh just one pound avoirdupois, or an average of only two thirds of an ounce each. A large variety of forms of this porcelain are produced, in both ornamental and useful designs. The larger vases are usually simple in outline and of the same comparative lightness as those of smaller size. They often possess pierced necks, feet, and handles, and are elegantly decorated in enamels, gold relief, and chasing.

A triumph of the potter's skill is a Belleek ostrich-egg *bonbonnière*, in two segments, which is exquisitely perforated or honey-combed over its entire surface.

92.—WHITE GRANITE JARDINIÈRE. OTT & BREWER COMPANY.

Illustration 91 represents a large vase of the " Bourne " pattern, decorated in raised gold and colors. The shape is graceful and the decoration is exceedingly artistic.

In addition to art porcelains, this factory produces a great quantity of granite ware and opaque china, in dinner, tea, and toilet sets, which are both print-decorated and hand-painted. A *jardinière* of white granite, which is here figured, is a refined example of artistic decoration in quiet tones (Ill. 92).

In presenting a biographical sketch of Mr. Brewer, we cannot do better than quote from the *Pottery and Glassware Reporter*, of June, 18, 1891 :

"In 1873 Messrs. Ott & Brewer bought out the interest of Mr. Bloor, who removed to East Liverpool, where he subsequently died. The young member of the firm, then in his twenty-ninth year, filled with enthusiasm for his business and inspired with the patriotic sentiments pervading the preparation for the 1876 Centennial Exposition, at once began to show the possibilities of his craft, and the result was a showing at Philadelphia that was a revelation both to the American people and their foreign competitors. In the preparation and organization of the American pottery display, Mr. Brewer took an active and leading part, and subsequently took a prize at the Paris Exposition, where he also exhibited. About this time he first manufactured vitrified hotel china, and several specimens still in his possession testify to its excellent quality. It was, however, left to others to make its manufacture a commercial success. Mr. Brewer, like the early potters of the English and French schools, has been more interested in achieving practical success than in making money, and, as a consequence, is not as wealthy as some of his more conservative contemporaries. He has spent many thousand dollars in arriving at the present stage, and the American industry generally has shared in its benefits.

"The United States Potters' Association, which has done much to unify, strengthen, and advance the pottery interests of this country, was suggested and successfully organized by Mr. Brewer, who was for some years its

93.—HON. JOHN HART BREWER.

secretary, and subsequently became its president. His familiar face is seen at every convention, and it is hard to tell when he is at his best, in the serious discussions of the convention, or when, as toastmaster at the banquet, the speakers are introduced with witty and appropriate remarks.

" In 1875 he was elected to the New Jersey House of Assembly in a district that usually went Democratic, and subsequently became a Representative in both the 47th and 48th Congresses, where he speedily became recognized as one of the most intelligent exponents and advocates of the tariff question, and gained a national reputation.

" Mr. Brewer is a thoroughly practical potter, familiar with all the details of the industry, acquainted with all its ups and downs during the past twenty-six years, and always taking an active interest in anything relating to its advancement. In the recent efforts to cultivate the spirit of practical art by offering prizes to the various art schools he has been prominent. His genial manners and kindly disposition have endeared him to all he has come in contact with, and even in the heat of political strife he has commanded the respect and friendship of his opponents. No employer is more popular among his employees, and no manufacturer more respected among his colleagues.

" Mr. Brewer was born in Hunterdon County, N. J., March 29, 1844, and is a lineal descendant, on his mother's side, of John Hart, one of the signers of the Declaration of Independence."

A short time previous to the Centennial Exhibition, Mr. Isaac Broome, an American sculptor, who had already gained considerable reputation as an artist of ability, was engaged by Messrs. Ott & Brewer to design and model a series of works in parian for that occasion. These at-

94.—Baseball Vase. Courtesy: New Jersey State Museum, Trenton.

tracted much attention, both on account of their originality of form and artistic treatment.   A tea set, ornamented
with raised designs and
portrait busts of Gen-
eral and Mrs. Washing-
ton, was particularly
n o t e w o r t h y.   His
" Fashion " vases, em-
bellished with figures
in low relief, illustrate
the styles of the last
and present centuries.
They are unique in
form and, like all of
Prof. Broome's work,
characterized by con-
scientious attention to
detail and careful finish.
One of the most spirit-
ed designs of the series
is the base-ball vase
(Ill. 94), which was sug-
gested by Mr. Brewer
and worked out by Mr.
Broome.   It is sugges-
tive throughout, in all
of its harmonious de-
tails, of the American
national game.   From
a pedestal rises a grad-

95.—Pastoral Vase and Bracket. Modelled
by Broome.

ually tapering vase, of which the lower portion is formed of a series of bats banded together by a strap, while the upper portion is embellished with figures of ball-players in low relief. The cover represents a base-ball, surmounted by the American eagle, and around the projecting ledge of the base are arranged three players in life-like attitudes. The modelling is faultless and the figures are full of action.

A pastoral vase, by the same artist, is no less meritorious, though of an entirely different character. The rustic decoration, in low relief, is well suited to the form, and the goat's head handles are in keeping with the other ornamental details. A faun's head bracket, of classic conception and excellently modelled, forms an appropriate support for the vase (see Ill. 95).

Probably the most pretentious piece of work which Prof. Broome has done for the Etruria Pottery is the parian bust of Cleopatra (Ill. 96). This alone would be sufficient to place him in the front ranks of American sculptors, and is one of a large number of heads which have been modelled by him. Busts of public men have been made from life or the best portraits obtainable, and are faithful likenesses of the originals. The parian ware of the Etruria Pottery is soft and mellow in texture and a close imitation of the finest statuary marble.

THE BURROUGHS AND MOUNTFORD COMPANY

commenced business in Trenton, in 1879, in what was formerly the Eagle Pottery. Their specialties are vitrified, thin, and hotel china, decorated table and toilet sets,

and underglaze printing on pottery and porcelain. The
mechanical application of decorations is the distinguish-

96.—Parian Bust—Cleopatra. Courtesy: New Jersey State Museum, Trenton.

ing characteristic of one line of their art potteries, which,
while closely imitating the more expensive methods of

hand-painting, enables them to produce highly artistic effects at a greatly reduced cost. The bold ornamentation of their *jardinières*, umbrella-jars, punch-bowls, and

97.—VASES. BURROUGHS & MOUNTFORD CO.

vases, after the Doulton, Royal Worcester, Limoges, and Adderley methods, bears a striking individuality of its

15

own. Probably their most beautiful pieces are those on which raised gold designs are applied by hand to an exquisite mazarine blue. One of the finest examples of this class is a large vase thirty-six inches in height, with silver and gold raised paste work, on a solid blue ground, executed by a Japanese artist. The accompanying illustration shows this piece mounted on a four-inch pedestal, between two vases of ordinary size (Ill. 97).

White tiles of a fine quality, with underglaze blue printed devices, as well as embossed and enamelled art tiles, are also made here to some extent.

One of their latest styles of ornamentation, as applied to panels in *jardinières* and vases, is the outline printing of human figures and scenes which are filled in by hand in colors, over the glaze. The effect is exceedingly rich and artistic, and by this process very creditable substitutes for the more expensive imported ceramic paintings are placed on the market at surprisingly low prices.

THE GREENWOOD POTTERY COMPANY

was incorporated in 1868, the present officers being Mr. James Tams, president, and Mr. James P. Stephens, secretary and treasurer. The business was established in 1861, under the style of Stephens, Tams, & Co. Mr. Tams came from Longton, Staffordshire, England, where, at an early age, he learned the pottery business in all of its branches. Until 1876 they made white granite or stone china ware, since which date they have been making a specialty of the manufacture of vitrified and translucent china for hotel, steamship, and railway uses. They are also producing at the present time thin china table ware of a superior quality, with overglaze and underglaze decorations, for domestic purposes, porcelain hardware trimmings, and electrical, telegraph, and telephone insulating supplies. Some years ago they added an art department to their extensive establishment, and their productions, consisting of vases, plaques, and other ornamental designs, richly decorated in the Royal Worcester style, are characterized by elegance of form, of which, it is said, no duplicates are made. The best pieces possess an ivory finish and white enamel, raised gold, silver, and bronze effects. Their mazarine blue is particularly noteworthy, being exceedingly rich in tone and remarkably fine and even in texture, and has been favorably compared with the *Bleu de Roi* of European factories. Another style of decoration, which has been practised here to some extent, is *pâte-sur-pâte* or clay upon clay.

98.—" IVORY " VASE, ROYAL WORCESTER STYLE. GREENWOOD POTTERY CO.

The plant of the company consists of seventeen large kilns, with an annual producing capacity of over half a million dollars. The experience of this company, in introducing their vitreous hotel china, reveals the extent of that deep-seated prejudice which existed in this country

some years ago against everything made in America, but
the superior merits of the ware were finally recognized,
and it has now largely taken the place of imported china.

The mark used from 1865 to 1876 was the coat-of-arms
of the State of New Jersey above the words " Ironstone
China," and " G. P. Co." This was printed in black
under the glaze. The first table porcelain made at this
pottery was stamped " G. P. Co."

MR. THOMAS MADDOCK

first made plumbers' sanitary ware in 1870, and still continues to manufacture it extensively. At the American
Institute Fair, held in New York in 1879, he exhibited an
interesting large Grecian vase of stoneware, decorated on
one side with a drawing of an ancient Egyptian potter at
work. The names of half a dozen governors of as many
States were written on the biscuit, who were present when
the piece was being made.

THE DELAWARE POTTERY.

In 1880 one of Mr. Maddock's foremen went to
the Enterprise Pottery and introduced these specialties
there. Mr. Oliphant was then interested in the latter
factory, but withdrew in 1884, and started the Delaware
Pottery in partnership with three of his sons, in conjunction with Mr. Thomas Connelly, recently from the
Belleek works, Ireland, and Mr. Charles Fay. Messrs.
Oliphant & Co. manufacture plumbers' appliances and
sanitary specialties, druggists' and jewellers' supplies.
These wares have justly acquired a wide reputation for

excellence of quality, design, and decoration. Their Wedgwood ware mortars and pestles are characterized by extreme hardness of body and smoothness of finish.

About 1886 Mr. Connelly commenced experimenting in Belleek china. He succeeded in producing some exquisitely thin trial pieces of the finest grade, but the ware was never made in sufficient quantity to place upon the market. The few pieces which were produced, consisting of small ewers, cups, and saucers, were fired in the large kilns with the sanitary ware. This branch of the business was not developed beyond the experimental stage, although at the time of Mr. Connelly's death, in 1890, success was assured.

THE INTERNATIONAL POTTERY.

In 1878 Messrs. James Carr, of New York, and Edward Clarke, of England, commenced the manufacture of cream-colored and white granite wares, as the Lincoln Pottery Company, in the old Speeler works, one of the first potteries built in Trenton for the manufacture of Rockingham and yellow wares. Mr. Carr retired within a few months, and Mr. Clarke, with others, founded the International Pottery Co. In 1879 the business was purchased by the present proprietors, Mr. William Burgess, now United States Consul at Tunstall, England, in the pottery district, and Mr. John A. Campbell, who have retained the corporate title. Porcelain was made here, with varying success, for some years previous to 1888, when a new body, of exceptional standing qualities, was produced, and has been made to the present time. The specialties of these works are toilet and dinner sets of artistic and novel shapes, in semi-porcelain body, in royal

blue, still blue, and gray underglaze colors. Their flown blue services, produced within the past two years, are of exceptional merit and have been pronounced equal in all respects to the best of the kind produced in England. While no special effort has been made in the direction of decorative designs, many of their pieces are characterized

99.—SEMI-PORCELAIN PLATE, COBALT BLUE BORDER AND GOLD PRINTED TRACERY. INTERNATIONAL POTTERY COMPANY.

by elegance of form and a richness and depth of blue ground seldom surpassed in this country or abroad. Their royal blue "Wilton" dinner service is especially praiseworthy. The International Pottery Co. also produces

porcelain of a fine quality, white granite, and other grades of ware, with embossed gold, enamelled, and vellum-finished decorations. The mark used on certain patterns

100.—SEMI-PORCELAIN TABLE WARE. INTERNATIONAL POTTERY COMPANY.

231

of underglaze ware is the circular stamp enclosing the names of the members of the firm, which is impressed in the clay. This and their Rugby flint china mark, which is printed under the glaze in brown, are here given.

They are now stamping all of their porcelain goods in blue color : Royal Blue

B—C

Porcelain.

The mark used on their ironstone china is the same which was formerly employed by Messrs. Carr & Clarke, and afterwards used in a modified form by Mr. Carr at his New York factory.

THE WILLETS MANUFACTURING CO.

Among the most extensive establishments in the Eastern States is that of the Willets Manufacturing Company of Trenton, N. J. The present proprietors, Messrs. Joseph, Daniel, and Edmund R. Willets, three brothers, succeeded to the business in 1879. The factory was erected in 1853 by William Young and Sons, who at first made Rockingham and common ware. At the Centennial Exhibition William Young's Sons made a display of crockery and porcelain hardware trimmings, at which time the plant included only four kilns. The business has since grown to such an extent, under the present management, that there are now thirteen large ware kilns besides those used for decorating. The products from these works include sanitary earthenware, plumbers' specialties, white and decorated pottery, opaque china, white granite, and art porcelain. A specialty in dinner and toilet services is underglazed decoration on white bodies.

After the Ott & Brewer Company had perfected the body and glaze of their Belleek ware and got it well under way, William Bromley, Sr., went with the Willets Manufacturing Company and instructed them in the process.

101.—SHELL AND CUPID PITCHER—BELLEEK. WILLETS MANUFACTURING COMPANY.

The manufacture of white egg-shell ware, to which they are constantly adding new designs, is another specialty of these works, and the company is now competing successfully with the Dresden, Limoges, and other foreign factories in supplying white art porcelain to decorators. In form their pieces are graceful and artistic, one of which is represented in Illustration 101. Some small picture frames, in Belleek body, decorated with delicately modelled flowers, are especially noteworthy.

102.—Large Vase, Chrysanthemum Decoration. Willets Manufacturing Company.

They also employ a number of competent artists to decorate their art goods, many of which are reproductions of the characteristic shell and coral forms of the Irish works. Illustration 102 represents a large Belleek vase with open-work handles and chrysanthemum decoration in delicate tints on an ivory, gold-stippled ground.

103.—Belleek Tray, Dresden Decoration. Willets Mfg. Co.

104.—Works of the Willets Manufacturing Company, Trenton, N. J.

THE CERAMIC ART COMPANY,

of which Mr. Jonathan Coxon, Sr., is president and Mr. Walter S. Lenox secretary and treasurer, was established in Trenton in 1889.   The first named gentleman became superintendent at the Ott & Brewer Company's works after Bromley left, and the latter was formerly in charge of their decorating department.   Here they learned the processes of manufacturing Belleek.   They are rapidly making a name by their constantly increasing patterns, many of which are exquisitely conceived and show the touch of thorough artists.   Their specialties are Belleek ware and " Indian china," many of their best pieces having been designed by Mr. William W. Gallimore. They have procured the best designers and painters that

105.—EGG-SHELL PORCELAIN—
THE "ENGAGEMENT" CUP AND SAUCER.
CERAMIC ART COMPANY.

can be found and employ both the overglaze and underglaze processes in decorating.   Their egg-shell ware is also furnished in the white to decorators.   Illustration 105 shows one of these undecorated pieces, a graceful lily-shaped cup and saucer.   In addition to vases and table pieces, they make many fancy patterns, such as thimbles, inkstands, parasol handles, menu slabs, and candelabra.

Among the most recent productions of the Ceramic Art Company are some beautiful pieces of carved ware, in Belleek body, which possess a high order of artistic merit. The decoration is entirely in relief, and is executed by carving the designs in the clay before burning, the only tool used being an ordinary jack-knife. This work is done by Miss Kate B. Sears, a young lady artist employed by

106.—Carved Vase. Ceramic Art Company.

the company. A spherical vase of this character, exhibited at the World's Columbian Exposition, is shown in Illustration 106. The interior is glazed, while the outside is porcelain bisque, entirely devoid of coloring in the decoration, which consists of elaborate designs of lilies and child figures extending around a central zone. The soft, white surface of the ware is admirably suited to the subject selected for decorative treatment.

THE TRENTON CHINA COMPANY

was incorporated in 1859, "to manufacture and sell porcelain, china, chemicals, drugs, and other articles of which clay, sand, and other earthy substances form the basis or principal ingredients." Of late years a specialty of this company has been vitrified china, white and decorated, for table uses. These works were closed in 1891. After undergoing a very troublesome experience before perfecting the quality of their china,—which was at last accomplished under the management of Mr. Duggan,—the money and patience of its backers became exhausted, and the company went into the hands of a receiver.

OTHER TRENTON POTTERIES.

By an Act approved February 9, 1865, the Trenton Pottery Company was incorporated for the manufacture of earthenware and crockery of various descriptions, the incorporators being Appollinaire Husson, James Taylor, John F. Houdayer, and Edmund Husson.

The Empire Pottery of Messrs. Alpaugh & Magowan was established in 1863, and was formerly owned by Messrs. Coxon & Thompson. In 1883 the business passed into the hands of the present proprietors. They manufacture thin porcelain, dinner, tea, and toilet, and decorated wares, principally in white granite body. They make a specialty of sanitary and plumbers' earthenware.

The Mercer Pottery Company was organized in 1868, and at the present time Mr. James Moses is the sole proprietor. The products of this pottery consist of a fine line of semi-porcelain dinner and toilet ware, both white and decorated; also white granite wares of the same kind. This firm was the first to produce what is now known as semi-porcelain earthenware in this country. Mr. Moses, we think, is fairly entitled to that credit. He has made a great success of it, and represents one of the leading firms in the United States to-day.

The New Jersey Pottery Company was organized in 1869, the incorporators being Elias Cook, John Woolverton, Caleb S. Green, Barker Gummere, and Nathaniel E. Britton.

The Fell & Thropp Company, known as the Trenton Pottery, was the old Taylor & Speeler pottery. It is now owned by Samuel E. Thropp and J. Hart Brewer. They manufacture a full line of white granite and C. C. wares. This pottery is the oldest white granite pottery in Trenton.

Messrs. Dale & Davis built the Pospect Hill Pottery in 1880, the latter having formerly been manager for Mr. John Moses at the Glasgow Pottery. They produce a large line of decorated semi-porcelain and white granite dinner and toilet wares.

The Crescent Pottery Company, composed of W. S. Hancock and Chas. H. Cook, was established in 1881. They manufacture sanitary earthenware and a full line of C. C. wares. At the present time they are one of the leading firms of Trenton.

The Crown Porcelain Works of Messrs. Barlow and Marsh were started in 1890. They produce a fine line of decorated *faïence* specialties. Mr. Marsh was formerly connected with Messrs. Robertson & Company of England, and is a practical potter and an artist of no mean ability.

The Trenton Terra-Cotta Company, of which Mr. Joseph McPherson is president, and Mr. O. O. Bowman is treasurer, manufacture an extensive line of fire-brick, vitrified salt-glazed sewer pipe, terra-cotta chimney tops and flues, and garden vases. The later are particularly elaborate and deservedly popular.

The American China Company of Trenton produced to a limited extent stone china decorated by the chromolithographic process, which has been employed in Europe for perhaps forty years. This process consists in the application of vitrifiable decalcomanie designs to the surface of the ware, either under or over the glaze, usually the latter. On a plate in my possession, made by the above-named company, is a central design of a crab, with marginal fronds of sea-weed in colors,—green, brown, black, and red. The effect is that of the ordinary decalcomanie transfer work, but, having been fired, the designs are permanently affixed, as in the other overglaze decorations. This process has been carried to great perfection, especially by the Doulton factory of Lambeth, England, and by some of the French potters, intricate and artistic designs being produced in delicate coloring which resemble fine hand-painted work, but the transfer printing can be distinguished by the dots and lines of the engraving, which can be readily detected on close inspection.

At the Arsenal Pottery of the Mayer Pottery Manufacturing Company, of which Mr. Joseph S. Mayer is president, decorated porcelain, underglazed and majolica wares are made. This is, probably, at the present time, the only concern in the United States which manufactures the so-called majolica ware. Their exhibit at the Chicago Fair included some finely modelled Toby pitchers or jugs, which are excellent imitations in form and color of the old English design so familiar to collectors.

The Union Pottery Company, which was closed in 1889, made for the political campaign of the previous year a quantity of six-inch tiles, dinner plates, etc., decorated with printed portraits of the Presidential candidates. This company was incorporated in 1869, the incorporators being Baltes Pickel, William White, Henry Smitn, Joshua Jones, and Elias Cook.

The American Art China Works were established December 1, 1891, in what was formerly known as the Washington Pottery, by Messrs. Rittenhouse, Evans, & Co. The ware made here is distinctively an American production, and is placed upon the market as American china. The body is thin, translucent, and strong, and resembles the Belleek ware made at other Trenton factories. The shapes are new, and the decorations artistic. The proprietors of these works are actuated by the laudable determination to demonstrate to the American public that it is possible to produce home goods fully equal in every respect to any that can be made abroad. White china, in all the shapes produced at these works, is sold for decorating.

16

In the latter part of 1892, Messrs. W. T. Morris and F. R. Willmore commenced the erection of a pottery in Trenton for the manufacture of art wares. The former was at one time connected with the Belleek works, Ireland, and the Royal Worcester Porcelain works, England, and recently with the Ott & Brewer Pottery of Trenton. Mr. Willmore was also for many years employed as decorator at the two last-named establishments. Their new works, which they have named the Columbian Art Pottery, were finished in the early part of 1893. Thin Belleek china and ivory ware, of a fine quality, are made here in original forms and decorations, and include articles of utility and ornamental pieces, such as candle-sticks, umbrella holders, *jardinières*, tea-pots, and specialties.

In addition to the Trenton establishments already mentioned are the East Trenton Pottery Co., which, during the Presidential campaign of 1888, produced plates with engraved portraits of the candidates; the Anchor Pottery; Enterprise Pottery Co.; Egyptian Pottery Co.; Equitable Pottery Co.; Warren Kimble; Imperial Porcelain Works of F. A. Duggan; C. W. Donaghue, potters' supplies; and a number of decorating establishments—Pope & Lee, Jesse Dean Decorating Co., W. C. Hendrickson, Tatler Decorating Co., and Poole & Stockton.

Other parties have also been engaged in the pottery industry since 1860 with varying success, some twenty establishments having discontinued business, with an aggregate loss of two million dollars.

Recently the Trenton Potteries Company has been incorporated, to acquire and continue the business heretofore conducted by the Empire, Enterprise, Delaware, Equitable, and Crescent potteries, with a capital stock of $3,000,000. Sanitary plumbing, toilet, and table wares will continue to be the staple productions.

The constant changes which are taking place in the pottery business in Trenton, through the closing of factories and the establishment of new ones every year, render it impossible to present a complete history of the industry to date, for even as these lines are being written word comes to us that new enterprises are being started ; and the wonderfully rapid advances in the art furnish evidence that no chronicler can keep pace with the progress of the American potter.

CHAPTER XII.

POTTERIES ESTABLISHED BETWEEN 1859 AND 1876.

A POTTERY was erected in Peoria, Ill., by Messrs. Fenton and Clark in 1859, who came from Bennington, Vt. They commenced the manufacture of white granite and cream-colored wares, but the venture did not prove a financial success and the factory was only operated about three years. Afterwards the works were continued by other parties, who made Rockingham and stoneware. We have seen some brown pottery tobacco jars which were made during this period, marked ^{PEORIA} ILLINOIS, of good form and excellent glaze.

In 1873 the Peoria Pottery Co. was organized and continued the manufacture of stoneware until 1889, when they took up the white-ware line and still continue to produce white granite, cream-colored, and decorated wares. At the Chicago Exhibition this company displayed some fine tinted table services in pale green, salmon, and other delicate colors.

THE NEW ENGLAND POTTERY CO.

Mr. L. W. Clark, son of Mr. Decius W. Clark, who was at one time superintendent of the United States Pottery,

Bennington, Vt., accompanied his father to Peoria, Ill., in 1859, and remained with the new firm of Fenton and Clark at that place for about two years, when he left to enter the army.   In 1875 he went to Boston, and, in partnership with Mr. Thomas Gray, assumed control of the New England Pottery.   This establishment was founded in 1854 by Mr. Frederick Meagher, who made Rockingham and yellow ware.   It was afterward taken by Mr. William H. Homer, from whom the plant was purchased by the present proprietors, who now produce the usual lines of useful services in cream-colored and white granite ware.   For the past five years they have been making a decorated product in colored bodies, to which they have given the name " Rieti " ware.   This is a semi-porcelain, finished and decorated chiefly after the Doulton, Adderley, and Worcester methods.   They also make porcelain of an admirable quality, and their goods are characterized by an artistic style of decoration and excellence of glaze, their mazarine blue and " old ivory " finish being especially praiseworthy.   The decorating branches are under the direct supervision of Mr. J. W. Phillips, who originates and engraves many of the best designs used in their printing processes.   Mr. Thomas H. Copeland designs and models most of their pieces which, from the line of trade they seek, are chiefly utilitarian rather than ornamental, but they possess a grace of outline and delicacy of coloring which render them objects of great beauty.   The chocolate jugs, *jardinières*, and cuspidors. of these works compare very favorably with the imported wares, after which they are to some extent patterned.   Of the few purely decorative forms which they have attempted, a semi-porcelain vase, twenty inches in height, made in 1889, is particularly meritorious. This is artistically painted in natural colors on raised paste, the top and base

being in solid dead gold. Mr. Bands, of the Royal Worcester works, England, was the artist (Ill. 108).

A two-handled cracker jar, made at this factory, is worthy of illustration. The body ground is polished ivory. The ornamentation consists of corn-flower grouping in embossed gold, with ferns and foliage in natural tints, outlined with

107.—TWO-HANDLED CRACKER JAR. NEW ENGLAND POTTERY CO.

gold. The fluted neck and base are tinted in robin's-egg blue with fleur-de-lis pendants, in relief gold. The form of the vessel is graceful and the handles are a convenient adjunct to the usually awkward form of cracker or rose jar (Ill. 107).

Mr. Clark's previous career as a potter will be found in connection with the history of other establishments, with which he was, at various times, associated. Porous cups for electrical purposes and other specialties in earthenware are also made here.

Among the most recent productions of the New England Pottery, of an ornamental character, are a *jardinière* and a chocolate jug, which deserve special description. The former is made of stone porcelain body and finished with bronze leaf scrolls on a white ground with buff shadings. The base is in clouded bronze and Roman gold. The form of the piece is graceful and the waving outlines of the upper edge produce an exceedingly ornate effect (Ill. 109).

The chocolate jug is also of stone porcelain. This is covered

108.—SEMI-PORCELAIN VASE.
NEW ENGLAND POTTERY COMPANY, 1889.

from shoulder to foot with a fine mazarine blue glaze, on which is laid a cameo decoration in raised white enamel. The subject of the decorative design, which is artistically conceived and admirably executed, is an "Interview between Bird and Bug" on a hawthorn bush. The shoulder of the piece is white, finished in relief gold filigree work, with small sectional panels of maroon, bearing raised gold rosettes. The borders and handle are finished in Roman gold. The contrast of the white design and the rich gold ornamentation against the deep-blue ground is particularly effective (Ill. 110.)

109.—JARDINIÈRE. NEW ENGLAND POTTERY CO.

POTTERY AT BATH, S. C.

In the spring of 1862, Col. Thomas J. Davies, a cotton planter in Edgefield Co. (now Aiken Co.), South Carolina, was induced by Anson Peeler, formerly of Bennington, Vt., who had been a resident of the former State for some six years, to embark in the manufacture of firebrick near Bath, on the South Carolina Railroad. Mr.

Peeler was a carpenter by trade and a skilled mechanic, and was placed in charge of the entire business. The necessary capital and the slaves for performing the labor were furnished by Col. Davies. Soon after the establish-

110.—Chocolate Jug. New England Pottery Company.

ment of these works large quantities of bricks were produced equal in quality to any that had previously been imported, which were marked "Bath, S. C., Fire-Bricks." The great furnaces for casting ordnance, and the powder mills of the South, procured their fire-bricks from these

works. From a small beginning an extensive business
was soon established, and crucibles and tiles for gas works
were also made extensively. In 1863 a great demand
sprang up for earthen jars, pitchers, cups and saucers, and
the fire-brick works were partially transformed into a
manufactory of such wares, which were produced in large
quantities by negro men and boys, who employed the old-
fashioned " kick-wheel " in their manufacture. The Confederate hospitals were supplied with thousands of these
articles of rude and primitive shape, the body being composed of three fourths to five sixths of kaolin and alluvium
earth from the swamp lands of the Savannah River, about
six miles distant. This composition made a tough body
which partially vitrified in burning. With sand and ashes
mixed thoroughly as a glaze, excellent results were obtained. The ware was black or brown, clumsy, and
entirely devoid of ornamentation, but strong and admirably adapted to the purposes demanded by the exi-
gencies of the time. In 1864 the products of the works
were insufficient for supplying the demand, although the
large horizontal kilns were devoted entirely to the burning
of these wares. At the termination of the war, in 1865,
operations at this pottery were suspended, and the enterprise passed into history.

Col. Davies was born in Georgia, and is a Southern
gentleman of the old school. He was graduated from
Princeton College, New Jersey, and has been a resident
of South Carolina for fifty years. Since his retirement
from the pottery business he has been engaged in the
mining of china clays.

So far as can be ascertained, there was but one other pottery in the South during the Civil War,—that of the Stevens brothers, near Milledgeville, Georgia, where crude earthenware was made.   These works have been extended, and are at present producing fire-bricks and tiles.

THE PHILADELPHIA CITY POTTERY.

These works were established by Messrs. J. E. Jeffords & Co., in 1868, as the Port Richmond Pottery Co.

III.—DECORATED COFFEE-POT, DARK-BLUE GROUND.   J. E. JEFFORDS & CO.

The pottery now includes two distinct factories, one of which turns out a high grade of Rockingham, yellow, and white-lined blue ware, mostly for culinary purposes, while the adjoining works produce an excellent variety of white and decorated pottery for table and toilet uses.   In Rockingham, some of the old English designs are reproduced, such as the "Toby" ale-jug and the cow creamer. The decorated white ware, such as tea-pots and gypsy kettles, ornamented with floral designs in gold and colors, on dark-red, blue, brown, and cream-colored grounds, possess considerable merit. A few years ago a more elaborate style of ornamentation was attempted in the painting of bird and floral subjects above the glaze (see Ill. 111), but this was soon discontinued as being too costly for the general market. Printing from copper plates is extensively practised here at the present time, and competent artists are employed in the decorative departments. Mr. Jeffords came from the New York City Pottery of Messrs. Morrison & Carr, where he learned the various branches of the business. He has fully equipped his factories with the most approved modern appliances, and employs about one hundred and eighty hands. Among other specialties extensively produced here are decorated *jardinières* and stoneware bottles for liquor baskets, which are sold largely for yachting and excursion purposes.

The only mark which has ever been used at this establishment is a diamond bearing the date of the establishment of the present firm, 1868.

THE UNION PORCELAIN WORKS.

Messrs. Thomas C. Smith and C. H. L. Smith are the proprietors of these works, which are situated at

Greenpoint, Long Island. They manufacture a true hard porcelain in table services, decorative pieces, electrical insulators, and hardware trimmings. The senior member of the firm, who is an American, was formerly an architect by profession, but owing to a peculiar combination of circumstances was forced to purchase these works about the time of the breaking out of the Civil War, without intending to engage in the business himself. During an absence abroad shortly afterwards, however, he conceived the idea of embarking in the porcelain business, and on his return he set to work to utilize the knowledge which he had acquired among the large factories of Europe and at once commenced his experiments. The composition which had been used by the German potters from whom he bought the works was the English bone body, which was abandoned by Mr. Smith in 1864, when he introduced the hard kaolinic body, which has since been

112.—BONE-CHINA MUG, RAISED DECORATIONS. UNION PORCELAIN WORKS, 1864.

made exclusively to the present time. An example of translucent bone porcelain, made in the latter year, is a beer mug with embossed figures of Bacchus, surrounded by vine-leaves, shown in Illustration 112. The earlier experiments made by Mr. Smith were attended with only partial success, but in 1865 he perfected a plain white ware for the market, and a year afterward he commenced to decorate his goods. But here he was met with the difficulty of finding underglaze colors which would stand the intense heat of the sharp fire necessary to vitrify the ware. So far as we have any knowledge, Mr. Smith was the first potter in America to apply the underglaze method of decoration to hard porcelain, for it has already been seen that Messrs. Tucker & Hemphill, in Philadelphia, used only overglaze colors from 1825 to 1838, during the existence of their porcelain factory. The Greenpoint works, however, have of late years used the overglaze method also, in order to obtain a greater variety of coloring in the production of decorative art pieces.

The late Karl Müller, a talented German sculptor and artist, who was educated in Paris, was employed for several years at the Greenpoint works as chief designer and modeller. Just previous to the Centennial Exhibition, Mr. Müller designed a number of vases and other pieces which exhibit a marked originality in conception and a high degree of excellence in execution. Of these we may mention the Century vase, in which appears a relief portrait of Washington against a mat blue ground, panels around the base representing, in white relief, an Indian, the Tea Scene in Boston Harbor, a Revolutionary Soldier, and other historical subjects. The handles of the vase represent the head of the American bison. A second vase is designed to illustrate Longfellow's poem, " Kéramos," with raised designs commemorating the history of the ceramic art from the most remote ages. Two busts in a buff body represent Edwin Forrest as *William*

Century Vase. · Greenpoint Porcelain.

Poets' Pitcher. Greenpoint Biscuit Porcelain.

Greenpoint Porcelain. Painted by J. M. Falconer.

Greenpoint Porcelain.

Greenpoint Porcelain. View of
Memorial Hall.

Greenpoint Porcelain.

" Kéramos " Vase.
Greenpoint Porcelain.

Greenpoint Porcelain.

Tell (Ill. 116), and Charlotte Cushman as *Meg Merrilies*,
modelled by Mr. Müller from photographs. A series of
statuettes, pitchers, and busts of prominent Americans,
in porcelain biscuit, reveal the highest art of the sculptor. A Poet's pitcher, in biscuit, designed by Mr. Müller,
is among the most highly artistic works produced at
this factory. It is of graceful form, embellished with
relief portraits of prominent poets of ancient and
modern times. The
"Liberty cup" is beau-
tifully modelled, with
embossed figures of
Mercury and Justice,
surrounded by the corn
plant of the North and
the tobacco plant of the
South, with handle rep-
resenting the Goddess
of Liberty standing on
an eagle with outspread
wings. It is finished in
mat gold traced with
color (Ill. 113).

113.—THE LIBERTY CUP,   MODELLED BY
MÜLLER. UNION PORCELAIN WORKS.

Among the artists engaged in decorating the Greenpoint porcelain, Mr. J. M. Falconer of Brooklyn has been
one of the most prominent. Some of his paintings on
plates and plaques exhibit a high degree of artistic merit,
as in some views of Centennial buildings, and a number
of ideal designs, in which the coloring is chaste and the
execution admirable.

The manufacture of hard porcelain tiles has become an important branch of the business of this factory. These tiles are made both thick and thin, in underglaze decoration, and are claimed to be the only tiles made in this country which will endure the heat of a hearth fire.

114.—GREENPOINT PORCELAIN VASE, IN EMBOSSED GOLD AND JEWEL WORK. GROTESQUE LIZARDS IN MAT GOLD.

They are decorated with figures of griffins and other fancy designs. The overglaze method has also been applied to tiles for mantel facings and wainscoting, and on the walls of the private office of the establishment may be seen a series of large tile panels embellished with paintings representing the ancient ceramic processes of Egypt, as depicted on the pyramids.

In table services the most noteworthy are those decorated in overglaze colors and white enamelled designs. A handsome dinner set in underglaze blue outlined with gold, is one of the latest achievements of this factory.

115.—TÊTE-À-TÊTE SET. UNION PORCELAIN WORKS.

The composition of the paste varies according to the purpose for which it is to be used. For the manufacture of hardware trimmings, which form an important part of the products of these works, a larger proportion of kaolin is introduced.

The porcelain made here is composed in body of kaolin, quartz, and feldspar.   It is fired in biscuit at a low
temperature, in the second story of the porcelain kiln,
using for its baking the surplus heat passing away after
having done its greater work in the first story or glost kiln
where the glazing is done.   At this first burning the ware

116.—BUST OF EDWIN FORREST AS WILLIAM TELL.
UNION PORCELAIN WORKS.

receives only sufficient fire to make it properly fasten
together in form.   It is quite fragile, easily broken with
the fingers, and porous, not having yet had sufficient heat
to commence vitrification.   In this condition it is what is

termed porcelain biscuit, and is ready for the glaze-tub. The glaze of porcelain is composed of the same materials as the body, and so compounded that those elements which are soonest fluxed by the influence of the heat are in greater proportion than they are contained in the body. The porous, low-fired biscuit is dipped into a liquid puddle of glaze. Upon being withdrawn its porosity quickly absorbs the excess of water, leaving a dry coating of the glaze compound, which has held the water in suspension, upon the surface of the piece. This piece of porous biscuit covered with glaze is now cleaned of glaze upon its foot, or that part upon which it rests, to prevent its sticking or burning fast to the clay sagger or firing case ; otherwise the glaze on the bearing parts would, at the time of flowing, form a cement, fastening the piece and the sagger together. The pieces are placed separately in the saggers. The heat in firing hard porcelain is carried to such a high degree that the ware touches the point of pliability, almost the melting-point. At this great heat the body is vitrified ; at the same time the glaze, from its slightly softer composition, is melted into the body of the ware, producing a hard, vitreous, and homogeneous material properly known as true, hard porcelain. This is the process used at Sèvres, Meissen, Berlin, and elsewhere.

THE MOORHEAD CLAY WORKS.

These works were established at Spring Mills, Montgomery Co., Pa., in 1866, by Messrs A. S. Moorhead and Wm. L. Wilson, and three years later were entirely destroyed by fire. New works were at once built on the same site, of much greater capacity. The products of these works are terra-cotta sewer pipes, ornamental chimney tops, drain tile, pipe flues, fire-brick and tiles, garden edging and border tile, flower-pots, terra-cotta window boxes, hanging vases, *jardinières*, garden vases, pedestals and statuary, rustic ornaments, fountains, aquarium ornaments, and terra-cotta shapes for decorators.

THE CHELSEA KERAMIC ART WORKS.

Mr. Alexander William Robertson started a small pottery in Chelsea, Mass., in the year 1866, for the manufacture of brown ware such as was made in Great Britain, and of lava ware similar to that of Germany. Two years afterwards Mr. Hugh Cornwall Robertson, a younger brother, who had served an apprenticeship at the Jersey City Pottery in 1860, was admitted to partnership in the business, the firm name becoming A. W. & H. C. Robertson, when the production of brown ware was discontinued and the manufacture of plain and fancy flower-pots was substituted. In the following year porous cones or filters were made for chemical purposes. In 1872 James Robertson, a practical potter of wide and varied experience in Scotland, England, New Jersey, and New York, and recently from the East Boston pottery, joined his sons, the firm style being changed to James Robertson & Sons, when work of a more pretentious character was undertaken. A red bisque ware, in imitation of the antique Grecian terra-cottas and Pompeiian bronzes was first produced in 1875. The factory adopted the name of the Chelsea Keramic Art Works. The red ware was characterized by a remarkably fine texture and smooth finish, the clay being peculiarly adapted to the faithful reproduction of the graceful classic forms, the fine polished grain offering an excellent surface for the most minute carving, showing the engraved lines as perfectly as on wood.

Some of the vases were decorated with red figures on a black ground, in the ancient Greek style, modelled after pieces in the Englefield collection. Of these the amphora, lecythus, œnochœ, stamnos, and krater were favorite forms. The ornamentation of this class of ware is the natural red clay, the black having been worked on with the brush around the designs. The process of polishing

117.—GREEK REPRODUCTION, CHELSEA KERAMIC ART WORKS. BOSTON MUSEUM OF FINE ARTS.

the surface completed the resemblance to the antique. One of the finest of these reproductions is a large vase, thirteen and a half inches high, in the Boston Museum of Fine Arts. It is the early work of Mr. John G. Low of Chelsea (Ill. 117).

On thirteen vases of fine red body, Mr. Franz Xavier Dengler, the talented young sculptor, who afterwards died at the age of twenty-five, modelled from life, in high relief, choosing child and bird forms. One of these, in the Boston Museum of Fine Arts, is shown in Illustration 119. It is a vase fifteen inches in height, of compact, red clay. The firm also received the benefit of advice from a number of capable artists, including John G. Low, G. W. Fenety, and others. For lack of public support, however, this branch of the art was soon abandoned. The next venture was the Chelsea *faïence*, introduced in 1877, which

118.—CHELSEA FAÏENCE. BARBER COLLECTION.

is characterized by a beautiful soft glaze. This ware soon attracted the attention of connoisseurs, and carried the firm to the front rank of American potters. The decoration consists of floral designs, either made separately by hand and sprigged on, or carved in relief from clay laid directly on the surface while moist.

A number of plaques about ten inches in diameter were modelled by Mr. H. C. Robertson, either engraved or carved in high relief, some of the latter being modelled after Doré's illustrations of La Fontaine's *Fables*, such as "The Wolf Turned Shepherd," etc.   They were made of a stone body, and generally covered with a quiet blue or gray glaze.

Some novel effects were produced by *hammering* the exterior of vases before burning, and afterward carving sprays of flowers in relief and applying them to the indented surface. The modelling was executed by Miss Josephine Day, a sister-in-law and pupil of Mr. H. C. Robertson, and by Mr. Robertson himself.   Being done by hand, from original designs, no duplicates were produced.   On some of the hammered pieces, the designs were cut into the surface and filled in with white clay, forming a mosaic, the bases of the vessels being colored buff, which formed a pleasing

119.—A "DENGLER" VASE, RED WARE, MODELLED DESIGNS. BOSTON MUSEUM OF FINE ARTS.

contrast beneath a semi-transparent glaze.   About the same time a variety of *faïence*, known as the Bourg-la-Reine of Chelsea, was produced by the process of painting on the surface of the vessel with colored clays and covering with a transparent glaze, on the principle of the Limoges *faïence*.

Mr. James Robertson died in 1880, after a long and useful life, at the ripe age of seventy years. The firm continued under the same name, and in 1884 A. W. Robertson retired from the business. In that year the remaining partner, Mr. Hugh C. Robertson, commenced

120.—INLAID, HAMMERED, AND EMBOSSED POTTERY.
CHELSEA KERAMIC ART WORKS.

to make a stoneware somewhat resembling parian in appearance, possessing a hard, vitrified body, which he worked into a variety of artistic forms.

From this time Mr. Robertson directed his efforts toward solving the secret of the famous Chinese *Sang de bœuf,* and after four years of sacrifice and patient investigation his labors were in a measure successful. He believes he has discovered the exact treatment necessary to produce the true ox-blood red, which with the Chinese was the result of accident rather than an established art. The body is the true stone, perfectly waterproof, and capable of resisting as high a degree of heat as any ware. The forms of the vases are simple, with curving outlines, and entirely devoid of ornamentation which would tend to impair the beauty of color, which is that of fresh arterial blood, possessing a golden lustre, which in the light glistens with all the varying hues of a sunset sky. In experimenting to obtain the blood-red of the *Sang de bœuf*, varieties were produced of a deep sea-green, "peach-blow," apple-green, mustard-yellow, greenish blue, maroon, and rich purple, the glaze being hard, brilliant, and deep. Examples of this ware now grace the cabinets of a number of collectors in the United

121.—Crackle Vase. Boston Museum of Fine Arts.

States, of which Mrs. F. S. Thomas, of New York, purchased four of the finest. Only three hundred pieces of the Sang de Chelsea were made, but the demand for works of this character being limited, some of the finest examples still rest on the dusty shelves in the Chelsea workshop.

Imitations of the Japanese crackle ware were also produced, and a specimen of this class, in the Boston Museum of Fine Arts, which is of a gray color, with blue underglaze decoration, compares very favorably with Oriental

122.—PLAQUE REPRESENTING "SPRING." DESIGNED BY H. C. ROBERTSON, 1879.

examples. This was executed by Mr. Hugh C. Robertson (Illustration 121).

In the collection of Dr. Marcus Benjamin of New York City is a pilgrim vase decorated after a drawing by Mr. James E. Kelly of New York, which originally appeared in the old *Scribner's Monthly Magazine* of May, 1878, the subject being the old-time post boy, mounted on a horse and heralding his approach to the village by blowing his trumpet, which afterwards developed into Kelly's statuette of Sheridan (see *Cyclopedia of American Biography*,—Sheridan). The figures were modelled by Mr. Hugh C. Robertson in low relief, to which an effective glaze adds depth and distance. They were worked in white clay and laid on the yellow body of the vase and then covered with a single glaze, producing the effect of a grayish-blue design against a yellowish-olive or mouse-colored ground. Only five or six copies were produced.

After more than twenty years of devotion to his art, Mr. Robertson was compelled to close his factory in 1888 for lack of means to carry his work further. A company, however, was incorporated on July 17, 1891, under the title "Chelsea Pottery, U. S.," of which Mr. Hugh C. Robertson was appointed manager. Here, with increased facilities at his command, Mr. Robertson will devote himself to the further development of American ceramic art.

POTTERY AT PHŒNIXVILLE, PA.

The Phœnixville Pottery, Kaolin, and Fire-brick Company was organized in 1867, and a few years later was succeeded by Messrs Schreiber & Co., who made yellow and Rockingham ware, and terra-cotta ornaments and wall-pieces. Heads of hounds and stags in several sizes, and large boar's heads, were made extensively here, and twenty years ago were in demand for decorating the in-

teriors of public-houses.   Some of these may still be seen
in country taverns.   These were considered works of considerable artistic merit when first produced.   The antlers
and horns of stags and antelopes were made separately
and afterwards inserted.   Messrs. Beerbower & Griffen
took the pottery in 1877 and commenced the manufacture
of white granite ware.   In 1879 the firm name was changed
to Griffen, Smith, & Hill, and in the following year

123.—TERRA-COTTA BOAR'S HEAD. PHŒNIX-
VILLE POTTERY. BARBER COLLECTION,

the   manufacture   of
" Etruscan " majolica
was added.   Through
their majolica ware
the firm became widely
known.   The model-
ling of some of the
pieces, such as *com-
potières* with supports
composed of three in-
tertwined   dolphins,
boudoir flower-shells
or jewel cups, and

other fancy shapes, was refined and artistic, the designer
being an English artist of the name of Bourne.   Some of
these designs bear a striking resemblance to the Irish
Belleek ware, not only in conception but in the extreme
thinness of the body and the tinted nacreous glazes which
cover them.   Coral, sea-weed (Fucus), and marine shells
were closely imitated and their commercial majolica for
table purposes was largely made in leaf forms from moulds
taken from the natural objects.   The impressed mark

used on this ware was a monogram composed of the initials of the firm (G. S. H.), sometimes surrounded by a circular band containing the words " Etruscan Majolica." These marks continued to be used after the retirement of Mr. Hill, when the style became Griffen, Smith, & Co. From 1880 to 1890 the factory produced a good grade of white and decorated ware, mostly in table services and toilet sets.   In 1890 a large portion of the works was destroyed by fire and the manufacture of majolica was dis-

124.—MAJOLICA.   PHŒNIXVILLE POTTERY.

continued.   Mr. Smith withdrew from the firm in 1889 and erected levigating mills at Toughkenamon, Pa., near which place are large beds of kaolin.   The firm style was then changed to Griffen, Love, & Co.

As early as 1882 experiments were commenced in the manufacture of hard porcelain, and a series of sample pieces were made for the New Orleans Exhibition.   The quality and designs of these trial pieces were creditable, and the experiment proved that this factory was capable of producing true porcelain of a high order.   One of the New Orleans pieces, a pitcher of thin semi-transparent body, was also made of white earthenware, glazed and gilded, the latter of which is reproduced in Ill. 125.   It is in the shape of a canteen, the mouth representing the head

125.—WHITE-WARE PITCHER.
PHŒNIXVILLE, PA.

of a Continental soldier. The raised designs are flesh-colored, on a solid gold ground.   The three-cornered hat is black.   Mr. Scott Callowhill, an English artist, was employed for a while in modelling and painting, but left to accept a position with the Providential Tile Works of Trenton.

At the beginning of the year 1891 a change was made in the proprietorship, and a new company incorporated, under the title of the Griffen China Company, for manufacturing fine translucent French china in plain white table services.

In 1892 these works were permanently closed.

THE HAMPSHIRE POTTERY.

Some original work of a high character is now being done at the Hampshire Pottery of Messrs. J. S. Taft & Co., Keene, N. H.   This pottery was started in 1871 for the manufacture of red ware, and afterwards stoneware. At a later date majolica was made quite extensively.

Recently the firm has been paying particular attention to art specialties, in new and graceful shapes and novel decorations, such as fancy baskets, jugs, cracker jars, and cuspidors, comb and brush trays, bon-bon boxes, rose bowls, tea sets, and umbrella stands. The ware is a white, opaque body, covered with a variety of effective glazes. I have seen at Niagara and other summer resorts pieces of Keene pottery with local views printed upon the surface for sale to tourists as souvenirs.

One of the best designs produced by these works is the " Witch Jug," of a graceful form and ivory tint. On one side is painted, in appropriate colors, a witch, with broom in hand, in pursuit of bats, against a ground of clouds. On the opposite side are three witch pins in black, and the lettering "Salem, 1692," in gold. The handle, foot, and border of lip are gilded. This souvenir jug was made especially for Mr. Daniel Low, silversmith, of Salem,

126.—The Witch Jug. Hampshire Pottery. J. S. Taft & Co., Keene, N. H.

Mass., to commemorate the witchcraft delusion which obtained in that place two hundred years ago, the sale being entirely controlled by him.

About forty hands are employed at the Hampshire Pottery, nearly half the number being engaged in decorating.

TERRA-COTTA WORKS, PHILADELPHIA.

Messrs. Galloway & Graff displayed at the Centennial terra-cotta statuary, tazzas, and vases in Greek shapes for decorators, pedestals, fountains, flower-pots, and garden edging.

Messrs. Harvey, Moland, & Co., successors to Wm. K. Black, are large producers of garden vases, statuary, sewer pipe, and drain tile.

CHAPTER XIII.

CINCINNATI.

A MONG the first potteries of Cincinnati was one which
was in operation for some time previous to the
middle of the present century, owned by a family
of the name of Kendall, father and sons, who were
remarkable for their great stature, being over six feet
in height. This pottery is said to have been the first in
that city to produce a fine grade of stoneware, yellow, and
Rockingham. About the year 1850 the Kendalls gave up
business and went farther west.

William Bromley, originally from Stoke-upon-Trent,
England, went to Cincinnati about 1842 and successfully
operated a pottery there for several years. At one time
the ware in one of his kilns met with a singular mishap in
the process of firing, which caused it to assume such a
novel appearance that it was sold at very high prices.
There was considerable demand for more of the same
character, which of course could not be furnished, because
Mr. Bromley did not know how the freak occurred, and
his excuse to those who desired it was that he could not
supply it *because it was too costly to make*. He died about
twenty years ago.

George Scott, of Staffordshire, England, came to this country about 1846, and shortly after settled in Cincinnati, where for some time he sold goods for William Bromley. It is said that, after saving some money, he imported a thousand dollars' worth of queensware from England, which he disposed of advantageously and with the proceeds purchased an old tavern on Front Street, and changed it into a pottery. With the able assistance of his wife, who was as capable a potter as he, a business was established which soon yielded him a competency, and after his death some years ago the firm's name was changed to George Scott's Sons, under which style the business is now carried on. This consists of the manufacture of a high grade of white granite, cream-colored, decorated, and printed table and toilet wares.

The Hamilton Road Pottery was founded by Messrs. M. and N. Tempest, and in 1865 was purchased by Mr. Frederick Dallas, who continued the business until his death a few years ago. Here were made stone china and the commoner wares. Some of the earliest experiments of the ladies of Cincinnati were conducted at these works, as we shall see hereafter, which marked the first step in the development of the industry in that city.

Messrs. Tempest, Brockmann, & Co. commenced the manufacture of common ware in Cincinnati in 1862, and five years later first produced white ware. In 1881 a stock company was organized, under the title of The Tempest, Brockmann, & Sampson Pottery Co., and so continued until 1887, when Mr. C. E. Brockmann, the only surviving member of the original firm, bought the entire business, and has since conducted it under the name of The Brockmann Pottery Co. The works cover an acre of ground, and are about to be further enlarged. The products of this factory embrace cream-colored, white granite, and decorated wares.

WOMAN'S WORK IN CINCINNATI.

The decorative pottery movement which has made Cincinnati celebrated as a ceramic art centre may be said to have had its inception in 1875, when Mr. Benn Pitman, of the Cincinnati School of Design, procured from the east some overglaze colors and invited a few of the ladies of that city, who were interested in the subject, to meet at his offices in the Carlisle Building to talk over the matter of forming a class to receive instructions in china painting. It was in these rooms that the first experiments in porcelain decoration were made, under the direction of a young German lady, Miss Eggers, who had previously acquired some knowledge of the art at Dresden. Following closely on these somewhat imperfectly successful efforts came a " Centennial Tea Party," held by the " Women's Centennial Executive Committee, of Cincinnati," for the benefit of the Mount Vernon fund. The pieces of china, which had been painted by the ladies especially for this occasion, were placed on exhibition and afterwards sold by auction. Good prices were realized, the highest being twenty-five dollars for a cup and saucer. This event marked the first step in the progress of the ceramic art in Cincinnati. In the same year, Miss M.

Louise McLaughlin painted some white porcelain plates in blue underglaze designs, which were sent to Messrs. Thomas C. Smith & Son, proprietors of the Union Porcelain works at Greenpoint, Long Island, by whom they were fired, and one of these first attempts is preserved in the Cincinnati Museum of Art.

During the Centennial Exposition, in the following year, Miss McLaughlin was particularly impressed with the exhibit of the then novel Limoges *faïence*, and on her return home she determined to discover, if possible, the method of its decoration. Her first experiments were attempted in the fall of 1877, after having procured colors from Paris, at the pottery of Messrs. P. L. Coultry & Co., where common yellow ware was made. These experiments were conducted under great disadvantages on account of the limited facilities at command. The first piece taken from the kiln, in September, 1877, demonstrated the practicability of the process. In May following some pieces were shown at a local loan exhibition, and others were exhibited in New York in October. Pieces were also exhibited at the Exposition Universelle at Paris in 1879, and received honorable mention.

The success attained by Miss McLaughlin stimulated other ladies to renewed efforts in the same direction, and soon a little colony of workers had sprung up in the Queen City. In April of 1879, Miss McLaughlin gathered around her a number of ladies who were interested in decorative art, and the Pottery Club, which afterwards became an important factor in the development of the ceramic art industry in Cincinnati, was organized, with

Miss McLaughlin, president, Miss Clara Chipman Newton, secretary, and Miss Alice Belle Holabird, treasurer. This was probably the first club of women, organized for such a purpose, in the United States. In addition to those already named, the following ladies constituted the

127.—VASES BY MRS. MARIA L. NICHOLS, 1880.

original membership: Mrs. C. A. Plimpton, Mrs. E. G. Leonard, Miss Mary Spencer, Miss Agnes Pitman, Mrs. Frank R. Ellis, Mrs. Wm. Dodd, Miss Clara Fletcher, Mrs. George Dominick, and Miss Laura A. Fry. Later the number was increased to fifteen, and finally to twenty. A room was rented in the pottery owned by Mr. Frederick Dallas, on Hamilton Road, where white and cream-colored wares were produced. Two kilns for firing underglaze and over-glaze ware were erected here, the cost being defrayed by Miss McLaughlin and Mrs. Maria Longworth Nichols. Experiments were prosecuted with greater vigor, and rapid improvement in methods was made, through the intelligent co-operation of Mr. Dallas and his foreman, Mr. Joseph Bailey, now superintendent of the Rookwood Pottery. Mrs. Nichols and other ladies, not members of the Pottery Club,

128.—PORCELAIN VASE, UNDERGLAZE DECORATION. BY MRS. M. L. NICHOLS, 1878.

worked in another part of the building which had been erected by the mother of Anthony Trollope for her country-house during her residence in Cincinnati.

Various styles of work were attempted here during 1879 and 1880.

129.—"Ali Baba" Vase, Underglaze Decoration by M. L. McLaughlin, 1880. On loan to the Cincinnati Art Museum.

Among Mrs. Nichols' best pieces of this period are three vases, shown in Illustration 127, the largest being thirty-two inches in height, in bold relief and underglaze color. Possessed of rare and versatile talent, she has since produced a great variety of pieces, original in conception, artistic in treatment, and bold in execution.

130.—White Clay Vase, Underglaze Decoration.
Miss Clara Chipman Newton, 1880.

Under the leadership of Miss McLaughlin the Limoges, or *pâte-sur-pâte*, method of painting the surfaces of unbaked pieces with colored slips was employed with gratifying results. One of the finest of her pieces finished during this period is the "Ali Baba" vase, thirty-eight inches in height, which is made. of red clay, decorated under the transparent glaze with colors mixed with white clay (Ill. 129). The design is the Chinese

Hibiscus, in dull red and yellow on a delicate sage-green ground, d a i n t i l y blending to a greenish white. Three of these vases were made from the mould, one of which is now in the Cincinnati Museum.

Other members of the club, of whom Miss Clara Chipman Newton was one of the foremost, directed their attention more particularly to painting on the bis-

131.—*Moorish Vase, Inlaid Decoration. L. F. Plimpton, Designer; Mrs. C. A. Plimpton, Decorator, 1881. Given to the Cincinnati Art Museum by the Women's Art Museum Assn.*

cuit in cobalt blue and other colors, and achieved a marked success. An example of this style, the work of Miss Newton, is here figured (Ill. 130). It is a vase of white clay body, twenty-one inches high, with arabesque design painted under the glaze, and finished with intersecting gilt lines and gold bands at top and bottom, above the glaze. This was produced in 1880, at the Hamilton Road Pottery, the coloring being a dark, rich blue, clean cut and sharp, without any trace of flowing.

132.—*Stoneware Jug with Incised Decoration by Miss Laura A. Fry, 1881. Given to the Cincinnati Art Museum by the Women's Art Museum Assn.*

Pottery Illustration 131 shows an exceedingly artistic example, with pierced handles. This vase was designed by Mr. L. F. Plimpton and decorated by Mrs. Plimpton, and is now owned by the Cincinnati Art Museum. The ground is yellow, with inlaying of red and other Ohio clays and a black clay from Indiana. In the Cincinnati

133.—Miss M. Louise McLaughlin.

room of the Woman's Building at the World's Columbian Exposition, this piece attracted considerable attention.

Miss Laura A. Fry also produced some excellent work in etched designs after the Doulton method. A stone jug, with incised decoration, outlined in blue, and made in 1881, is also the property of the same museum (Ill. 132).

Another style, consisting of relief work in parian paste, received attention from several members of the club, notably Mrs. E. G. Leonard and Miss Agnes Pitman. It is not possible to review at length the individual work of each interested worker in this field. All followed out ideas more or less original and each accomplished work of genuine merit. We must refer those who desire to pursue this subject further to the excellent article in the May number of *Harper's Magazine* for 1881, by Mrs. Aaron F. Perry. The Pottery Club continued a successful and harmonious existence until 1890, when, on account of a lack of financial support, it was disbanded by mutual consent. Miss McLaughlin and Miss Newton have continued their work in overglaze decoration, and the former has embodied the results of her investigations in a series of valuable treatises on Pottery Decoration and China Painting.

After the Pottery Club had disbanded, a few of the former members organized a club which they called *The Associated Artists of Cincinnati*, of which Miss McLaughlin became president and Miss Newton secretary. Many beautiful examples of overglaze decoration, as well as metal work, executed by the members of this association, were exhibited at the Chicago Fair, among which some large porcelain vases, artistically painted in dainty colors and gold tracery, will rank with the best professional work.

ROOKWOOD.

It is safe to assert that no ceramic establishment which has existed in the United States has come nearer

fulfilling the requirements of a distinctively American institution than the Rookwood Pottery of Cincinnati, Ohio.
For this reason, and because of the additional fact that
the founding of this factory was due to the intelligent and
well directed efforts of a woman, the history of Rookwood, from its inception, cannot fail to have a peculiar
interest for American collectors and patrons of art.

The ceramic display of Japan, at the Philadelphia
Exhibition of 1876, inspired the venture which resulted
in the establishment of these works, in 1880, by Mrs. Maria
Longworth Nichols (now Mrs. Bellamy Storer), whom
we have already seen as an
enthusiastic investigator and
student in some of the Cincinnati potteries. She began
her work at the Dallas white-
ware pottery, where she and
several other amateurs continued for two years. The

134.—Old Rookwood.

heat being found to be too intense for firing underglaze
colors, at the granite ware factory, first suggested to Mrs.
Nichols the idea of building a place of her own. Her experiments were continued at the new establishment, which
she had erected at 207 Eastern Avenue, and which,
through the wise liberality of her father, Mr. Joseph Longworth, was afterwards furnished with the necessary means
for its maintenance while its products were finding a
market and until financially it could stand alone. The
name selected for the works was that of the country place
of Mr. Longworth, at East Walnut Hills, in the suburbs

of the city, so called on account of the great number of crows which frequented the adjacent woods.   In the more congenial quarters of the new pottery Mrs. Nichols sur- rounded herself with skilled workmen and able artists, and the first kiln of ware was fired in November of 1880. A specialty was first made of commercial ware for table

135.—MRS. MARIA LONGWORTH STORER.

and household purposes, the principal body used being intermediary between cream-colored and white granite wares.   In 1881 considerable quantities of this ware were produced in breakfast and dinner services, pitchers, plaques, vases, wine-coolers, ice-tubs, water-buckets, um- brella jars, and a variety of other patterns, which were sold either in ivory finish or decorated with underglaze blue and brown prints of birds, fishes, and other animal subjects. These, being artistic in form and now difficult to procure, are much sought for by collectors (see Ill. 136). All of the forms made in white during this period were also furnished in blue, sage-green, and red bodies, which were often ornamented with devices carved in the paste. The border work on white tea-sets was painted

136.—ROOKWOOD PLATE, PRINTED DECORATION.

over the glaze by an Englishman named Broomfield. Yellow ware of a superior quality was also made about the same time.

During the last-named year, Mr. Ferdinand Mersman, at present modeller for the Cambridge Art Tile Works at Covington, Ky., just across the river, designed some fine pieces for the Rookwood works, including a Garfield

Memorial pitcher and several vases with figures in high relief, the latter being modelled entirely by hand and never duplicated. The pitchers, with relief portrait of President Garfield, were made of sage-green clay with "smear" or dull glaze, in two sizes, of which less than a hundred were issued.

The printing processes were soon entirely abandoned

137.—Japanese-Style Punch Bowl. Underglaze Decoration by M. L. Nichols (Rookwood), 1882. Given to the Cincinnati Art Museum by the Women's Art Museum Assn.

and table wares were gradually superseded by the more elegant decorative forms which have since attracted so much attention. Methods were adopted which tended to the development of original work and the copying of other wares was entirely discontinued.

The ware produced at Rookwood is a true *faïence* and may be classed under three heads : *Cameo*, or shell-tinted ware, generally of a beautiful pink color, gradually

No. 138.—Group of Rookwood Vases.

shading into white, and highly glazed. *Dull Finished* ware, similar in color to the former, possessing a surface soft in texture and having the appearance of being unglazed, but susceptible of being easily cleaned ; and lastly, the most characteristic of all, the richly glazed *Rookwood faïence.* The distinguishing feature of all of these varieties is the tinting and harmonious blending of the grounds beneath the heavy, transparent, colored glazes, producing the effect of rich tones of black, yellow, red, olive, green, brown, and amber of great brilliancy, mellowness, depth, and strength.

The highest achievements in glazing are the so-called tiger's-eye and gold-stone, which glisten in the light with a beautiful auriferous sheen.   In several pieces which we have seen, the decorator has ingeniously utilized certain iridescent points, where the shining particles of the glaze have concentrated, for the eyes of fishes which have been painted around them.   The accompanying engraving (Ill. 138) will give a fair idea of some of the graceful forms of vases produced here, but no adequate conception of the great beauty of the glazing can be conveyed in black and white.

Several distinct bodies are employed, one of which may be described as a true earthenware.   It has been discovered by costly experiment that the point of complete or nearly perfect vitrification injures, more or less, the underglaze colors, but in the finer bodies that point is approached as closely as possible to obtain the best results. The chief body now in use partakes of some of the qualities of stoneware and some of the properties of semi-porcelain.   A piece of well fired Rookwood biscuit will practically hold water but will absorb more or less of it, and far surpasses regular earthenware in vitreous ring. The clays used are found mainly in the Ohio valley, including a red variety from Buena Vista, Ohio, yellow from Hanging Rock, Ohio, and a white or cream-colored clay from Chattanooga, Tenn.,—artificially tinted bodies being also employed to some extent.

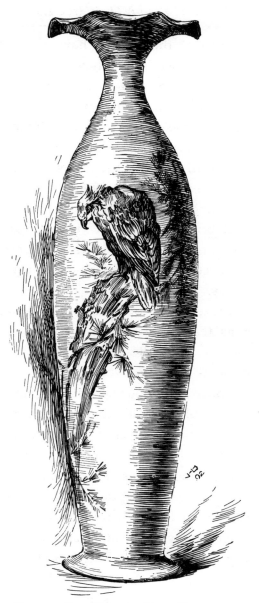

No. 139.—Dull-Finished Vase, Decorated
by Mr. A. R. Valentien. Pennsylvania
Museum, Philadelphia.

The workmen of this factory have all been especially trained in their respective branches. Excepting in the preparation of the clays, no machinery is used save the primitive potter's wheel, which gives more freedom and greater variety to the outlines of vessels than the more mechanical processes of moulding, the shapes produced being mainly variations of classic forms, possessing marked individuality of treatment. Only one thrower is employed at the pottery, and his graceful creations have obtained a world-wide celebrity. Each piece is afterwards passed to a turner, who carefully trims off the surfaces on a lathe which is attached to an old-fashioned throwing wheel turned by a boy.

For the more rapid production of certain standard forms, such as tea-pots, jars, and pitchers, which are still made to some extent, the casting method is practised, being the same as that discovered at Tournay, France, in 1784. This consists in pouring the prepared liquid clay or "slip," into a hollow mould and allowing it to stand for a few moments until the plaster has absorbed the super-abundant moisture from the parts in contact, forming a thin shell of uniform thickness which adheres to the mould after the slip has been emptied out, and is allowed to stand a while longer before being removed.

Mr. Joseph Bailey, now superintendent at the Rook-wood Pottery, came to the United States in 1848 from Tunstall, Staffordshire, England. He belongs to a family of potters, one of his uncles being Taylor Booth, son of Ward Booth, both of whom were prominent members of the craft in England during the early part of the present century. Mr. Bailey entered the pottery of Mr. R. Bagnall Beach in Philadelphia, where he remained for about six months, and afterwards worked for Messrs. Harker and Taylor, of East Liverpool, Ohio. In 1850 he went to Cincinnati, where he has remained almost continuously.

140.—Mug decorated by E. P. Cranch, 1891. Cincinnati Art Museum.

The late Mr. E. P. Cranch, a well-known lawyer of Cincinnati and an exceedingly clever artist, was connected with the pottery from the first day of its existence, and helped it by his fine taste and criticism, as well as by his excellent work.   His old-time humorous sketches in black and brown possess uncommon merit.   The quaint style which characterizes his work is perhaps seen at its best in a set of mantel tiles painted by him to illustrate the old American ballad of *Isaac Abbott*, which is a

141.—Tile from Isaac Abbott Set.
Painted by E. P. Cranch.
Rookwood Pottery.

sample of the traditionary lore of New England country life during the eighteenth century, having been handed down from father to son, unrecorded until Mr. Cranch transcribed the air and words, as heard by him, more than fifty years ago, from the lips of a nephew of Dr. Noah Webster, of New Haven, Conn.   These, with the original descriptive designs used on the tiles, were published in booklet form by Robert Clarke & Co., of Cincinnati, in 1886, and dedicated to the Cincinnati Literary Club.

No less meritorious is a similar series of tiles painted by Mr. Cranch, to illustrate the ancient ballad of *Giles Scroggins' Ghost*.   He also decorated a variety of other pieces, such as beer-mugs, pitchers, etc., which find a ready sale. These are generally finished with a " smear " glaze, and present a pleasing contrast to the other productions of this factory. Mr. Cranch died in November, 1892, in his eighty-third year.

While no serious attempt has as yet been made to manufacture art tiles in a business way, experiments have been essayed in this direction from time to time, which have amply shown that the Rookwood methods are peculiarly adapted to the production of artistic tiling for cabinet inserts and mantel facings. We figure a six- by

142.—HAND-PAINTED TILE. ROOKWOOD.

twelve-inch hand-painted tile that was made here recently to show the possibilities in this direction (Ill. 142). The decoration in pure white is applied to a cameo-tinted body, —a pink ground gradually shading into white. The dainty and delicate coloring, the brilliancy of the glazing, and the superior quality of the body, together with the originality of the decorative treatment, point to the early establishment of this branch of the art.

The Rookwood Pottery was the first in this country to demonstrate the fact that a purely American art-product, in which original and conscientious work is made paramount to commercial considerations, can command the appreciation of the American public. Owing to the many experiments undertaken, it was operated at an annual loss until the year 1889, when it paid off all its indebtedness and became a financial success. At that time, no longer needing pecuniary aid, it was turned over by Mrs. Storer to Mr. W. W. Taylor, who soon afterwards organized a stock company under the name of the Rookwood Pottery Co. Under the efficient management of Mr. Taylor, the enthusiastic president, rapid strides are

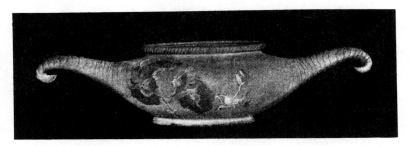

143.—RAM'S HORN FLOWER BASKET.   ROOKWOOD.

constantly being made in the improvement of methods, shapes, bodies, and glazes.

A new structure, with all modern equipments, has recently been erected on the summit of Mount Adams, overlooking the city, where, with vastly improved facilities, the capacity of the factory has been greatly increased. Here the kilns are fired with crude petroleum, which insures better and more certain results. A room has been set apart for the especial use of Mrs. Storer, where she can continue her work when so inclined.

Ten years ago Rookwood was scarcely known outside of Cincinnati. To-day its exquisite ceramic creations may be found in almost every home of culture and refinement and in every prominent art museum in the land. The evolution of Rookwood *faïence* was the result of a combination of conditions peculiarly favorable to the development of a new art product. It was the conception of a talented woman, representing the third generation of a family widely known in cultured social circles as patrons of the arts, who devoted her rare abilities and her abundant means to the realization of an idea. Fostered by the sentiment of a community long noted as an art centre and rich in private collections of ceramic treasures, aided by the advice of competent critics, assisted

144.—VASE. DECORATED BY MR. SHIRAYAMADANI. PENNSYLVANIA MUSEUM.

by the intelligent co-operation of artisans and artists who came almost at the beginning and have ever since been identified with the gradual development, the venture was peculiarly favored and the result has been particularly gratifying, both to the founder herself and the community to which she belongs. Such were the conditions which operated in combination to perfect the Rookwood pottery

as it comes to us to-day, and without which such results
could not have been attained.   But we may expect still
greater achievements in the future, under the efficient
direction of Mr. Taylor, who is devoting his energies to
the still higher perfection of underglaze decoration.

The Installation of the Rookwood pottery at the
World's Columbian Exposition was the conception of
Mr. Taylor.   The space occupied by the Rookwood dis-
play was bounded on the two sides by heavy walls four

145.—THE NEW ROOKWOOD.

feet high, and three feet in width, faced with large panels
of fire-clay body decorated with symbolical and appropriate designs, such as the whirling globe, typifying the potter's wheel, the dragons of fire, and the vase emerging
from the glow of the kiln.   The walls were of a warm
yellow color.   On each side rose three slender columns of
the same material twelve feet in height, and of a rich
malachite green, terminating in flame points of red and

orange. At the back of the enclosure stood a handsome cabinet containing the treasures of Rookwood, such as exquisite pieces of " tiger-eye " and " gold-stone," while on the walls and placed around the enclosed platform were many larger pieces showing the best work of this kind which has thus far been produced. One of the most effective pieces, which was prepared especially for the Exposition, was a large pottery boat of Columbian form, three and one half feet in length, supported on a pedestal artistically modelled to represent the idea of water and waves. The pieces which attracted most attention, however, were some vases and plaques decorated with ideal and grotesque heads, figures of monks, and other designs after engravings and photographs, painted under the glaze. This style of work evinces such a degree of artistic feeling and intelligent treatment of colors as to occasion considerable surprise to all who had the fortune to examine it. Among the foremost of those who have attempted this new style of decoration are Messrs. M. A. Daly, A. Van Briggle, and W. P. McDonald. It is understood that not only fancy heads, but actual portraits, have been attempted with most gratifying results, and the day is not far distant when it will be possible to procure from the Rookwood Pottery painted portraits equal in all respects, and more satisfactory in some, to the oil painting.

THE CINCINNATI ART POTTERY COMPANY.

Mr. Thomas J. Wheatley commenced experimenting in clays and glazes at the pottery of Messrs. P. L. Coultry

& Co., in 1879, and in 1880 established a workshop on Hunt Street, where, under the firm name of T. J. Wheatley & Co., underglaze work was produced to some extent after the style of the Limoges *faïence.*

In 1879 a joint-stock company was organized under the title of the Cincinnati Art Pottery Company, of which Mr. Frank Huntington was made president, and Mr. Wheatley continued his connection with the works until 1882, when he withdrew to engage in other business. For several years the company confined its operations to

146.—"HUNGARIAN FAÏENCE." CINCINNATI ART POTTERY COMPANY.

underglaze work, and some of the pieces produced were remarkable for beauty and originality of form and excellence of workmanship. Later, barbotine ware, in applied work, was manufactured for a time, but this was soon dropped for a more artistic style of overglaze decoration on white bodies. The " Hungarian *faïence* " made here soon became popular with the purchasing public. The " Portland blue *faïence* " was so called on account of the rich dark-blue glaze, of the color of the famous Portland vase, which formed a peculiarly striking ground for gold

decorative effects. The highest achievement of this
manufactory, however, and the most distinctive in style,

147.—Canteen-Shaped Vessel. Kenzota Pottery. Cincinnati Art Museum.

is the ivory-colored *faience* in the forms of vases and
bowls decorated with gold scroll-work and chrysanthe-

mums in natural colors. Of the latter several artistic examples may be seen in the Cincinnati Art Museum, including a daintily painted vase of canteen shape (Ill. 147) and a fan-shaped flower-holder or wall piece decorated by Rose (Ill. 148). The name *Kezonta* has been selected to designate these wares. The origin of the

148.—Fan-Shaped Vase. Kenzota Pottery. Cincinnati Art Museum.

word is interesting. The trade-mark adopted was the figure of a turtle, and when it was ascertained that the Indian name for turtle was *kezonta*, this was afterwards added to the device and printed on decorated pieces. Pottery in the biscuit, in deep blue and white glazes, has been largely sold to decorators, the forms being generally modifications of the ancient Roman and Greek. Many ladies found profitable employment in painting these pieces for the market, and it is with regret we learn that the Cincinnati Art Pottery has recently been closed. In design and treatment much of the ware produced here is characterized by originality and a high degree of artistic merit.

Within the past few years other potteries have attempted in Cincinnati to make decorated ware, with varying success. One founded by Mr. Matt Morgan produced a *faïence* modelled in low relief in Moorish designs, and a variety of ware with incised designs, touched with color. As a designer he displayed unmistakable talent, and his work was original and strongly characteristic.

The Avon Pottery commenced the manufacture of a ware somewhat resembling the earlier efforts of Rookwood. Dr. Marcus Benjamin, of New York City, possesses a gracefully modelled cup or mug of Avon ware with ram's horn handle, undecorated save in the tinting of the ground, which shades from white to dark pink. Other examples in the collection of the Pennsylvania Museum, Philadelphia, exhibit the same characteristic, a gradual shading of color—pink, olive, light blue, or brown, and some small covered vases are furnished with handles modelled in the form of elephants' heads. Both of the above mentioned potteries were closed after a brief existence.

CHAPTER XIV.

DEVELOPMENT OF THE CERAMIC ART
SINCE THE CENTENNIAL.

THE revelations of the Centennial Exhibition set our potters to thinking and stimulated them to greater competition. Never before was such an impetus given to any industry. The best productions of all nations were sent here and exhibited beside our own modest manufactures, and it was only too apparent that America had been left behind in the race. Up to that time there had been a few sporadic instances of attempts at originality, but comparatively little had been accomplished of a really artistic nature. The existence of a true ceramic art in this country may be said to have commenced with the Fair of 1876, because greater progress has been made since that important industrial event than during the two centuries which preceded it. We have already reviewed the wonderful recent advancement of the principal potteries established before the Centennial. We shall now briefly outline the history of those started since, not already mentioned.

Among other prominent American exhibitors at Philadelphia in 1876 were the Empire China Works, Greenpoint, N. Y., manufacturers of porcelain hardware and cabinet trimmings; Isaac Davis, Trenton, N. J., white granite and decorated crockery; Messrs. Astbury & Maddock, Trenton, sanitary earthenware and china; Messrs. Yates, Bennett, & Allen, Trenton, table and toilet wares; Brunt, Bloor, Martin, & Co., East Liverpool, Ohio, white granite and decorated table and toilet services; and the American Crockery Co., Trenton, N. J., makers of stone china, bisque, and white granite goods.

BENNETT FAÏENCE.

Mr. John Bennett, formerly director of the practical work in the *faïence* department of the Lambeth Pottery of Messrs. Doulton & Co., of London, England, came to the United States in the Centennial year and settled for a time in New York City, where he introduced his method of decorating *faïence* under the glaze. He built his first kiln in Lexington Avenue, and afterwards erected others in East Twenty-fourth Street near the East River. At first he imported English biscuit, but after a time he employed potters to make the common cream-colored body, as the tint imparted a warmth to his colors. He also used, to some extent, a white body, made in Trenton, N. J. His work was soon in great demand and brought high prices. The shapes were simple and generally devoid of handles or moulded ornaments. The decorations consisted chiefly of flowers and foliage, drawn from nature in a vigorous and ornate style, and painted with very few touches. A background was worked in after the painting, in loose touches and delicate tints, and finally the whole design was boldly outlined in black or very dark color. The glaze was brilliant, even, and firm, and the coloring exceedingly rich, the mustard yellows, deep blues, and browns tinged with red giving the ware a bright and attractive appearance. A cylindrical vase decorated with red and white trumpet flowers impasted on a blue mottled ground (Ill. 149), and a small spherical vase with apple

149.—BENNETT FAÏENCE.
WM. LYCETT COLLECTION.

blossoms on a glossy black ground (Ill. 150), in the possession of Mr. William Lycett, of Atlanta, Georgia, are excellent examples of Mr. Bennett's most characteristic work. He also produced some pieces in the style of the so-called Limoges *faïence*, by applying colored slips to the unfired clay.

During the half dozen years that Mr. Bennett devoted to this work in New York many attempts were made to imitate his style.

It seems proper at this point to quote what Mrs. Aaron F. Perry has written in her paper on "Decorative Pottery of Cincinnati" in *Harper's* concerning Mr. Bennett's relations to the Lambeth Pottery before coming to this country :

"Mr. Bennett's attitude toward Mr. Doulton is so respectful and deferential, and in regard to what he has himself done is so modest, that his own statement in answer to an inquiry on this point is not without interest. It is as follows : 'Your impression respecting Doulton Lambeth *faïence* is right. I introduced it, and taught all the pupils, glazed and burned ; but in justice to Mr. H. Doulton, the principal, I must say it is very doubtful whether I would have brought it to the success it attained had I not been engaged by him. His natural good taste and desire to improve in art pottery always had a stimulating effect upon me. You will gather from the above that I think the Lambeth *faïence* ought to be called *Doulton ;* at the same time, I have felt slighted by no mention being made of my name in Mr. Sparkes's paper on Lambeth pottery.' " In his last statement, however, Mr. Bennett is clearly in error, as Mr. Sparkes, in his article, dated June, 1876, distinctly states that about fifty young ladies were employed " at the pottery of the Messrs. Doulton, painting and otherwise decorating the ware, under the

150.—Bennett Faïence. Wm. Lycett Collection.

immediate superintendence of Mr. John Bennett, the able Director of all the practical work in the Faïence Department."

About 1882 Mr. Bennett sought retirement on his farm in the Orange Mountains of New Jersey, and although he built a kiln there, he has since done but little in the way of *faïence* decoration. The mark used on the earlier pieces was " J. Bennett, N. Y.," and later, " West Orange, N. J."

At Tarrytown, N. Y., a pottery was started about 1878, under the style of Odell & Booth Brothers. They made majolica and *faïence*, decorated under the glaze. A few years ago they closed the works, which, after remaining idle some time, were opened and operated by the Owen Tile Co., manufacturers of decorative tiles.

WHEELING, WEST VIRGINIA.

In November of 1879 the Wheeling Pottery Company was organized, the officers being George K. Wheat, president, William A. Isett, secretary, and Edward Meakin Pearson, general manager. To Mr. Pearson's untiring energy and practical knowledge of the business the success of the company is largely due. In 1887 the same gentlemen organized a new company known as the La Belle Pottery Co., and the same officers were chosen to manage the latter, and in January, 1889, the two companies were merged into one. Mr. Pearson was elected president of the concern a year later, and has held the position continuously until the present time. The products of the original works are plain and decorated white granite ware, while at the La Belle works adamantine china, plain and decorated, is made. The entire plant consists of fifteen large kilns and thirteen decorating kilns, and forms one of the most extensive potteries in the United States. The large decorating department is under the efficient management of Mr. Charles Craddock, who has been connected with the company since 1882. He is a native of Burslem, England, and was for years in the employ of Messrs. Minton & Co., of Stoke-on-Trent.

151.—Mr. Edward Meakin Pearson.

Mr. Edward M. Pearson, the president of the company, was born in Burslem, Staffordshire, England, on May 6, 1848, at which time his father owned the Abbey Pottery at Cobridge, old established works, which, it is said, were built in 1703, where young Pearson afterwards learned the trade. He was admitted to partnership with his father in 1869 under the firm name of Edward Pearson & Son. In 1867 and 1868 the son had visited the United

States in the interest of their English house, which was engaged exclusively in the American trade. The partnership was continued until 1873, when Mr. Edward M. Pearson came to this country to remain permanently, and in July of the same year he went to East Liverpool to ascertain if white ware could be successfully made there. Nothing was then being attempted in that direction save some trials which Messrs. Knowles, Taylor, & Knowles were then making. These gentlemen permitted Mr. Pearson to carry on some experiments in their factory,

152.—MAZARINE BLUE AND WHITE PITCHER, RAISED GOLD DECORATION. WHEELING POTTERY CO.

which proved highly successful. The citizens of the town offered to donate the land and $10,000 toward the establishment of a white ware factory if Mr. Pearson would accept the management. Accordingly, in conjunction with Messrs. Homer and Shakespeare Laughlin, Mr. Pearson accepted the offer, and in 1874 erected the plant which is now operated by Mr. Homer Laughlin. Several other potteries were afterwards planned and built by Mr. Pearson in East Liverpool, and of the eight which made white ware in that town while Mr. Pearson resided there, to the year 1879, he has been connected with five. In the last-named year he moved to Wheeling, W. Va., as we have already seen, where he has been prominently identified with the pottery industry ever since.

Mr. Pearson is connected on his mother's side with the prominent Meakin family of potters of Staffordshire, England, from which source he receives his middle name.

Although a native Englishman, Mr. Pearson has become thoroughly Americanized and has been prominent in the advocacy of tariff matters before both houses of Congress. He is an active member of the U. S. Potters' Association, has held a number of prominent offices in that organization, and is now a member of several important committees.

THE OHIO VALLEY CHINA COMPANY,

of Wheeling, W. Va., manufacture porcelain in striking shapes and decorations. The exhibit of this company at the World's Columbian Exposition was a surprise to the public. The modelling shows jagged or coarsely serrated edges with points projecting from handles, feet, and prominent parts, somewhat after the style of certain French and German wares. The decorations are of great variety and generally over the glaze, and in many instances handles and zones are perforated in an artistic manner. Fine effects are obtained by moulding Cupids in high relief in irregular alcoves or panels on the sides of vases.

THE STEUBENVILLE POTTERY CO.

In November, 1879, a meeting was called by representative business men of Steubenville, Ohio, to meet Mr. A. B. Beck, an English potter, to consider the matter of forming a joint-stock company for the purpose of manufacturing white granite and other wares. The existence of beds of excellent coal within the city limits, and the natural advantages of the location on the Ohio River

153.—" CANTON CHINA " PITCHER.
STEUBENVILLE POTTERY CO.

and the great Pan Handle Railroad system, convenient to the markets of the north and east, decided the projectors of the enterprise in organizing a company under the name of the Steubenville Pottery Company. The necessary buildings were accordingly erected and the first kiln was drawn on February 18, 1881. The present officers are Mr. W. B. Donaldson, president, Mr. R. Sherrard. Jr., vice-president, and Mr. Alfred Day, secretary and treasurer, who has also been for several years the popular secretary of the United States Potters' Association.

About five years ago, coal was superseded by natural gas as a fuel, which insures a superior finish of the ware and better results in the baking. The products of this factory are white granite and decorated ware, in table and toilet services. The works now furnish employment to about two hundred hands, and annually produce $175,000 of finished goods.

A new departure has recently been made at this pottery

in the adoption of a semi-vitreous, opaque body of a rich cream color and exceedingly light weight, which is called "Canton china." It is made in vases, *jardinières,* and toilet sets, with overglaze dec-orations on tinted and gold-stippled grounds. A graceful ewer vase, with openwork handle formed of forget-me-nots, is particularly effective. This is sold in a number of pleasing decorations, or fur-nished plain for decorators, and is already becoming popu-lar on account of being par-ticularly well adapted for this

154.—"CANTON CHINA" VASE. STEUBENVILLE POTTERY CO.

purpose (Ill. 153). The stamp used on the "Beula" pattern, in white granite dinner ware, is an outline map of the State of Ohio.

The Louisiana Porcelain Works of Messrs. Hernandez & Saloy were started in New Orleans about 1880, or pos-sibly earlier, for the manufacture of French china. The ware was made by French workmen, from French ma-terials, and was similar in quality to the Limoges porcelain. It was sold white, but at the time of the closing of the establishment, about 1890, a decorating department was about to be added.

THE FAÏNCE MANUFACTURING COMPANY

of New York began in 1880 to make, at Greenpoint, Long Island, pottery decorated with hand-modelled flowers ap-

plied to the surface and painted under the glaze, to which
the name barbotine was incorrectly given, this term being

in France used synon-
ymously with "slip"
or liquid clay. When
the temporary demand
for this class of ware
had subsided, the com-
pany made for a time
so-called majolica
ware. Plain shapes,
without the moulded
flowers, were dipped
in colored glazes, some
pleasing results being
obtained by blending
the various tints in
streaked and marbled
effects.

Mr. Edward Ly-
cett, formerly of Staf-
fordshire, England,
who had since 1861
carried on an exten-
sive decorating busi-
ness in New York

155.—FAÏENCE VASE. FAÏENCE MANUFACTURING CO.
BY EDWARD LYCETT.

City, where he em-
ployed from thirty to
forty people in painting and gilding imported wares,
joined the Faïence Manufacturing Company in 1884,

156.—PORCELAIN VASE.   FAÏENCE MANUFACTURING CO.
BY EDWARD LYCETT.

and assumed the direction of the factory. Being a practical potter, as well as an artist of ripe experience, he at once set to work to compound better bodies and glazes and to design new shapes and decorations, and soon began the manufacture of richly embellished pieces, such as vases and other articles of ornamental character. One of the finest examples made at this factory, which is shown in Illustration 155, is a large granite vase, in the Persian style, designed and painted by Mr. Lycett. While entirely covered with rich ornamentation, the effect is subdued and pleasing. The ground is a dark bronze, over which conventionally treated flowers, the poppy on one side and the clematis on the other, are executed in dull tones of color and outlined with raised gold, while the embossed and perforated work, handles, and foot, are covered with gold of different tints. The height of this vase is forty-two inches, and it is claimed that it was sold for probably the highest price yet paid for any single piece of American pottery.

A fine grade of porcelain was introduced by Mr. Lycett, its peculiarity being that, although a true porcelain, entirely devoid of bone, it is fired in the reverse of the usual method, being burned hard in the biscuit and softer in the glaze, in which no lead or borax is present, thus possessing all the advantages, in placing and firing, of a *faïence* or earthen body and the superior glaze of hard porcelain. Vases up to twenty-six inches in height were made of this body, which is very white and of a pleasing softness to the eye. The example here figured is modelled and painted in the Moorish style, with openwork handles, collar, and cover, decorated in raised gold and bronzes of brown, olive, and other tints, on a pale ochre ground (Ill. 156).

A dolphin-handled vase, twenty-eight inches high, is a fine example of artistic treatment. The ground is of a pale ivory tint, on which aquatic plants are painted in subdued tones, enriched and re-heightened with vein-ings and outlines of raised work in gold and bronzes (Ill. 157). This is the work of Mr. Joseph Lycett, a son of the former director of the works. The handles are cov-ered with mat gold and a peculiar dark gold bronze which pro-duces a singularly mas-sive effect. The body is a fine *faïence*, which may be described as

157.—FAÏENCE VASE. FAÏENCE MANUFAC-TURING CO. BY JOSEPH LYCETT.

a superior quality of white granite ware. Illustration No. 158 represents a fine *faïence* vase with painting of "A Flight of Storks" in gold and bronze on an ivory ground. The handles and cover are pierced. The height of the vase is about eighteen inches. The decoration is the work of Mr. Edward Lycett.

In testing various materials for improving the glazes, Mr. Edward Lycett was fortunate in observing effects of iridescence on some of his experiments, which, being continued on new lines, resulted finally in the discovery of a method of making the reflecting glaze, or *Reflêt métallique* of the ancient Persian tiling, which has been so much admired for its brilliant reflections of prismatic and opalescent colors. Specimens of Mr. Lycett's *Reflêts nacrés* and *métalliques*, now before me, fully merit the description of the Oriental *Reflêts* given by our late Minister to Persia, the Hon. S. G. W. Benjamin, in his book, *Persia and the Persians*, and is a remarkable result of patient research. An example submitted to the South Kensington Museum, in London,

158.—Fine Faïence Vase, "A Flight of Storks." Decorated in Gold and Bronze on an Ivory Ground. Faïence Manufacturing Co.

was pronounced a "marvellous piece of lustre," and at the late Piedmont Exposition in Atlanta, Ga., a special medal was awarded for tiles treated with this glazing.

Mr. Lycett has also recently sent a few of these tiles to the Technical Museum of Hanley, Staffordshire, England, and in acknowledging their receipt, Mr. William Burton, the able chemist of the Wedgwood works, and lecturer on pottery, writes : " I have just unpacked them and am surprised and delighted with the beauty and perfection of their iridescence. You have rightly named them Persian lustres, for they have exactly the qualities of the old Persian lustred ware, some of which happen to be displayed in an adjoining case."

Mr. Lycett severed his connection with the Faïence Manufacturing Company in 1890, when it became the agent in this country for a French manufactory. Mr. Lycett has now retired from active business, but his three sons, Mr. William Lycett of Atlanta, Georgia, Mr. F. Lycett of Bridgeport, Connecticut, and Mr. Joseph Lycett of Brooklyn, N. Y., who have for many years enjoyed the benefit of their father's instruction, are still actively engaged in teaching and decorating.

A pottery was erected at Evansville, Ind., in 1882 by Mr. A. M. Beck, who came from England. He built three kilns and commenced the manufacture of majolica ware. At Mr. Beck's death, two years later, the works were sold to Messrs. Bennighof, Uhl, & Co., who commenced making white ware. In 1891 the Crown Pottery Co. was organized and the plant was increased to six kilns and four enamel kilns. The present products are white granite specialties in table and toilet goods, plain, white, and decorated. The trade-mark used by the company is a crown.

THE CHESAPEAKE POTTERY,

of Baltimore, Md., although among the youngest of the American potteries, has achieved a high reputation for the variety of excellent and novel bodies and glazes it has produced, and has won still greater distinction by the beauty and originality of its designs, both in form and decoration. The works were started in 1881 by Messrs. D. F. Haynes & Co., and were continued without change until 1887, when the style was altered to The Chesapeake Pottery Company, and in 1890 Messrs. Haynes, Bennett, & Co. assumed control and are still operating the pottery with marked success.

Mr. David Francis Haynes, the senior partner, has stood at the head of the business since its inception. He was born in 1835, in the town of Brookfield, Mass., and sprang from a sturdy Puritan race, his emigrant ancestor, Walter Haynes, having landed in Boston, from the ship *Confidence*, in 1638. Mr. Haynes spent his early life on a New England farm, attending the public schools of the vicinity until the age of sixteen, when he entered a crockery store in Lowell, Mass. Here he rose rapidly, and before attaining his majority was sent to England by his employer in charge of an important trust. Possessing a natural taste for decorative work, he displayed at an early age marked talent for construction and ornamentation, and his visits abroad, among the art treasures of England and the Continent, proved a revelation and an education to him. Returning to his native land in the autumn of 1856, Mr. Haynes soon moved to Baltimore and entered the employ of the Abbott Rolling Mills, a large concern engaged in the manufacture of plate iron. In 1861 he was placed in charge of these extensive mills, in which armor plates for the ironclads were made. At the close of the war he was sent to Virginia to manage a large iron property, where he became interested in the mining of iron ores and clays. In 1871, the offer of an

159.—MR. DAVID FRANCIS HAYNES.

interest in a crockery jobbing house brought him back to Baltimore and to the handling again of the wares for which he had always retained a fondness.

On purchasing the Chesapeake Pottery property, Mr. Haynes entered at once into the congenial work of producing a variety of wares, being greatly aided by the knowledge gained in the jobbing trade of the productions of the Old World and the wants and tastes of the American people. Finding that but little attention had been paid in this country to original designing for pottery purposes, and that practical, trained modellers, who possessed artistic sense, were difficult to procure, he commenced to design wares for the Chesapeake Pottery himself. The result of his patient study and constant practice are revealed in his wealth of beautiful creations which have been copied extensively both in this country and abroad. No one of our potters has done more to refine the wares for daily household use than Mr. Haynes. He has always held it to be of much greater importance to elevate the quality, as far as possible, of the entire pottery product of the country, than to produce a few fine pieces that should be within the reach of only the wealthy. To make the cup and jug of the plainest home a thing of beauty has been his ruling motive. With this in view, he has been constant in his endeavor to have the United States Potters' Association take up the work of establishing a pottery training school, the benefits of which would be shared by the entire craft.

Mr. Edwin Houston Bennett, the junior member of the firm, is a son of Mr. Edwin Bennett, one of the pioneer potters of this country. The former was born in Baltimore and his business life has been spent in pottery work. His painstaking experiments in the firing of kilns and the making of wares have placed him prominently among the rising practical potters in this country, and made his share in the progressive work which is being done at the Chesapeake Pottery an important one.

When this factory was started, majolica ware was in great demand. Its first product was called "Clifton" ware, and belonged to the majolica family, but was superior in body and glaze, and was pronounced by judges equal to the famous Wedgwood ware of that grade. Following this came the "Avalon" ware, which was of a fine body, of ivory tint and soft rich glaze, ornamented

160.—"SEVERN" WARE. CHESAPEAKE POTTERY.

with sprays of flowers in relief, which were touched with color and gold, making a pleasing decoration. The "Calvertine" ware, made about the same time, was similar in its composition to the "Avalon," but quite different in decorative treatment, being turned upon the lathe, with spaces for bands, upon which were overlaid conventional relief ornaments, which produced a refined effect when treated with delicate colors and outlined with darker tints of gold.

In 1885 parian wares were produced, with modelled flowers, panels with heads in relief, medallions of Thor-

161.—CASTILIAN AND ALSATIAN SEMI-PORCELAIN TOILET WARE. CHESAPEAKE POTTERY.

waldsen's " Seasons," and similar works, which received the commendations of experts for the mellow tone, sharpness, and rich translucency of the body.   Some cattle-head plaques in high relief, modelled by Mr. James Priestman, from studies of typical animals in the noted herd of Mr. Harvey Adams, were especially praiseworthy.

The most original and perhaps, all things considered, the most refined and beautiful of the various Chesapeake bodies was the so-called "Severn" ware, first brought out in 1885. This was a fine, thoroughly vitreous body of a subtle grayish-olive tint, which was secured, without any artificial coloring, by a combination of American clays and

162.—USEFUL AND DECORATIVE SEMI-PORCELAIN WARES. CHESAPEAKE POTTERY.

other materials. Dr. William C. Prime, author of *Pottery and Porcelain of All Times and Nations*, said of it : "No one who is interested in the art of pottery can fail to note this ware as marking an era in the history of American ceramics."

All of these bodies, excepting the parian, were made into a great variety of useful and ornamental articles, such as jugs, plates, mugs, cups, lamps, vases, pilgrim and Ghooleh bottles. During the greater part of this time the Chesapeake Pottery was making a varied line of toilet ware, in a fine ivory body. The so-called " Roman " set, which had an embossed surface with an ornamentation of grape leaves, was one of the first produced. In 1886, the manufacture of fine semi-porcelain was commenced, and

the " Arundel " dinner service was put upon the market, the first work of the kind designed by Mr. Haynes, which has since been extensively copied by American, English, and German potters, and sent to this country for sale in china and cheaper grades of ware. Then came the " Clifton " and " Severn " dinner w a r e shapes, and in toilet ware the " Breton," " Castilian," "Aurelian," "Alsatian," and " Montessan," all noted for their originality, excellence of construction, and beauty

163.—" Merchant of Venice " Vase. Chesapeake Pottery.

of form and decoration. The "Castilian" set is worthy of special mention, being Moorish in form, in relief ornamentation, and in color,—a well-conceived adaptation of barbaric ideas to the use of the modern household.

The " Alsatian " toilet set is embellished with circular panels on opposite sides of each piece, bordered with rich relief ornamentation, forming appropriate frames or settings for pictures. Mr. Haynes has introduced, for one of the decorations in these panels, a beautiful, conventional design of interlacing leaves ; for another, some well drawn peasant heads, and for a third, scenes from the *Merchant of Venice*, executed by a well-known artist, and printed in delicate vellum tints. On one side the trial scene is depicted, where Portia says, " The quality of mercy is not strained—it droppeth as the gentle rain from

164.—Montessan Semi-Porcelain Toilet Set. Chesapeake Pottery.

heaven," and on the other the scene between Antonio, Bassanio, and Shylock, in which the latter exclaims, " And for these courtesies I 'll lend you thus much monies " (see Ill. 163).

The Montessan toilet set is quartered with strips of pleasing relief work and the handles bear a grotesque head, full of life and spirit. The color decorations are suited to the form, and in treatment suggest the Rococo style which prevailed about the beginning of the present century.   This set was not exhibited until late in January, 1892, but was copied by a celebrated English firm and displayed in their London warerooms in May following,— a decided compliment to American work.

The latest achievements of the Chesapeake Pottery are a line of parlor and banquet lamps, clocks, and large decorative vases, all characterized by originality of design, grace of form, and delicacy of execution.

165.—LAMPS AND VASES.   CHESAPEAKE POTTERY.

Mr. Haynes has also recently designed a porcelain "Pompadour" clock case, with Rococo relief ornamentation and finished in rich gold (Ill. 166).   It measures fourteen and one-half inches in height.

At the exhibition of American pottery held in Memorial Hall, Philadelphia, in the autumn of 1889, Miss Fannie Haynes, daughter of Mr. D. F. Haynes, entered in competition a large vase which attracted considerable attention and took one of the prizes, and was afterwards purchased by the trustees of the Museum for the permanent collection. The chief merit of the work lies in the genuine Moorish feeling in the relief ornament and its color treatment, but the Arabic character of the English inscription, " In the History of Pottery Read the Story of the Race," which forms part of the decoration, is particularly marked, and strongly resembles, at a short distance, a real bit of Oriental lettering. Miss Haynes has inherited a fondness for decorative work. She studied in design at the Maryland Institute Art Schools, and afterwards in the Metropolitan Museum Schools in New York, then gave instruction in modelling in the Pratt Institute Schools of Brooklyn, New York. At present she is engaged in making designs

166.—PORCELAIN CLOCK. CHESAPEAKE POTTERY.

for leading manufacturers of silks and silkoline fabrics in New York.

The most important, and perhaps the most artistic, piece of ware thus far produced by Messrs. Haynes, Bennett, & Co. is the " Calvert " vase, shown at the Columbian

Exposition for the first time. It measures twenty-eight inches in height and twenty-six in width, including the handles, which are in the resemblance of winged female figures terminating at the base in a richly foliated ornament. The lid or cover of the vase is surmounted by a well executed flame-point, which emphasizes the Renaissance treatment of the entire piece. Bands of rich relief ornamentation around the neck, on the shoulder, and about the foot and lower portion, enhance the beauty of the fine lines in the form. This vase was designed by Mr. Haynes, and the handles were modelled after ideas of his and under his direction by Mr. Fred E. Mayer, a young man of considerable talent, who studied under Prof. L. W. Miller in the Pennsylvania Museum and School of Industrial Art, Philadelphia.

167.—MOORISH VASE DESIGNED BY MISS FANNIE HAYNES. COLLECTION OF THE PENNSYLVANIA MUSEUM OF ART, PHILADELPHIA.

Several copies of the "Calvert" vase have been made, and decorated in widely divergent styles. One of these shows a delicate tinting of the handles and all the relief work in a pale marine or turquoise green of mat or satin finish, enriched with dead gold, the contrast of this combination with those parts of the body and cover that are left white producing a refined and beautiful effect. The entire treatment of the vase is characteristic of Chesapeake Pottery work.

Another example is entirely covered with a rich dark Pompadour red, the raised horizontal lines of the orna-

168.—"CALVERT" VASE. CHESAPEAKE POTTERY.

mentation being overlaid with gold, combining richness and strong color effect with simplicity. A third style of decorative finish is after Worcester methods, the treatment having been left to Mr. Scott Callowhill of Trenton, an artist formerly employed at the Worcester works, who found in this vase a subject worthy of his best effort.

Mr. Haynes has also recently worked out a strong design for a water filter of large proportions, one of the decorations for it being an effective all-over pattern made up of the fleur-de-lis and a quartered rosette, employed alternately, applied in deep underglaze blue.

THE PAULINE POTTERY COMPANY.

In 1883 Mrs. Pauline Jacobus started a small workshop in Chicago under the name of the Pauline Pottery, which consisted of one small kiln and employed a single presser and a couple of decorators. In the spring of 1888 the works were moved to Edgerton, Wisconsin, and considerably enlarged. At present the products of the factory are porous cells for electric batteries and underglaze art ware. Thirteen ladies find employment here, under the direction of Mrs. Jacobus, in painting on the biscuit. On the removal of the works to Edgerton the Pauline Pottery Company was incorporated under the laws of Wisconsin and the business has steadily increased, until at present thirty-five hands are engaged in producing the wares for the market. The decoration of the art wares is entirely underglaze, and the forms of the pieces are ornate and graceful. Ewers, vases, flower jars, bon-bon boxes, candlesticks, lamp stands, and fancy designs are produced to a considerable extent. The painting is done entirely with the brush, frequently in the Japanese style. The body of the ware is light and porous, resembling the ordinary Japanese Kioto ware. The resemblance is particularly apparent in examples in which the entire surface of the glaze is covered with fine crackling. Modern Italian majolica ware is also imitated here to some extent.

The Onondaga Pottery Company, of Syracuse, N. Y., produce white granite and cream-colored wares, in plain and decorated dinner and toilet services.

The Mayer Pottery Company, of Beaver Falls, Pa.,

169.—Pauline Art Pottery, Edgerton, Wis.

manufacture stone china, lustre band, sprig ware, and decorated goods.

Messrs. Goodwin Brothers operate an establishment at Elmwood, near Hartford, Conn., where they own extensive clay beds. They produce cream-colored, Rockingham, yellow, and terra-cotta goods. The latter include an extensive variety of fancy flower-pots, hanging baskets, vases, both ornamental and plain for decorators, cuspidors, *jardinières*, umbrella jars, and fancy lamp-stands, hand decorated in colored and rustic designs, bronzed, silvered, and lustred. They also have salesrooms in New York City.

The Nashville Art Pottery was making in 1886 a fine red ware with good brown glaze, in artistic shapes. Examples may be seen in the Trumbull-Prime collection, now on exhibition at Princeton College.

The Charles Graham Chemical Pottery Works, Brooklyn, N. Y., one of the most extensive in this country, produce chemical stoneware of every description, porcelain-lined earthenware wash-trays, fire-bricks, and acid receivers up to 500 gallons capacity.

The Akron Stoneware Agency, of Akron, Ohio, of which the Boston Pottery Co. is a branch, manufactures extensive lines of stoneware, Rockingham, and yellow wares, in the usual utilitarian forms, such as jugs, jars, pitchers, flower-pots, bottles, spittoons, and household utensils. In Akron there are fifteen establishments where clay and pottery products are made.

The Warwick China Company was organized in Wheeling in 1887, of which Mr. J. R. McCourtney was the first president and Mr. George Bradshaw, formerly foreman for Mr. Homer Laughlin, of East Liverpool, manager. Mr. O. C. Dewey succeeded to the presidency in the following year, and in 1889, on the resignation of Mr. Dewey, Mr. Charles W. Franzheim, then vice-president of the Wheeling Pottery Company, became president of the Warwick China Company, and still holds that position. The products of this factory are semi-porcelain dinner, tea, and toilet ware.

In 1887 or 1888 the West Virginia China Company was established, with Mr. Wm. L. Hearne president and Mr. James Clarke, formerly of the Trenton China Company, manager. This company was re-organized about two years ago under the name of the Ohio Valley China Company (which see).

Summer visitors to Martha's Vineyard are familiar with the peculiar earthenware which is made at the Gay Head Pottery of Mr. W. F. Willard, Cottage City, Mass., which is fashioned in plain vase forms from variegated clays found at the west end of the island. These deposits are bright red, light blue, and drab, and the peculiarity of the ware is that it is not burned, but *sun-dried*, and consequently not intended for use, but merely for ornament. The different colored clays are ground separately, placed together in a ball, and turned into shape, and when partially dry the vessel is shaved and then allowed to harden in the sun. The surface presents the appearance of striped stoneware, without glazing, the bands of red, blue, and slate-colored clays being distinct and remarkably brilliant. Articles are also made from the red clay and burned, but the coloring disappears in the kiln, and consequently much of the ware is sold in an unbaked state to curiosity hunters, in order to preserve the natural hues of the clays. This pottery gives employment to several hands and has been in operation for about fourteen years.

THE LONHUDA POTTERY CO.

An art pottery has been recently established in Steubenville, Ohio, for the manufacture of underglaze *faïence*. The firm, which is known as the Lonhuda Pottery Company, is composed of Mr. W. A. Long, chemist, Mr. W. H. Hunter, editor of the Steubenville *Daily Gazette*, and Mr. Alfred Day, secretary of the United States Potters'

170.—LONHUDA POTTERY.

Association. Mr. Long has for some years been engaged in experimenting with clays and colors suitable for underglaze decoration, with a view to producing a high class pottery which should be characteristically American.

The forms of vessels have, in a great measure, been suggested by examples of Chiriqui and other Indian wares in the collection of the Smithsonian Institution at Washington. In addition to the monogram of the company, which has been used as a factory mark, the impressed figure of an Indian's head has been adopted for use on such pieces as are distinctively American in shape.

The colors used are mixed with clays to heighten or soften the lights, and applied in colored slips to the green body, over the tinted and blended grounds of refined tones of reds, warm browns, yellows, and neutral grays. After the first firing the ware is covered with a brilliant tinted glaze. Foreign clays are used almost exclusively in the body, which is more or less vitreous and of a yellowish color. The product is ornamental rather than utilitarian, consisting mainly of vases, *jardinières*, and small articles for household use. The shapes are simple and graceful in outline, and the decorations are the work of competent artists, among whom is Miss Laura A. Fry, formerly of Cincinnati.

CHAPTER XV

EARLY BRICK- AND TILE-MAKING.

THE belief that all of the bricks which were used in the construction of houses in this country previous to the middle of the eighteenth century were imported from Europe is widespread but erroneous. It is true that bricks were brought from Holland to New York in the seventeenth century, and some of the ancient buildings in the New England States and Pennsylvania were built of bricks procured from Great Britain, yet it is equally certain that brick-making had become an established industry in America a few years after the arrival of the first white settlers. It is stated by Dr. J. Leander Bishop, in his *History of American Manufactures*, that bricks were burned in Virginia as early as the year 1612, and so rapid was the development of this art that " tyle-makers " in this new Colony were living well by their trade in 1649. Two years previous to the latter date, brick- and tile-making were being carried on in New England as independent callings. Daniel Pegg and others manufactured bricks in Philadelphia in 1685, and, shortly after, numerous brickyards were in operation along the shores of the Delaware. Many residences throughout the country, particularly in certain sections of Pennsylvania, were built of brick early in the eighteenth century. The cost of importing these supplies from England and transporting them to the rural districts, far removed from tidewater, would have been prohibitory. That building-bricks were extensively manufactured here previous to 1753 is indicated by a statement of Lewis Evans, of Philadelphia, who wrote to a friend in England in that year: " The greatest vein of Clay for Bricks and Pottery, begins near Trenton Falls, and extends a mile or two in Breadth on the Pennsylvania side of the River to Christine; then it crosses the River and goes by Salem. *The whole world cannot afford better bricks than our town is built of.* Nor is the Lime which is mostly brought from White Marsh inferior to that wherewith the old castles in Britain were formerly built."

When burned, as formerly, in " clamps," the bricks formed their own kiln, piled on edge, a finger's breadth apart, to allow the heat to circulate between. Those which came in direct contact with the wood-fire in the kiln were blackened and partially vitrified on the exposed ends; while the opposite extremities, which were farthest from the heat, were only partially baked, and consequently too soft for external use. The bricks which were uniformly surrounded by heat came out red. To utilize all of the bricks produced, the black ends of the former were laid outward in the wall, thus combining utility with ornamentation. Many of the older buildings were constructed in this manner, the black binders and red stretchers alternating, each layer breaking joints with that immediately

above and below.   This method of laying bricks was the
most common in use and was known as the Flemish bond.

The first roofing tiles used in America were in all
probability brought from Holland.   Peter Jagou built
three houses on the Burlington Islands in the Delaware
River, about 1668, of brick and tile.   In 1670 he was
plundered by the Indians and his dwelling was destroyed.
Among the ruins of one of these structures Dr. Charles C.
Abbott discovered, in November, 1891, some red and
yellow bricks and examples of curled or "pan" tiles which
were apparently of Dutch workmanship, though Prof.
Edward S. Morse, who has devoted much time to the
study of the roofing tiles of the world, has suggested to
me that as there is no evidence that these were imported,
they may have been made in this country.   In his instruc-
tive article on Roofing Tiles, published in *The American
Architect and Building News,* of April 23, 1892, Prof.
Morse, referring to the flat roofing tile which has been
found extensively in Eastern Pennsylvania, makes use of
the following statement : " As the form of this tile and
its dimensions correspond to the average flat tile seen in
Germany, it is almost certain that the tile was introduced
by the early German emigrants to that region."

Flat terra-cotta roofing tiles were made to a considerable extent in certain parts of this country, particularly in
the German settlements of Eastern Pennsylvania, early in
the last century, and were commonly used on smith-shops
and out-buildings, but rarely on dwellings.   The art was
brought from Germany, where the same methods of manufacture are, to some extent, still practised.   In this con-

nection the statements furnished by Prof. Morse possess considerable interest. He says : " The making of flat tiles, as I saw it near Wurtzburg, was of the simplest description. An iron frame having the outline of the tile to be made was the only important implement involved in the process. This frame represented the mould. The table upon which this rested consisted of a thick piece of

26.—PENNSYLVANIA ROOFING TILES (EIGHTEENTH CENTURY).

plank, over which was spread a piece of woolen cloth, one edge of which was nailed to the lateral edge of the plank, while the opposite edge of the cloth had secured to it an iron rod, the weight of which kept the cloth drawn smoothly over the plank. The iron frame was now placed upon the cloth and clay was packed into it with the hands, and then pounded down with a wooden mallet such as a moulder might use. A straight-edge was used to scrape away the superfluous clay, a little mass being left at the head of the tile which was afterwards shaped into the nib which was to hold the tiles to the laths or battens. This being done, a square piece of board notched at one end to admit the nib was placed on the frame. The workman then grasped the iron rod attached to the free end of the cloth, and with the other hand holding the board in its place, lifted the cloth and inverted the whole thing, transferring the soft tile to the board. The iron frame was then removed, and the board with its unbaked tile was placed in the sun to dry." Such was substantially the method resorted to by the early tile-makers in this country, with the difference that rain grooves were added to the upper surface of the tile by the finger of the workman before the clay had dried. The grooving, however, was not always accomplished in this primitive manner. Mr. Solomon Grimly of Schwenkville, Pa., informs me that his grandfather, in describing the process employed by the Montgomery County (Pa.) tilers in the early part of the eighteenth century, stated that the frame or mould in which the tile was formed was grooved in the bottom and into this the clay was pressed and the superfluous material was cut away by passing a strong thread or wire across the top, a lump being left at the upper margin which was drawn up with the fingers to form the catch or knob. The uniformity of grooving which is sometimes noticed in tiles from the same source would seem to prove this statement to be correct.

CHAPTER XVI.

ORNAMENTAL TILES.

THE first wall and paving tiles produced in the United States were probably made at the factory of Abraham Miller in Philadelphia. About 1845 one of his workmen, Mr. Thomas F. Darragh, who, in 1838, when a lad of fourteen, went to Mr. Miller to learn the potting trade and remained with him for twenty years as apprentice and journeyman, now with the firm of Hyzer & Lewellen, of Philadelphia, made for Mr. Miller some Rockingham tiles of large size, probably measuring nine by eighteen inches, which were used for facing the outside of the warehouse. Mr. Darragh also produced some mottled tiles of various colors for paving in front of Mr. Miller's residence, on the north side of Spruce Street east of Broad. Miller was making at that time an octagonal spittoon for the market. By cutting these horizontally in half he procured an ornamental pattern of novel effect which he utilized as wall tiles, by forming a border of them around the ceiling of his office. The idea was original and characteristic of the man.

At the United States Pottery, Bennington, Vt., experiments were made with inlaid tiles in 1853, and a sufficient number were produced to cover a floor space of seven feet square, underlying the exhibit of this factory at the Crystal Palace Exhibition which was held in New York in that year. These tiles were about ten inches square and made by the wet-clay process. The body was white, inlaid with variegated colors, the designs consisting of ornamental centre-piece and border with the American flag in each corner. It is not known what disposition was made of this tile floor after the exhibition, and it seems that the difficulties encountered in making these examples deterred the company from continuing experiments further in this direction.

173.—Some of the First Fancy
American Tiles.
Hyzer & Lewellen.

Previous to 1872, Messrs. Hyzer & Lewellen, of Philadelphia, were experimenting in floor tiles, and I have before me some interesting examples of these early attempts. Their first efforts were directed to the manufacture of encaustic tiles of geometrical shapes,—square, diamond, and triangular,—with natural and artificially-colored American clays, mainly buff, red, and black, the designs being inlaid to the depth of about a quarter of an inch. While these attempts proved partially successful, the wet-clay method employed at that time was unsatisfactory, because the shrinkage was found to be irregular and the pieces came from the kiln of different thickness. The next experiments were made by the damp-dust process, which has been employed ever since. The accompanying illustration will show two forms of geometrical wall tiles which were made previous to 1876. They are plain tiles of yellow clay, of great hardness, the glaze being also hard and entirely free from " crazing," and fully equal in all respects to anything of the kind which has since been produced in this country. The hexagonal specimen figured is decorated with painted designs above the glaze, consisting of a green vine on a buff ground, with a red centre outlined in black. The lozenge-shaped example is painted with a black device on a lemon-colored ground. Later, several patterns of six-inch unglazed mantel tiles, with conventional floral decoration in low relief, were produced, but the manufacture of ornamental tiles was only carried on a short time. At present this firm makes a specialty of plain geometrical floor tiles of different colored bodies and of exceeding hardness. The clay used is fine and homogeneous, and when burned almost approaches stoneware. They also manufacture fire-brick, furnaces, cylinders, dental muffles, and stove-linings. Furnace tests of the standing-up power of the best known fire-bricks, instituted by the Second Geological Survey of Pennsylvania, in 1876, at Harrisburg, showed that the productions of Messrs. Hyzer & Lewellen were superior in heat-resisting qualities to all others that were submitted for examination.

THE LOW ART TILE COMPANY.

174.—A " Low " Tile.

Mr. John G. Low, the founder of the Low Art Tile Works, was born in Chelsea, Mass., in 1835, where five generations of the same name had preceded him. From the age of sixteen until the year 1877 he devoted himself to various lines of painting, commencing with fresco and decorative work. In 1858 he went to Paris, where he studied with Thomas Couture and with M. Troyon, the celebrated cattle painter, for three years. In 1877 he became deeply interested in ceramic manufactures, and, in the following year, formed a copartnership with his father, Hon. John Low, and at once commenced the erection of a tile manufactory in his native place. Having never seen a tile made in any factory, he began experimenting on purely original lines and soon overcame the mechanical difficulties which presented themselves. A novel method was resorted to in the ornamentation of his earlier productions, which he patented and called the " natural " process. To secure accurate impressions of delicate objects, such as grasses, leaves, laces, etc., the article to be reproduced was placed on the surface of the lightly shaped and unburned tile and forced into the clay by means of a screw press. On this impression was spread a piece of tissue paper, and over this was piled a quantity of the prepared dust, which was subjected to a second

175.—VIEW OF THE LOW ART TILE WORKS, CHELSEA, MASS.

pressure. The tile, or pair of tiles, of double thickness, was then separated and the paper removed, when the impressions of the objects appeared in relief and intaglio, showing every minute detail of marking. These Mr. Low called " natural tiles."

The method employed in making embossed or relief tiles is that now used by all tile works in this country, which was patented by Mr. Richard Prosser, in England, in 1840, for making buttons, and shortly after applied by Mr. J. M. Blashfield to the manufacture of tiles, called the "dust" process, which consists in slightly moistening the dry, powdered clay and subjecting it to great pressure in dies containing the designs to be impressed upon

176.—AN F. S. A.

them. They are then burned and afterwards glazed or enamelled in delicate colors.

In a little more than a year after the works were started, we find this firm competing with English tile-makers at the Exhibition at Crewe, Stoke-on-Trent, which was conducted under the auspices of the Royal Manchester, Liverpool, and North Lancashire Agricultural Society, one of the oldest in England. There they won the gold medal over all the manufacturers of the United Kingdom for the best series of art tiles exhibited. This record, probably unsurpassed in ceramic history, serves to illustrate the remarkably rapid development of an industry new in America but old in the East, and shows the vast resources at command of the American potter.

In 1883 Hon. John Low retired from the firm and Mr. John F. Low became associated with his father under the style of J. G. & J. F. Low.

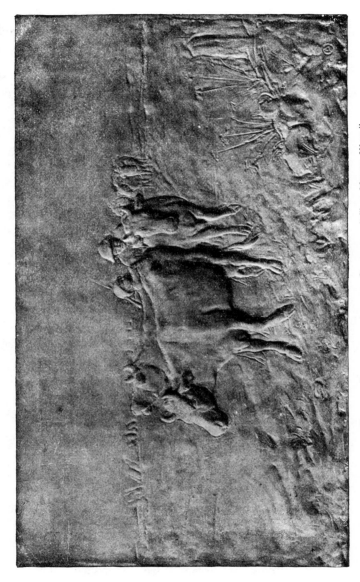

177.—Plastic Sketch, by Arthur Osborne. "The Milky Way."

349

Mr. Arthur Osborne, who has designed the majority of the tiles produced here, joined the Lows a few months after they commenced experimenting, and is still connected with the factory.   He is a talented and versatile

No. 178.—Tile Stove.

young artist, whose conceptions are chaste and classic and possess marked originality.   Among his numerous designs are ideal heads, mythological subjects, portraits, Japanese sketches, and an almost endless variety of animal, bird, and floral studies. His "plastic sketches," on a larger scale, are particularly meritorious, some of the most pleasing being a group of sheep in a pasture, a drove of swine entitled " Late for Dinner," a herd of cattle wending their way homeward (Ill. 177), and " The Old Windmill." These are made of plastic clay, called the " wet-clay " process, and vary in size to upwards of eighteen inches in length. A beautiful conceit is the " Fleeting Moments,"

No. 179.—Panel for Soda Fountain.

in which three cupids hover around an hour-glass, one being depicted in the act of winging his way upwards. In the high-relief tiles the undercutting is done by hand after the designs have been stamped in the press.

The Low Art Tile Co. also manufacture mantel-facings, panels, stove-tiles, calendar tiles, clothes hooks, paper-weights, inkstands, clock cases, candlesticks, bon-bon boxes, and at one time made to some extent ewers and vases with relief ornamentation, or in plain colors, enamelled and glazed. They at one time also made tile stoves. Lately they have been making a specialty of the manufacture of art-tile soda fountains, in which work Mr. Osborne has found a broader field for the exercise of his talents.

180.—Hon. John G. Low.

A superb fountain made by this firm, and exhibited at the Chicago Exhibition, is probably the most elaborate piece of work produced by them. As an example of tile-modelling it has not been surpassed. The centre panel, measuring about six feet in width by five in height, is arched at the top, and on each side is a smaller panel of the same form. The design of the central piece consists of a group of human figures in high relief surrounding a fountain, and Cupids form the subject-design of the lateral panels. The delicate olive glaze which covers the tile-work produces a rich and harmonious effect.

The Lows have never imitated other work, either domestic or foreign. They have never made hand-painted, mosaic, printed, encaustic, or floor tiles, and they have never employed men who were trained in other tile works. Consequently their products are characterized by a marked originality, both in style and design, which has caused them to be extensively imitated, both at home and abroad.

THE AMERICAN ENCAUSTIC TILING CO.

was projected in 1875 at Zanesville, Ohio, by a former resident of that place, who, while engaged in business in New York, had succeeded in interesting some capitalists of that city in the manufacture of flooring tiles from Ohio clays. The first experiments not proving satisfactory, Mr. George A. Stanbery, a mechanical engineer, who had been a commissioner to the Vienna Exposition, was engaged to take charge of the works, and through his energy and ability, with the financial aid of Mr. B. Fischer of New York, the president of the company, and his associates, the enterprise was finally placed upon a paying basis.

In 1880 glazed or enamelled tile were first made here. Encaustic or inlaid floor tiles are made by both the plastic and the damp-dust processes, and the geometrical designs for these are prepared by competent designers, who are employed by the company for this purpose.

Relief tiles are also made here to a large extent, designed by Mr. Herman Mueller, modeller for the company, who studied in the Industrial Academy and Preparatory Art School of Nuremburg, and in the Art Academy of Munich. Special designs have been produced in single

181.—ENCAUSTIC TILE DESIGN.

panels, twelve by eighteen inches in dimensions, of which we have seen some female water carriers of Grecian type. Plastic sketches of large size have also been executed for special orders. Among other styles produced at this factory are imitation mosaic tiles, damask, and embossed damask-finished tiles. By a peculiar treatment, pictures and portraits are also reproduced on a plain surface. This consists in modelling on a smooth surface of clay in intaglio and filling the carved portions with a colored glaze, the shadows being regulated by the depth of the carving, the high lights being raised to near the level of the tile. The relative thickness of the glaze produces the corresponding depth of tint, and the effect is that of a photograph or flat picture instead of a design in relief. In this manner ideal heads and faithful portraits have been successfully executed. The method is clearly shown in the accompanying illustration, which represents a six-inch tile in the biscuit state, and the same filled in with glaze, the latter being an excellent likeness of Mr. John Hoge, a director of the company (Ill. 183).

182.—"OLD AGE."

Mr. Karl Langenbeck, the efficient chemist of the works, has had considerable experience in analyzing clays, and has charge of the laboratory of the company, in which experimental tests are made.

In the manufacture of tiles many chemical and mechanical problems are involved, such as the proper selection and combination of clays to insure sufficient cohesiveness to dry without warping or cracking ; the selection of a temperature in burning that will be suitable to all the different clays ; the preparation of a glaze for enamelled tile which will possess the same co-efficient of expansion and shrinkage as the clay bodies upon which it is placed.

In the "dust" process the prepared materials are made

coherent by the application of enormous pressure, which, in this factory, is obtained by mechanical presses, automatic in action, which are controlled by the company, and constructed in the machine shops connected with the works.

Some of the most artistic productions of this factory

183.—Intaglio Portrait.   Modelled Tile.

184.—Six- by Eighteen-Inch Panel—" Swallows."

are the eight, ten, and fifteen tile facings, with raised designs of classic female and child figures.

Before the new works were finished, eleven large kilns were in operation. Recently the producing capacity has been very largely increased by the addition of twenty-eight kilns, which have been built on a tract of thirty-five acres in the city of Zanesville, making in all thirty-nine kilns.

The new works are located on the western bank of the Muskingum River, in the northern part of the city, and

185.—Twelve- by Eighteen-Inch Panel—"Summer." Designed by Mr. Herman Mueller.

186.—Ten-Piece Panel—Six-Inch Tiles, 12 x 30 Inches. Designed by Herman Mueller.

consist of twenty-four separate buildings. They were formally dedicated on the 19th day of April, 1892, when the schools of the city were closed, and the business of

187.—FIFTEEN-PIECE TILE DESIGN, 18 x 30 IN. BY HERMAN MUELLER. AMERICAN ENCAUSTIC TILING CO.

the place entirely suspended, the citizens giving themselves up to the celebration of the event. A handsome souvenir tile was designed for this occasion by the company, of which fifteen thousand were distributed.

This company has recently produced a new style of unglazed floor tiling, in elegant designs and attractive coloring, which is designated by the name and trade-mark of "Alhambra." Beautiful soft effects in carpet patterns have been obtained on a vitreous body of great hardness. The tinted arabesque designs are inlaid to the depth of about one eighth of an inch, simulating mosaic work.

THE STAR ENCAUSTIC TILE COMPANY.

The experimental period of the present Star Encaustic Tile Company, Limited, of Pittsburgh, Pa., dates back at least twenty years. In 1876 a factory was built by the Pittsburgh Encaustic Tile Company, Limited, which was merged into the present concern in 1882. The products of this factory are gas-burned, unglazed encaustic tile for geometric and tesselated pavements, floors and hearths. The great variety of shapes and colors admits of almost unlimited combinations, resulting in rich and pleasing effects. Mr. John C. Alrich is chairman of the company and Mr. Samuel Keys manager.

THE UNITED STATES ENCAUSTIC TILE COMPANY

of Indianapolis, Ind., was organized soon after the Centennial Exposition with Mr. J. G. Douglass, president, Mr.

188.—VIEW OF THE NEW WORKS OF THE AMERICAN ENCAUSTIC TILING CO., ZANESVILLE, OHIO.

360

W. W. Lyon, secretary and treasurer, and Mr. F. H. Hall, superintendent. The building soon afterwards burned down and larger and more suitable ones were erected in 1879. In 1886 the present management purchased the business and changed the name to the United States Encaustic Tile Works. The plant now includes six biscuit and twelve muffle kilns, the products being plain, encaustic, enamelled, and relief tiles for flooring, mantel facings, wainscoting, hearths, and other interior decoration. The clays used for white bodies come from South Carolina and Kentucky, and those for dark bodies are obtained from Indiana. The burning is done by means of natural gas. Miss Ruth M. Winterbotham, who models for this manufactory, has produced many beautiful designs, notably some three- and six-section panels.

189.—SIX-INCH RELIEF TILE.
U. S. ENCAUSTIC TILE WORKS.

A series of three mantel panels, representing Dawn, Midday, and Twilight, are particularly deserving of mention. Recently this factory has produced some effective tiles in raised blue designs on a white ground. Mr. Robert Minton Taylor, of England, was connected with these works from 1881 to 1883. The present officers are Mr. John J. Cooper, president, Mr. Jackson Landers, vice-president, and Mr. John Picken, secretary and treasurer.

In the Woman's Building, at the Chicago Fair, Miss Winterbotham exhibited a series of tiles and panels which she had designed and modelled for this company. A panel measuring perhaps fifteen by eighteen inches, decorated with three well executed female figures in relief, apparently representing the March zephyrs, attracted considerable attention, as did also a circular tile plaque, fifteen inches in diameter, with relief design showing a frontier scene with wood-chopper, bison, mountains, and setting sun.

THE TRENT TILE COMPANY.

In 1882, the Harris Manufacturing Company was organized for the production of tiles, and shortly afterwards the name was changed to the Trent Tile Company. In 1883 Mr. Isaac Broome, who had formerly been connected with the Etruria Pottery, of Trenton, returned to that city from the West to accept the position of designer and modeller for the new company. He continued in this capacity for about two years, during which period he stocked the works with many excellent designs, some of which are still being produced there.

The Trent Tile Company is now making a specialty of dull-finished or " Trent finished " tiles in alto-relievo, which are treated by the sand-blast process after being glazed. The effect is a soft, satin-like finish, exceedingly pleasing to the eye. The process is protected by patents. This style of finish forms a striking contrast to the glazed and enamelled varieties also made here, of which effective panels, six by eighteen inches, in one piece, are manufactured extensively. Larger tiles have also been produced here for special work, some of them being twelve by twenty-four inches. The company has also recently been making soda-water fountains with modelled panels.

Over twenty kilns are at present operated by the Trent Tile Company, including six round biscuit kilns, and upwards of a dozen enamelling kilns. The English muffle kilns are used for enamelling, but the firing is done at a pretty high temperature. The present officers of the

190.—BACCHANALIAN PANEL. NINE BY EIGHTEEN INCHES. DESIGNED BY MR. W. W. GALLIMORE. TRENT TILE WORKS.

company are Mr. Benjamin F. Lee, president, Mr. Alfred Lawshe, treasurer, and Mr. DeWitt C. McVay, manager.

In 1886, Mr. William Wood Gallimore became designer and modeller for these works, having previously acquired an enviable reputation as a modeller of portrait busts and vases. Mr. Gallimore is an Englishman with thirty years' experience as a potter and designer. His father, Mr. William Gallimore, was an artist, engraver, and color maker, and under his instruction the son obtained a complete knowledge of the manufacture of potters' colors. The younger Gallimore began his career in the office of Mr. John Ward, solicitor, Burslem, Staffordshire, and his evenings and leisure hours were devoted to the study of art in the Art School of Stoke-upon-Trent. While in the law office he executed his first model, a group of figures, representing a Neapolitan fisherman and family, after an engraving which appeared in the *Illustrated London News.* This work attracted consider-

191.—NINE- BY EIGHTEEN-INCH PANEL.—FISHING BOYS.   DESIGNED BY W. W.
GALLIMORE.   TRENT TILE CO.

able attention among the artists of the district, and Mr. George Reade, a modeller of reputation, at once tendered the young artist a position in his studio at Burslem, which was accepted. Here, under Mr. Reade's instruction, young Gallimore became proficient in modelling pieces of useful ware, and was entrusted with much of the outline drawing for the establishment. On Mr. Reade's retirement from business, his pupil continued his studies in figure modelling under M. Louis Kremer, a French artist of ability. Subsequently Mr. Gallimore became connected with a number of the prominent potteries in England. For six years he was at the Belleek potteries in Ireland, where he lost his right arm by the bursting of a gun. He afterwards was commissioned by Mr. William Henry Goss, proprietor of the London Road, Stoke-upon-Trent, potteries, an eminent author, to execute some busts of prominent Englishmen, which were afterwards produced by Mr. Goss in fine parian. These portrait busts were pronounced admirable likenesses of the originals, including a head of the late Mr. Llewellynn Jewitt, which serves as the frontispiece to the latter's *Ceramic Art of Great Britain*, a bust of Mr. S. C. Hall, editor of *The Art Journal*, another of the present Earl of Derby, and one of the Earl of Beaconsfield.

Since the loss of his arm, Mr. Gallimore has done his modelling with his left hand, and he has accomplished better work with one arm than he did when in possession of both. All of the designs produced by the Trent factory during the past six years are his work, the dies being made in his workshop by his son, under his supervision. Mr. Gallimore is a versatile and prolific sculptor, and an artist of fine ability. His style is vigorous and characteristic; his portrayals of boys and Cupids are especially pleasing. Among the more pretentious of his recent productions are a finely modelled coat-of-arms of the State of New Jersey, designed for architectural embellishment, and a six-foot panel with figures in relief. In addition to his work for the Trent Company, he has designed some of the best vases and other pieces for the Ceramic Art Company of Trenton, makers of Belleek china, and other establishments. The tile portrait which forms the frontispiece to this volume was modelled and kindly volunteered by Mr. Gallimore, and is pronounced an excellent likeness.

Mr. William Gallimore, the father, was a designer and engraver of the old school, and did considerable work for the Wedgwoods, Enoch Wood, John Alcock, and other English potters. He died at his son's house in Trenton, N. J., in 1891, aged eighty-four, the last piece of work which he did, a short time previous to his death, being a chrysanthemum design for transfer printing, for the house of J. E. Jeffords & Co., Philadelphia. Among his papers he left a large and interesting collection of proofs from the original copper plates which he and others had engraved for the above named firms during the first half of the present century, together with many of the original drawings from which the engravings were made, and some proofs of curious old engravings for " bat-printing."

Mr. W. W. Gallimore's sons, William and Jesse, have recently commenced business on their own account, under the supervision of their father, as designers and modellers of useful, ornamental, and figure subjects,—the sons having inherited the artistic talents of their father and grandfather. Miss Flora and Miss Marian Gallimore, the daughters, are also clever modellers of floral designs for applied ornamentation, and have done considerable work of this character.

THE PARK PORCELAIN WORKS.

In 1884, Mr. H. R. Mitchell, of the Park Porcelain Works, West Philadelphia, experimented in glazed relief tiles, examples of which are on exhibition in the Pennsylvania Museum of Art. He modelled a number of designs from natural objects, such as leaves and turtle-shells, the latter being exact reproductions, both in form and coloring, of the original models. The manufacture does not seem to have advanced beyond the experimental stage, although the workmanship was creditable and some of the glazes excellent.

THE PROVIDENTIAL TILE WORKS.

of Trenton, N. J., were projected about 1885 and the first goods were turned out in the spring of 1886. Mr. Isaac Broome, who had previously been with the Trent Tile Company of the same place, was the first designer and modeller of the new establishment, and some of his designs are still being produced.

The products of this factory are glazed tiles, plain and in relief. At one time embossed tiles were made in two colors, the raised ornamentation being of a different color or tint from the ground, and some good results were obtained by this treatment. Underglaze decoration was also employed for a time, but both styles were abandoned as being unsuited to the American market. The present output consists principally of embossed tiles for mantels, hearths, and wall decorations. Some of the newest designs are relief tiles, measuring six by twelve and six by eighteen inches, and among the most popular pieces are hunting panels for mantel facings, with representations of fighting bucks, stag's heads, sportsmen, and dogs.

The present designer and modeller is Mr. Scott Callowhill, recently, for a short time, connected with the Phœnixville (Pa.) pottery. He came to this country in

192.—RELIEF PANEL—" MIGNON."
BY SCOTT CALLOWHILL, AFTER
LEFEBVRE.

1885, from the Royal Worcester works, England, where with his brother, Mr. James Callowhill, now of Roslindale, Mass., he had charge of two of the principal decorating-rooms in which the finer class of decoration, in raised paste and gold bronze, was done. He also while in England worked for the Doultons at Lambeth. Mr. Callowhill has recently executed some artistic panel designs, one of which is a six- by twelve-inch tile, " Mignon," after Jules Lefebvre, and another, a six- by eighteen-inch piece, after Mr. Benjamin W. Leader's picture, entitled " February fill Dyke," in intaglio. This panel is glazed in a single color and is one of a set of three intended for a mantel facing.

Among the latest productions of this factory are gilded and decorated tiles in the style of the Royal Worcester *cloisonné*, exceedingly rich and pleasing in effect. One variety consists of raised designs, glazed and outlined in gold, the relief portions being finished in shades lighter or darker than the ground, while another style possesses arabesque reliefs painted in delicate overglaze colors and

193.—INTAGLIO—"FEBRUARY FILL DYKE." BY CALLOWHILL, AFTER LEADER.

gold against glazed grounds of white, ivory, pale pink, and French gray shades. The general effect is that of metal *cloisonné*. The works are under the management of Messrs. James H. Robinson and C. Louis Whitehead.

THE BEAVER FALLS ART TILE COMPANY, LIMITED.

of Beaver Falls, Pa., was organized in 1886 by Mr. F. W. Walker, who is secretary, treasurer, and manager.

194.—BEAVER FALLS STOVE TILES.

The works started with the manufacture of plain enamels, and a few months later added embossed and intaglio tiles, as well as tiles for stove decorations, of which this company has since made a specialty. The discovery of natural gas and the advantages to be obtained by its use as a fuel for the burning of all pottery wares was the inducement for Mr. Walker, who had been very much interested in the investigation of tiles and their manufacture, to organize the company, and his ability as a chemist soon enabled him to place the works in a position to manufacture a line of glazes of soft, rich tones, and their remarkable freedom from crazing soon won for the fac-

195.—Six-Inch Relief Tile—
"Sappho." By Broome.

tory a high reputation in the trade. Their delicate tints of pale blue and greenish and purplish grays are particularly beautiful examples of transparent colored glazing.

These works have always employed the best designers that could be obtained. Prof. Isaac Broome, a sculptor of rare artistic ability, became connected with the factory in 1890. Among his most highly admired pieces is a six-inch tile with a classic female figure (Sappho) in relief, leaning on a harp.

The factory is now making a specialty of artistic tile designs suitable for solid wall decorations, in all the leading styles, for libraries, dining-rooms, and bath-rooms. One of the most chaste patterns recently produced is a dado in Romanesque style, of which a section is here represented (Ill. 198). The examples figured are characteristic illustrations of the geometric, floral, and figure embellishment of the Beaver Falls productions.

A circular four-and-a-half-inch likeness of Mrs. Grover Cleveland was executed here a few years ago, which is an excellent example of tile portraiture. Among the most recent productions of the works are a series of six- by eighteen-inch panels, representing Poetry, Music, and Painting (Ill. 197), and some twelve- by twelve-inch heads, including one of Washington.

Prof. Isaac Broome is one of America's most versatile artists. He was born at Valcartier, Quebec, on May 16, 1835. He first became interested in the subject of ceramics when, as a young man, he visited the museums of Europe to study the collections of Grecian and Etruscan vases for archæological material for use in his chosen professions of sculpture and painting. After some years he turned his attention to the potter's art, and about the close of the Civil War he established a terra-cotta manufactory at Pittsburgh,

196.—Passion-Flower Panel. By Broome.

where he made vases, fountains, and architectural designs. His productions, however, were in advance of the public taste, and the venture had to be abandoned. After a period of portrait-painting, frescoing, sculpturing, and modelling, he started architectural terra-cotta works in Brooklyn, N. Y., about 1871, and produced some large pieces of artistic work, but he was finally compelled to relinquish this second enterprise by the arbitrary ruling of the city Board of Health which, under the pretext that the firing of his kilns endangered the safety of the adjacent buildings, ordered him to close the works.

Just previous to the Centennial, as we have already seen, Mr. Broome was engaged by the Etruria Pottery of Trenton, N. J., to prepare some special designs for the

197.—RELIEF PANEL— "MUSIC," FROM PAINTING, POETRY, AND MUSIC FACING. BY BROOME.

approaching exhibition. In 1878 he was appointed a special commissioner on ceramics to the Paris Exposition, and, in conjunction with General McClellan, made a thorough study of the ceramic art as it exists abroad. While connected with the Ott & Brewer Company at Trenton, he made some original drawings on stone for some special and general work which were printed in black, in colors, and in gold, said to be the first lithographic printing on pottery ever done in America.

In the year 1880, on his return to Trenton from abroad, he utilized the time in recovering from an attack of illness in putting into practical application some ideas which he had previously thought out in the production of a variety of ware never before attempted in this country. The body was a well vitrified porcelain with underglaze color effects, the paste, colors, and glaze being thoroughly incorporated together by a single firing. The result was a ware difficult to describe, but most pleasing in its modest

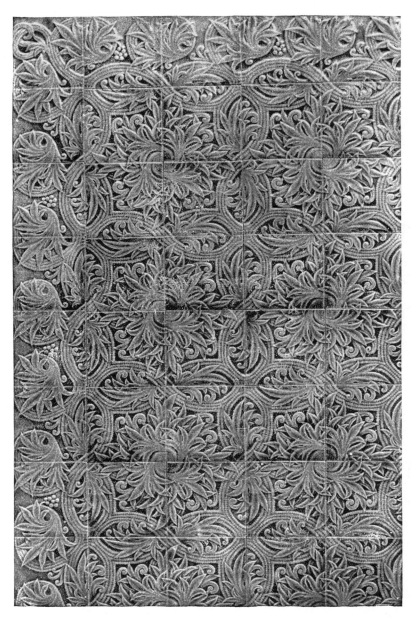

198.—Dado in Romanesque Style. Beaver Falls Art Tile Co.

tones and the softness and depth of translucent effect. Only about one hundred of these vases were made, for the most part of small size, ranging from three to ten inches in height, the forms being simple but full and rich in outline, and particularly adapted to the peculiar style of coloration in analogous or contrasting harmonies. These pieces were made entirely by Prof. Broome, assisted by his young son, the clays being prepared in the basement of his residence, dried in plaster moulds in the sun, thrown, turned, glazed, and colored on the green clay in a second-story room, and finally taken to Davis' pottery in Trenton and fired in a regular ware kiln.   All of these interesting pieces were sent to a dealer in New York and scattered in collections throughout the country (see chapter on Marks).

In 1883 Mr. Broome became connected with the Harris Manufacturing Company, now the Trent Tile Company, as designer and modeller, and afterward, in 1886, was instrumental in establishing the Providential Tile works, of Trenton, and designed many of their best works.   He is an indefatigable worker and a prolific artist, his sculptures being characterized by exquisite conception and the most painstaking execution of details.

Among the more important works of Prof. Broome are a marble bust of Dr. Ducachet, in a niche in St. Stephen's Church, Philadelphia, executed in 1858 ; a semi-colossal marble bust of Washington in the Philadelphia Club-house, Thirteenth and Walnut streets, made from the most authentic portraits in the same year ; and a ceramic bust of Hon. Joseph D. Bedle, New Jersey's Centennial Governor, now in the State Library at Trenton.

THE CAMBRIDGE ART TILE WORKS

were established at Covington, Kentucky, in March of 1887, by Messrs. A. W. Koch, F. W. Braunstein, and Heinrich Binz, all of Cincinnati, for the manufacture of enamelled and embossed tile, since which date the plant has been enlarged from year to year to accommodate the constantly increasing business. These works are producing to-day an extensive line of high-grade art goods of various shapes for interior decoration—friezes, moulding, and

199.—" KING LEAR."

mantel facings—ranging in size from one half inch square to six by eighteen inches. In addition to relief work for mantel and wall decoration, the intaglio treatment has also been employed to some extent, whereby photographs may be reproduced with good effect by filling in the depressions with colored glazes. Imitation mosaic work is also a specialty of this factory. The glazes used on the various productions are remarkably free from crazing.

From a large number of excellent designs we have

selected for illustration a six-inch head, representing King
Lear, which was modelled by Mr. Clem. Barnhorn, who
recently received the European scholarship offered by the
Cincinnati Art School.

200.—"WINTER." MODELLED BY MERSMAN.

The principal designer and modeller for the works is
Mr. Ferdinand Mersman, formerly connected with the
Rookwood Pottery of Cincinnati, who studied at the

Academy of Fine Arts in Munich. One of his designs, a six- by eighteen-inch panel, representing Winter, is here figured, and of his more pretentious works we give an illustration of a ten-piece design entitled " Daughters of the Sea."

201.—" DAUGHTERS OF THE SEA " FACING. MODELLED BY MERSMAN.

THE MENLO PARK CERAMIC COMPANY

was started at Menlo Park, N.J., in October, 1888, by Mr. J. T. Smith and Mr. Charles Volkmar, for the manufacture of art tiles and other interior ceramic decorations.

Mr. Volkmar, who came from Baltimore, Md., springs from a family of artists. His father's reputation as a portrait painter and restorer of pictures is well known, and his grandfather was an engraver of considerable prominence. The younger Volkmar began his art studies in his native city, and as early as 1859 attracted attention as an etcher of merit. Before reaching his majority he went to Paris and studied under Harpignies and others. Here he remained for a number of years, acquiring an enviable reputation as an animal and landscape painter in oils and water colors, and his works were exhibited in several of the salons. During this period he became greatly interested in the Limoges method of underglaze painting in clay, and, entering a pottery in one of the suburbs of Paris, devoted himself to the study of the various processes of manufacture, the composition of glazes, and the mysteries of the kiln. Later he became connected with other potteries, in the capacity of an ordinary workman, and in this manner acquired a knowledge of the art of underglaze decoration which could not have been obtained in any other way. Returning to America about 1878, he built a kiln at Greenpoint, Long Island, and subsequently another at Tremont, near New York City, where he began to make decorated tiles and art pottery. The " Volkmar *faïence* " of that period was of the same character as the Haviland slip-decorated ware. In 1883 he produced a limited number of so-called " barbotine " vases, decorated on plain surfaces or modelled in relief. His process differs from that in vogue elsewhere, in that the colors are applied to the thoroughly dried surface of the unbaked ware instead of to the moist or green clay, by which method he claims that he can obtain better results in the avoidance of unequal shrinkage of the body and the securing of greater brilliancy of effect.

Recently Mr. Volkmar has been devoting himself to architectural work. One of the most important pieces of special work executed by him in the last two years is the interior decoration of the William Rockafeller mansion at Tarrytown, N. Y., consisting of enamelled terracotta, or *faïence*, in a vestibule with groined arches and loggia, the latter embellished with a five-foot frieze, heavy cornice, and panelled ceiling. This work was modelled after special designs of the architects, Messrs. Carrere and Hastings. The style of decoration is Italian Renaissance

2.)2.—PORTION OF FIVE-FOOT FRIEZE IN LOGGIA OF THE ROCKAFELLER MANSION, TARRYTOWN, N. Y.

in high relief, the color of the enamel being in such perfect harmony with the wainscoting of Tennessee marble that at a short distance no difference in shading is perceptible. This terra-cotta body is white in color and of a somewhat sandy nature, fired hard, and covered with a glaze or enamel.

Mr. Volkmar's method of decorating tile consists in the use of enamels instead of transparent glazes, which he is able to shade to the most delicate and subdued tints, to match any variety of marble, onyx, or other material. His "old gold" and "old ivory" are just now particularly popular for decorative purposes, to harmonize with the light furnishings which have recently been revived.

Another peculiarity of his tiles is the employment of slightly relieved lines, to indicate the design, in place of high-relief effects, which are often decorated in two shades of the same color, or in two harmonious colors of low, broken shades.

Some of Mr. Volkmar's tile work may be seen in the ceiling of the Boston Public Library, in light gray-blue coloring. In the Market and Fulton National Bank building, New York City, over eight thousand six-inch Volkmar tiles were used for wall decorations, in Romanesque style, the color scheme being old ivory, pale blue, and light maroon. Mantel facings and hearths, with raised designs, of artistic conception, finished in old ivory and gold, have also been made by Mr. Volkmar for many of the residences of prominent people.

Mr. Volkmar has taken steps to organize a new company, which will be established in Menlo Park, to be known as the Volkmar Ceramic Company. The manufacture of artistic tiling will be a specialty of the new establishment, as well as high-grade architectural clay work of every description.

The Menlo Park Ceramic Works are still being operated by Mr. J. T. Smith.

THE ROBERTSON ART TILE COMPANY

was formed at Morrisville, Pa., opposite Trenton, N. J., in 1890, by Mr. G. W. Robertson, who had been assistant manager at the East Boston Pottery from 1865 to 1871, and for several years afterwards associated with his father and brothers, James Robertson & Sons, at the Chelsea

203—Panel after the French.   Robertson Art Tile Co.

Keramic Art Works, Chelsea, Mass., and from 1878 to 1890 connected with the Low Art Tile Works, of the same place. Morrisville was selected for the new venture by reason of its many natural advantages. The new factory was called the Chelsea Keramic Art Tile Works, and Mr. Robertson became general manager for the company.

The business started with the manufacture of a fine grade of glazed brick, and for some time plain enamelled wall tiles have been produced. The glazes and enamels are of most excellent quality and remarkably free from a

tendency to craze, and the color scale possesses a wide range. A specialty is the manufacture of rough tiles with stucco finish for interior decoration. Recently some excellent etched and relief art tiles have been made, of which two six-by twelve-inch panels are here illustrated, one of which, in high relief, is a reproduction, probably, of a French design. The other, in low relief, was modelled by Mr. H. C. Robertson of Chelsea after one of Doré's illustrations of La Fontaine's fables.

204—PANEL MODELLED BY H. C. ROBERTSON AFTER DORÉ.

THE COLUMBIA ENCAUSTIC TILE COMPANY,

of Anderson, Indiana, manufacture natural-gas burned tiles, their specialty being plain enamelled tiles. Inlaid floor tiles and, to some extent, embossed tiles for mantels and ornamental purposes are also made here. Of the latter some twelve-by thirty-inch panels are now under experiment. The officers of the company are Mr. B. O. Haugh, president, Mr. George Lilly, vice-president and treasurer, and Mr. Samuel Hughes, secretary.

Some of their best six-inch designs are those with boy figures representing the seasons, and some children's heads. A mantel facing representing "The Return of the Swallows" is worthy of notice.

TYPICAL NINETEENTH CENTURY POTTER'S WHEEL

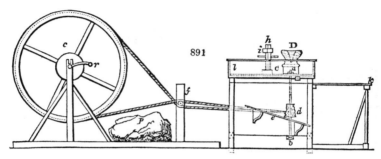

A profile of a potter's bench, also called a potter's lathe. Used for blocking out round ware. (a) Head of the potter's wheel: (d) pulleys with several grooves of different diameters for receiving the driving cord or band; (k) bench which the potter sits astride; (e) treadle footboard; (l) ledge-board for catching the shavings of clay which fly off from the lathe; (h) is an instrument with a slide-nut (i) for measuring objects in the blocking-out; (c) is a fly-wheel with its drive handle; (r) turned by an assistant; the sole-frame is held in place by a heavy stone; (f) is the oblong pulley-guide, having also several grooves for converting vertical movement to rotary movement; (d) is one of the intermediate forms given by the potter to the ball of clay, as it revolves upon the head of the lathe. From *Ure's Dictionary*, 1842.

TOOLS OF THE POTTER

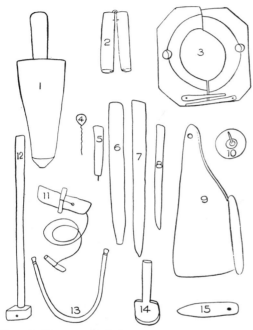

FIG. 1. Former of wood.

FIG. 2. Hinged mold for tubular spouts.

FIG. 3. Lifters for handling green ware.

FIG. 4. Plumb bob of clay and string.

FIG. 5. Awl.

FIG. 6. Former for mouths of jugs, etc.

FIG. 7. Wooden spatula.

FIG. 8. Wooden spatula.

FIG. 9. Arm rest. In use fastened by a bolt at the side of the wheel-box and covered with sheepskin as a cushion.

FIG. 10. Gauge for jar mouth. Lid of preserve jar fitted with handle to allow of placing it over the mouth of the jar being thrown to ascertain gauge.

FIG. 11. Wire for cutting ware from the wheel. Copper wire with wooden handle and leather guard.

FIG. 12. Gauge for height of ware. Planted in a lump of clay in the wheel-box.

FIG. 13. Bow for wire used in cutting ware from the wheel.

FIG. 14. Scraper for removing clay.

FIG. 15. Former for mouths of jugs, etc.

CHAPTER XVII.

ARCHITECTURAL TERRA-COTTA.

IT is interesting to note what the fifth edition of the *Encyclopædia Britannica*, published in 1815, contains relative to this subject : " Worlidge, and others after him, have endeavored to excite brick-makers to try their skill in making a new kind of brick, or a composition of clay and sand, whereof to form window-frames, chimney-pieces, door-cases, and the like. It is to be made in pieces, fashioned in molds, which, when burnt, may be set together with a fine red cement, and seem as one entire piece. The thing should seem feasible." And so we shall find that it was.

Terra-cotta, the most enduring of all building materials, has been used to a greater or lesser extent from a high antiquity in continental Europe, and in England terra-cotta trimmings were used in building as early as the fifteenth century. In the United States this material does not seem to have been introduced until after 1850. Experiments were made in this direction in 1853 by Mr. James Renwick, a prominent New York architect, but the innovation was not received with favor by builders. In 1870 the Chicago Terra-Cotta Company brought over from England Mr. James Taylor, superintendent of the well known works which were established by Mr. J. M. Blashfield in 1858. By the introduction of the English methods, the Chicago establishment soon turned out better work than had been produced before in the United States.

The Southern Terra-Cotta Works of Messrs. P. Pellegrini and Z. Castleberry were established in Atlanta, Georgia, in 1871, for the manufacture of architectural and horticultural terra-cotta. Their red and buff garden vases and statuary are justly noted for excellence of design, and their architectural work, for exterior and interior decoration, is of a superior character. Some of their terra-cotta mantels, supported by female figures, and their fire-place and chimney panels are especially meritorious.

The Perth Amboy Terra-Cotta Company, of Perth Amboy, N. J., was incorporated in 1879, and at once embarked in the manufacture of large designs for architectural purposes, from clay obtained in the neighborhood. The plant of this company has expanded so rapidly that at present it includes twenty-two kilns, some of them measuring forty-eight and one third feet in height by twenty-four and one sixth in diameter, which are among the largest of the kind on this continent, if not in the world.

This company has in its employ a number of eminent artists in this particular line, and has furnished terra-cotta details for many prominent buildings throughout the country. Of these may be mentioned the Ponce de Leon Hotel, St. Augustine, Florida ; Biological Laboratory,

206.—Panel in Warehouse, Jersey City, N. J. Perth Amboy Terra-Cotta Company.

387

Princeton College ; the Produce Exchange, Cotton Exchange, Washington Market, *Post* Building, *World* Building, Century Club, Racquet Club, Freundschaft Club, Tiffany House, and Mills Building, New York City ; Long Island Historical Building, Brooklyn, N. Y. ; Pennsylvania Railroad Station, Philadelphia, Pa. ; Iroquois Hotel, Buffalo, N. Y. ; Dearborn Station and Rialto Building, Chicago, Ill. ; Hastings Hall, Boston, Mass. ; De Soto Hotel, Charleston, S. C. ; the Montgomery County Court House, Birmingham, Alabama ; Adams Express Company, Cincinnati and St. Louis ; and Masonic Hall, Trenton, N. J.

In addition to the red and buff terra-cotta employed in brick structures, this company also manufactures a white terra-cotta which has been used in the Madison Square Garden, Imperial Hotel, *Judge* Building, Edison Building, New York City, and many other large edifices.

The officers of this company are Mr. E. J. Hall, president, Mr. W. C. Hall, vice-president and Mr. G. P. Putnam, secretary and treasurer.

The Winkle Terra-Cotta Company, of Cheltenham, St. Louis, Mo., commenced business in 1883. They manufacture a high grade of architectural terra-cotta in a variety of shades to match the different colors of building bricks. The officers are Mr. Joseph Winkle, president, Mr. Andrew Winkle, vice-president and Mr. John G. Hewitt, secretary and treasurer.

The New York Architectural Terra-Cotta Company, of which Mr. Walter Geer is president, was organized in the latter part of 1885, and the services of Mr. James

207.—THREE KILNS. PERTH AMBOY TERRA-COTTA COMPANY.

Taylor were secured to superintend the works. On the
10th of May following, the first kiln of terra-cotta was
burned, in the newly completed works at Long Island
City, opposite 58th Street, New York. The main building is 170 by 115 feet in extent, and six stories in height,
and is built of brick and terra-cotta. In 1891 an addition,
95 by 80 feet, was erected in the rear, to accommodate
the rapidly increasing business of the company. The
twelve kilns are situated on the second floor and the walls
ascend through the third, fourth, and fifth floors, thus

208.—BAS-RELIEF IN THE ST. ANTHONY CLUB-
HOUSE, PHILADELPHIA, PA. PERTH
AMBOY TERRA-COTTA COMPANY.

helping to warm the
apartments and fur-
nishing surplus heat
for drying the plastic
work in the pressing
and finishing depart-
ments, which are lo-
cated there.

Designs for archi-
tectural purposes are
made usually in
moulds, except in
special work, then turned out on the floor of the drying-
room, and, if requiring extra finish, or undercutting, are
afterwards carved or modelled by hand. The larger
designs are made in sections, of a size that can be con-
veniently handled by two men. After being sufficiently
dried, the pieces are placed in the kilns, where they remain
about seven days in the burning and cooling processes.

The Long Island City Works have furnished details

for more than two thousand buildings, scattered throughout the principal cities of the Union. Among these may
be mentioned the McIntyre Building, Manhattan Athletic
Club, Music Hall, Plaza Hotel, and Colonial Club, of
New York City, and the Montauk Club of Brooklyn.
The latter, designed by Mr. Francis H. Kimball, architect, is an elaborate Venetian Gothic structure, in a combination of three colors. The terra-cotta is of a pure
yellow, in surface ornamentation, upon a soft, brown
ground, with columns of Indian red, the whole framed in
a setting of bright buff brickwork.

209.—Military Panel, G. A. R. Memorial Hall, Wilkes Barre, Pa.
New York Architectural Terra-Cotta Company.

A medallion portrait of Jahn is an example of vigorous
treatment in terra-cotta sculpture and is one of a set of
three made for the Turn Hall, Trenton, N. J. The others
are portraits of Goethe and Schiller. These heads, made
of white terra-cotta, form a harmonious and pleasing contrast with the light Pompeiian color of the brickwork,
and the semi-glazed old-gold color of the adjacent terra-
cotta.

The New York Architectural Terra-Cotta Company
have lately produced a white terra-cotta which is said to

be fully equal to the red in durability and hardness, which has been used recently in the rebuilding of Harrigan's

210.—PANEL IN FIFTH AVENUE THEATRE, NEW YORK. N. Y. ARCHITECTURAL TERRA-COTTA CO.

Theatre and in the Fifth Avenue Theatre, New York. The effect is novel and pleasing. The latter is one of the best examples of the new development of white terra-cotta in New York. The color of the brickwork, which forms the ground, is lemon or pale yellow. The lower story is constructed of white marble from Vermont, and the effect is peculiarly appropriate in tone and richness of detail for a structure devoted to the higher order of histrionic amusement. In Illustration 210 may be seen one of a pair of panels in this theatre emblematic of dancing and singing which are used in the upper foyer windows. The experiments already made by this company and others in the production of a white terra-cotta have proved highly satisfactory, and it now seems only a question of time when the more perishable marble, as a building material, will be superseded by this more enduring substitute.

The color of terra-cotta is governed by the character of the local clays used in its manufacture. Until recently the red brick used almost exclusively in the Eastern States necessitated the employment of blood-red terra-cotta, but since the low rates of freight have of late years enabled our architects to use extensively different colored bricks from various localities, the demand for other tints of terra-cotta has increased. It has been ascertained that the color

211.—Panel in Residence of Mr. George Alfred Townsend, Gapland, Md. New York Architectural Terra-Cotta Company.

of the material has little relation to its strength or durability. The weather-resisting quality of burned clay is due to the presence of metallic oxides, which act as fluxes in the process of burning, thus cementing the particles of silica and alumina together, the color being imparted by the predominating oxide. Iron produces red, manganese black or gray, and white calcium creates a buff or light tint. The entire absence of oxides results in a white body which is difficult to vitrify on account of the want of fluxes, hence it is not suited for a building material, but by the use of a good weather clay for the body and the application of a skin of fine white clay, the

212.—WORKS OF THE NEW YORK ARCHITECTURAL TERRA-COTTA CO.,
LONG ISLAND CITY, N. Y.

terra-cotta is made equally hard and durable, as the skin takes up enough of the flux from the main body to render it of an equal weather value without seriously affecting its purity of color. That the New York Architectural Terra-Cotta Company has succeeded in producing a material answering to these requirements is amply demonstrated in a specimen which is now before me, which is of a

beautiful creamy whiteness, fine texture, and of the necessary hardness.

The Boston Terra-Cotta Company, of Boston, Mass.,
manufacture architectural and decorative terra-cotta, also
faïence or glazed terra-cotta for interior and exterior embellishment. Probably the most notable work of the latter
class thus far produced is the interior decoration of the cor-

213.—MEDALLION OF GENERAL WINFIELD S. SCOTT.

ridors of the Charlesgate and the Adams House of Boston.
Of the many prominent buildings throughout the country
for which architectural terra-cotta has been furnished by this
company, the Barnum Institute of Science and History, of
Bridgeport, Conn., may be mentioned as a fair example.
This structure contains a frieze divided into panels repre-

senting the different epochs in the history of Bridgeport, with figures about half the size of life. Medallion busts of eminent men, of heroic size, are inserted between the panels, which are remarkable for their fidelity to nature.

214.—FLORAL PANEL. STEPHENS, ARMSTRONG, & CONKLING.

Those of the late Mr. P. T. Barnum, the donor of the building, and General Winfield S. Scott, are especially praiseworthy as examples of lifelike portrait-modelling. Messrs. Fiske, Coleman, & Co. are the managers of the

Boston Terra-Cotta Company, as well as managers and agents of the Boston Fire-Brick Works, and associated with them are Messrs. Atwood & Grueby, in the production of architectural *faïence*.

In 1886 Messrs. Stephens & Leach started a factory for architectural terra-cotta in West Philadelphia, and later the firm name was changed to Stephens, Armstrong, & Conkling. During the six years of the works' existence they have furnished material for hundreds of important structures in Philadelphia and other cities, of which particular mention may be made of panels and gable work in the library of the University of Pennsylvania, and the Drexel Institute, West Philadelphia. A series of animal-head medallions, in high relief, are particularly excellent, and some bas-relief portraits of eminent men, modelled by such sculptors as H. J. Ellicott, John Boyle, and

215.—MEDALLION OF COLUMBUS.

E. N. Conkling, are among their best productions. A medallion of Columbus by Mr. Conkling, and a Cupid and floral panel by Thomas Robertson, are here represented. Admirable work is also being produced by other establishments in Boston, Chicago, and most of our larger cities.

The Indianapolis Terra-Cotta Company, located at Brightwood, Indiana, commenced business, under its

present management, in 1886. Mr. Benjamin D. Wal-
cott is president and treasurer, Mr. William F. Stilz,
vice-president, and Mr. Joseph Joiner, secretary and
superintendent.   The latter is a gentleman of large experience in this field, and a highly qualified architect.

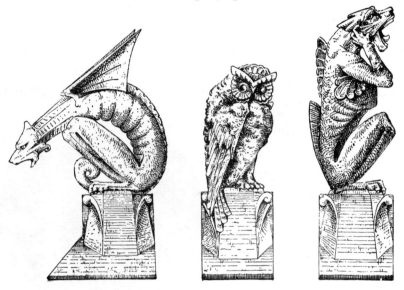

216.—Finials.   Indianapolis Terra-Cotta Company.

The products of these works are architectural and
horticultural terra-cotta, of excellent quality and workmanship.

Since about 1880 the demand for architectural terra-
cotta has rapidly increased, and to-day many manufactories
are in operation in various parts of the country.

CHAPTER XVIII

TILES FOR DECORATIVE EFFECT.

NEXT to paintings, etchings, and engravings, nothing can be more effective for wall decoration than artistically modelled tiles, in which color and shading are replaced by contour. The tile designer combines the arts of the painter and the sculptor, and his ceramic creations, partaking both of the nature of pictures and of delicate carvings, are well deserving of a place among the objects of art which adorn the dwellings of the cultured.

It is a remarkable fact that, while the art of tile making in this country is practically not more than fifteen years old, the United States to-day excels the world in the manufacture of relief figure tiles and tile panels. True it is that we have had the benefit of the skill and knowledge of some of the foremost modellers of Europe, who have come to our shores, but we have also developed a number of American sculptors, whose work, in this direction, has fully equalled the best that has yet been accomplished. Within the past year or so we have progressed with such marvellous rapidity in the mechanical, as well as the artistic, treatment of clays and glazes, that we are now able to produce tile panels of eighteen to thirty inches in length, in a single piece, with almost the same facility with which it was possible formerly to make six-inch tiles. Many of these tile sculptures are genuine works of art, and should be displayed in a tasteful and appropriate manner.

What we call taste is merely the ability to recognize that which is beautiful. We are endowed with what is commonly termed good or poor taste according to the degree of perfection to which this faculty has been developed. He who is said to possess poor taste is that one who is deficient in this perceptive faculty, and is therefore unable to appreciate the harmonious relation of conditions which constitute the beautiful. Fashion is often the perverter of taste, and fashions frequently change, but beauty is ever governed by fixed laws of nature. And so, when we see a beautiful picture in clay, modelled with the skill of a true artist, it is not a mere " matter of taste," or, in other words, a question of individual opinion as to the manner in which it shall be mounted to bring out its beauties the most effectively. We are too prone to accept the dictates of fashion in such matters, without regard to the suitability of contrasting materials, but experiment will often point out to us the path which leads to good taste. Thus custom has almost succeeded in convincing us that a glazed art tile, when used for decorative effect, should always be placed in a perishable, plush-covered frame, instead of in a light, graceful setting. Fashion might seek to persuade us that a fine oil painting would appear to the best advantage in a framework of incongruous velvet, but good taste could never be thus deceived. The coloring of the canvas requires the plain, rich contrast of the gilded frame. On the other hand such a setting would prove unsuitable for tiles, except in rare instances, as where white or cream-colored designs are mounted in light openwork frames of gold.

We see in the window of one of the foremost art stores a modelled tile surrounded with a broad plush frame, decorated with brass mountings. The whole appears stiff, dull, and unattractive. We place a similar panel in a light wooden frame of soft ivory white, deli-

217.—Light Blue Double Panel, Oxidized Silver Frame. Low Art Tile. Designed by Arthur Osborne.

cately carved and pierced, and the surface at once lights up with life, and its beauties are fully revealed.

The coloring of the glaze or enamel which covers the tile sculptures must largely govern the character of their setting. In general, dark-colored tiles should be framed in ivory white. Light-blue may be, with good effect, placed in wooden frames of oxidized silver, but in all cases the moulding should be chased or carved to produce the appearance of lightness. In some instances a border of delicately tinted silk plush may be inserted between the frame and picture, as, when the former is of old ivory and the latter of a cool gray color, a narrow line of pink or light terra-cotta may be added with excellent results. An ochre or burnt umber glaze will often harmonize with a terra-cotta moulding, but the ivory-colored frame will produce a dainty effect in combination with almost any tint of glazing.

Beautiful as are the highly glazed and enamelled

218.—" SAPPHO." PURPLISH-GRAY GLAZE, IN IVORY FRAME AND PINK PLUSH BORDER. BEAVER FALLS ART TILE CO. DESIGNED BY PROF. ISAAC BROOME.

products of the tile kiln, they sometimes acquire an additional charm when subjected to the sand-blast process, which imparts a softness and delicacy of effect to the sculptures not otherwise obtainable. The achievement of a dull finished surface on decorative tiles is a distinct step forward in the direction of artistic treatment, just as the dull gold ornamentation of a porcelain vase is generally a vast improvement over the harsh burnished gilding which is so often suggestive of commercial cheapness. To this latter style of tile finish the judicious application of plush mountings would be more harmonious than to a glazed surface, and, in certain instances, as where a tile of a delicately tinted, velvety surface is framed in plush of a darker shade of the same color, a rich effect may be secured.

A six- by eighteen-inch pastoral panel, made by the Trent Tile Company, of Trenton, N. J., in their " Trent finish," is here figured. The glaze is of a dainty shade of claret, the frame of old ivory (Ill. 220).

The framing of art tiles should be governed, in a large degree, by the subject of the design, and the same may be said of the tinting of the glazes employed. Panels symbolical of the four seasons should be colored, as a general rule, in keeping with the idea intended to be conveyed. Thus " Spring " should be finished in a delicate apple-green or apple-blossom pink ; " Summer " in azure blue ; " Autumn " in light red-brown or umber, and " Winter " in a dainty shade of French gray. Suitable frames for these tones of glazing are white or blue, oxidized silver with pink ornamentation, dark terra-cotta, and pink, respectively. A set of twelve- by eighteen-inch " Season " panels, so finished,

219.—Olive-Green Glaze in Old Ivory Setting. Low Art Tile. Designed by Osborne.

by the American Encaustic Tiling Company, of Zanesville, Ohio, and mounted in accordance with these suggestions, are among the most beautiful works of art in our collection.

In hanging framed tiles, it would be well to choose subjects which are in keeping with the positions selected.

220.—PASTORAL PANEL IN DULL FINISH.   GLAZE OF PALE CLARET, FRAMED IN
OLD IVORY.   TRENT TILE COMPANY.   MODELLED BY GALLIMORE.

221.—"SPRING" PANEL.   PALE APPLE-GREEN GLAZE, FRAMED IN PINKISH
WHITE.   AMERICAN ENCAUSTIC TILING CO.   DESIGNED BY
HERMAN MUELLER.

Ideal heads, modellings of child and female forms, and designs after paintings may with propriety be placed in the parlor ; portrait tiles and plastic sketches, in the library ; game and sporting tiles, in the dining-room or hall ; while designs of a more general character, such as pastoral and season panels, may, with good taste, be hung in any part of the house.

Art tiles may also be utilized in other ways for interior decoration. A good effect may be obtained by attaching a set of three framed panels to the woodwork of the mantel facing, a vertical design being hung or nailed on each side and a horizontal one across the top. When so utilized, the tile frames should harmonize, in material and carving, with the background.

222.—Three-Tile Panel—" Twilight." Blue Glaze, Cream White Frame. United States Encaustic Tile Works. Designed by Miss Ruth Winterbotham.

By thus applying æsthetic principles to the preparation of art tiles for interior decoration, incongruous combinations of colors and materials, which detract from the beauty of the objects themselves, are avoided and we have genuine works of art which are creditable alike to the modeller, the manufacturer, and the purchaser. Already our tile-makers have produced many of these "pictures in clay," which, as examples of the fine arts, are worthy of a place in any home, and the rapid development of this branch of the ceramic art promises to furnish us, at an early day, with works of a still higher art value, which are destined in a great measure to replace the more expensive paintings and water-colors on the walls of our dwellings.

Abraham, Evelyn, "The Pottery of Greensboro and New Geneva," *The Antiquarian* (September 1931).

Allen, R J., Son & Company. *Art Pottery* (Philadelphia, 1888).

Altman, Violet and Seymour. *The Book of Buffalo Pottery* (N. Y.: Crown, 1969).

Armstrong, A. R., "The Norwich Pottery Works," *Antiques,* IV, iv (October 1923), 170-172.

Audsley, George Ashdown. *First National Porcelain Painting Competition Inaugurated by the Ceramic Art Company, Trenton, New Jersey* (N. Y., 1897).

Austin, John C., "Williamsburg Ceramic Collection," *Antiques,* XCV, i (January 1969), 112-120.

Barbeau, Marius, "Canadian Pottery," *Antiques,* XXXIX, v (June 1941), 296-299.

Barber, Edwin AtLee. *Artificial Soft Paste Porcelain: France, Italy, Spain, and England* (Philadelphia: Pennsylvania Museum, 1907). "United States," 28-29.

. . . ., *Catalogue of American Potteries and Porcelains in the Pennsylvania Museum* (Philadelphia, 1893).

. . . ., *Catalogue of Mexican Maiolica belonging to Mrs. W. DeForest* (New York: The Hispanic Society of America, 1911).

. . . ., *The Ceramic Collector's Glossary* (N. Y.: Walpole Society, 1914).

. . . ., "Contemporary Imitations of Wedgwood," *Old China,* I, x (July 1902), 153-158.

. . . ., "The Earliest Decorative Pottery of the White Settlers in America," *House & Garden,* II, vi (June 1902), 233-239.

. . . ., "Early Ceramic Painting and Modeling in the United States," *Old China,* III, iii (December 1903), 50-55.

. . . ., "Enamels," *Old China,* III, vii (April 1904), 121-125.

. . . ., *Exhibition of Tiles* (Philadelphia: Pennsylvania Museum, 1915). "American," 41-48.

...................., *Hispano-Moresque Pottery in the Collection of the Hispanic Society of America* (N. Y.: The Hispanic Society of America, 1915).

...................., "How to Collect," *Old China,* III, xii (August 1904), 207-213.

...................., *Illustrated Catalogue of the Barber Collection of China, Pottery, Porcelains and Glass* (Philadelphia: Samuel Freeman, 1917).

...................., *Lead Glazed Pottery: Plain Glazed, Sgraffito, and Slip-decorated Wares* (Philadelphia: Pennsylvania Museum, 1907). "The United States," 24-30.

...................., "Lowestoft," *Old China,* I, i (October 1901), 5-18.

...................., *Marks of American Potters* (Philadelphia: Patterson & White, 1904).

...................., *Mexican Maiolica in the Collection of the Hispanic Society of America* (N. Y.: The Hispanic Society of America, 1915).

...................., "Mocha Ware," *Old China,* II, iv (January 1903), 71-73.

...................., *The Maiolica of Mexico* (Philadelphia: Pennsylvania Museum, 1908).

...................., "A New Series of Dark Blue Views," *Old China,* I, iii (December 1901), 37-39.

...................., "Old American Cream Ware and Yellow Ware," *Old China,* II, ix (June 1903), 171-174.

...................., "Old Tulip Ware of the Pennsylvania Germans," *Old China,* I, viii (May 1902), 112-114.

...................., "Painted Decorations of Old Staffordshire Potteries, as Shown by Old Copper Plate Proofs," *Old China,* II, vi (March 1903), 116-120.

...................., "The Phoenixville Pottery," *Clay Worker* (August 1897).

...................., "The Pioneer of China Painting in America," *Ceramic Monthly,* II, ii (September 1895), 15-20.

...................., "The Pioneer of China Painting in America," *New England Magazine* (1895).

...................., *Salt Glazed Stoneware: Germany, Flanders, England, and the United States* (Philadelphia, 1906).

................., "Some Ceramic Puzzles," *Old China,* I, iv (January 1902), 48-49.

................., "Some Rare Pieces of Early Pottery," *Old China,* I, vii (April 1902), 101-103.

................., "Some Rarities in Printed China," *Old China,* I, ii (November 1901), 22-25.

................., "Some Recently Discovered American Porcelains," *Old China,* III, ii (November 1903), 22-24.

................., *Spanish Glass in the Collection of the Hispanic Society of America* (N. Y.: G. P. Putnam, 1917).

................., *Spanish Maiolica in the Collection of the Hispanic Society of America* (New York: The Hispanic Society of America, 1915).

................., *Spanish Porcelains and Terra Cottas in the Collection of the Hispanic Society of America* (N. Y.: The Hispanic Society of America, 1915).

................., *Tin Enameled Pottery: Maiolica, Delft, and Other Stanniferous Faience* (Philadelphia: Pennsylvania Museum, 1906). "United States," p. 35.

................., *Tulip Ware of the Pennsylvania German Potters* (Philadelphia: Patterson & White Company, 1903).

Barons, Richard I. *An Exhibition of 18th and 19th Century American Folk Pottery* (New Paltz, N. Y.: College Art Gallery, State University College, 1969).

Barret, Richard Carter. *Bennington Pottery and Porcelain: A Guide to Identification* (N. Y., 1958).

................., *A Color Guide to Bennington Pottery* (N. Y.: Crown, 1966).

................., *How to Identify Bennington Pottery* (Brattleboro, Vermont: Stephen Greene, 1964).

................., "The Porcelain and Pottery of Bennington," *Antiques,* LXIX, vi (June 1956), 528-531; LXX, ii (August 1956), 142-145.

[Batchelder & Brown Tile], "The Beauty of the Modern Tile and its Place in Architecture," *The Craftsman,* XXV, v (February 1914), 491-493.

Batchelder Tiles: A Catalogue of Mantel Designs (Los Angeles, 1922).

Bayer, Ralph E., "Van Briggle Pottery," *Western Collector*, VII, iii (March 1969), 110-115.

Beckwith, Arthur. *Pottery: Observations on the Materials and Manufacture of Terra-Cotta, Stoneware, Fire-brick, Porcelain, Earthenware, Brick Maiolica, and Encaustic Tiles* (N. Y.: D. Van Nostrand, 1872).

Belknap, Henry W. *Artists and Craftsmen of Essex County, Massachusetts* (Salem: Essex Institute, 1927).

.... *Trades and Tradesmen of Essex County* (Salem: Essex Institute, 1929).

Bennett, C. A. *History of Manual and Industrial Education up to 1870* (Peoria, Illinois: Manual Arts Press, 1926).

Bigler, Lola Schell, et al. *Indexes to Publications of the American Ceramic Society, 1918-1955* (Columbus, Ohio, 1957).

Bingham, Robert Warwick, "George Washington in Liverpool Ware," *Antiques*, XII, i (July 1927), 32-35.

Binns, Charles Fergus, "The Art of the Fire," *The Craftsman*, VII, ii, 205-210.

.................., "The Arts and Crafts Movement in America," *The Craftsman*, XIV, iii, 275-279.

.................., "Building in Clay," *The Craftsman*, IV, iv, 303-305.

.................., "Clay in the Potter's Hand," *The Craftsman*, VI, ii, 162-168.

.................., "The Craft of the Potter," *The Craftsman*, IX, vi, 854-856.

.................., "Education in Clay," *The Craftsman*, IV, iii (June 1903), 160-168.

.................., "The Future of Ceramics in America," *The Craftsman*, VII, v, 563-566.

.................., "In Defense of Fire," *The Craftsman*, III, vi, 369-372.

.................., "Inspiration in Material," *The Craftsman*, V, iii, 260-263.

.................., (ed.). *The Manual of Practical Potting* (London: Scott, Greenwood, 1901). Third Edition, revised and enlarged.

.................., *The Potter's Craft: A Practical Guide for the Studio and Workshop* (N. Y.: D. Van Nostrand, 1910).

. . . ., "Pottery in America," *American Magazine of Art,* VII (1916), 131-138.

. . . ., *The Story of the Potter* (London: Newnes, 1901).

Binns, R. W. *Catalogue of a Collection of Worcester Porcelain in the Museum at the Royal Porcelain Works* (Worcester: Royal Porcelain, 1882).

Bishop, J. *History of American Manufactures, 1608-1850* (Philadelphia, 1861-1864). Two volumes.

Blair, C. Dean. *The Potters and Potteries of Summit County, 1828-1915* (Akron, Ohio: The Summit County Historical Society, 1965).

Blake, William P. *Ceramic Art: A Report on Pottery, Porcelain, Tiles, Terra-Cotta and Brick* . . . (N. Y.: D. Van Nostrand, 1875).

. . . ., "Report on Ceramics," *State Department Report, Paris Universal Exposition,* III, 113-224. (Washington, D. C., 1878).

Blasberg, Robert, "Arequipa Pottery," *Western Collector,* VI, x (October 1968), 7-10.

. . . ., "Newcomb Pottery," *Antiques,* XCIV, i (July 1968), 73-77.

Bobbitt, Mary Reed. *A Bibliography of Etiquette Books Published in America Before 1900* (N. Y.: New York Public Library, 1947). An overlooked source for the social history of pottery and porcelain in the United States.

Bogue, Dorothy McGraw. *The Van Briggle Story.*

Boicourt, Jane, "Design in American Pottery," *Antiques,* LIX, ii (February 1951), 134-135.

Branner, John Casper, "Bibliography of Clays and the Ceramic Arts," *United States Geographical Survey Bulletin,* 143 (Washington, D. C., 1896).

Brannon, Peter A., "Earthenware and Silver from the Tallapoosa River," *Antiques,* XXXIII, ii (February 1938), 84-85.

Bric-a-Brac: A Handbook for use of Visitors to the Loan Collection, Inter-State Industrial Exposition (Chicago: Rand McNally, 1877).

Buffalo Pottery: The Potter's Art (Buffalo, N. Y.: Larkin Co., 1905).

Bunt, Cyril G. E., "Gibson Picture Plates," *Antiques,* XXXVI, iii (September 1939), 122-124.

Burbank, Leonard F., "Lyndeboro Pottery," *Antiques,* XIII, ii (February 1928), 124-126.

Burgess, W., "English Pottery and Pottery Trade," *U. S. Consular Reports,* 136 (Washington, D. C., 1892).

..........., "Staffordshire *versus* American Pottery," *U. S. Consular Reports,* 132 (Washington, D. C., 1891).

Burty, Philippe. *Chefs-d'oeuvre of the Industrial Arts* (London: Cassell, Petter, and Galpin, 1869).

Buxton, Bessie W., "The Making of a Flower Pot," *Antiques,* XXVIII, ii (August 1935), 62-63.

Camehl, Ada Walker. *The Blue-China Book: Early American Scene and History Pictured in the Pottery of the Time* (N. Y.: Dutton, 1916). Note: "The White House Collection of Presidential China," pp. 245-266.

..................., "Mehwaldt, a Pioneer American Potter," *Antiques,* II, iii (September 1922), 113-116.

Campana, Dominick Mathew. *Book of Monogram and Fancy Letters* (Chicago, ca. 1924).

........................., *Decorative Designs for Decorations of All Kinds* (ca. 1911).

........................., *Designs and Color Schemes* (A/B/C/D: 1908/9; E/F/G/H: 1909/10).

........................., *Enamel Decorations for Porcelain & Glass* (Chicago, ca. 1921).

........................., *Firing of China and Glass* (Chicago nd.).

........................., *Novelties for the Ceramic Artist* (Chicago, 1909). Mostly Art Nouveau designs for China Painting.

........................., *100 Lustres: Colors-Combinations* (Chicago, nd.).

........................., *The Teacher of China Painting* (Chicago, 1940). Fifth edition.

Catalogue and Price List of Materials For China Decoration (N. Y.: The Cosmopolitan China Co., 12 W. Fourteenth Street, nd.).

Catalogue and Price List of China for Amateur China Decoration (N. Y.: Cosmopolitan China Co., nd.).

"Ceramics and Glass at Williamsburg," *Antiques,* LXIII, iii (March 1953), 243-249.

"Ceramics at Old Deerfield," *Antiques,* LXX, iii (September 1956), 238-242.

Chaffers, William. *The Collector's Handbook to Keramics of Renaissance and Modern Periods* (N Y.: Scribner's, 1909).

Chandler, L. Reginald, "The Methods of the Early American Potters," *Antiques,* V, iv (April 1924), 174-178.

China and Pottery Works (N. Y.: Gilman Collamore & Company, ca. 1900?).

China Painter Instruction Book (Chicago: Thayer & Chandler, 1914).

Clark, Edna Maria. *Ohio Art and Artists* (Richmond, Virginia: Garrett & Massie, 1932).

Clark, J. M. *The Swiss Influence in the Early Pennsylvania Slip-Decorated Majolica* (Albany, N. Y., 1908).

Clark, Victor S. *The History of Manufactures in the United States, 1607-1860* (Washington, D. C.: The Carnegie Institution, 1916).

Clarke, Isaac Edwards. *Education in the Industrial and Fine Arts in the United States* (Washington, D. C.: GPO, 1885).

Clement, Arthur, "Bonnin and Morris Porcelain," *Antiques,* LIX, ii (February 1951), p. 139.

. . . ., "Ceramics in the South," *Antiques,* LIX, ii (February 1951), 136-138.

. . . ., and Robert J. Sun, "The Cheesequake Potteries," *Antiques,* XLV, iii (March 1944), 122-124.

. . . ., *Notes on American Ceramics, 1607-1943* (Brooklyn: Brooklyn Museum, 1944).

. . . ., *Notes on Early American Porcelain, 1738-1838* (New York: Privately printed, Court Press, 1946).

. . . ., *Our Pioneer Potters* (N. Y.: Privately printed, 1947).

Collamore, Davis & Company.*Rookwood Pottery, Cincinnati* (N. Y., 1889).

Collard, Elizabeth. *Nineteenth-Century Pottery and Porcelain in Canada* (Montreal: McGill University Press, 1967).

Comstock, Helen (ed.). *The Concise Encyclopedia of American Antiques* (N. Y.: Hawthorne, 1958).

Cook, Albert, "Early Rhode Island Pottery," *Antiques,* XIX, i (January 1931), 37-38.

Cook, Charles D., "Early Rhode Island Pottery," *Rhode Island Historical Society Collections*, XVIII (1925), 81-83.

.............., "Unusual Bennington Pitchers," *Antiques*, XIV, vi (December 1928), 544-546.

Cook, Mary Elizabeth, "Our American Potteries: Weller Ware," *Sketchbook*, V (1906), 340-346.

Cox, George J. *Pottery for Artists, Craftsmen and Teachers* (N. Y.: Macmillan, 1914).

Cox, Warren E. *The Book of Pottery and Porcelain* (N. Y.: Crown, 1944).

Craig, James H. *The Arts and Crafts in North Carolina, 1699-1840* (Winston-Salem, North Carolina: Museum of Early Southern Decorative Arts, 1965).

Crawford, Jean, "Jugtown Pottery," *Western Collector*, VI, vii (July 1968), 7-11.

.............., *Jugtown Pottery: History and Design* (Winston-Salem, North Carolina: John F. Blair, 1964).

Crooke, E. E. *Crooke's Manual of Marks on Antique Pottery and Porcelain* (Indianapolis, Indiana, 1937).

Crutcher, Jean, "The Art Pottery of America: Shawsheen Ware," *Antique News*, II, vii (February 1965), 1 ff.

Cummin, Hazel E., "Old Bristol Ware in American Cupboards," *Antiques*, XXVII, vi (June 1935), 223-225.

Davidson, Mary E., "William H. Farrer, Potter," *Antiques*, XXXV, iii (March 1939), 122-123.

Davis, Theodore R., "Presidential Porcelain of a Century," *Ladies Home Journal* (May 1889).

DeKay, Charles, "Art From the Kilns," *Munsey's Magazine*, XXVI, i (October 1901), 46-53. Features Rockwood, Grueby, Newcomb, and Dedham.

.............., "Pottery from the Durant Kilns: Some Recent Work of Jean Durant and Leon Volkmar," *Arts and Decoration*, III (1913), 96-97.

Dieter, Gerald W. and John Cummings. *The Bible in Tile: The Story of the Mercer Biblical Tile in the Sanctuary of Salem Church* (Doylestown, Pennsylvania: Salem United Church of Christ, 1957).

Dow, George Francis. *The Arts & Crafts in New England, 1704-1775* (Topsfield, Massachusetts: Wayside Press, 1927).

Drepperd, Carl W., "Origins of Pennsylvania Folk Art," *Antiques,* XXXVII, ii (February 1940), 64-68.

Dyer, Walter A., "Early Pottery of New England," *Antiques,* I, i (January 1922), 19-22.

Earle, Alice Morse. *China Collecting in America* (N. Y.: Scribner's, 1892).

"East Liverpool, Ohio, Potteries," *Crockery & Glass Journal* (December 18, 1924).

Eaton, Allen H. *Handicrafts of New England* (N. Y.: Harper & Brothers, 1949). "New England Pottery," 152-167.

. . . ., *Handicrafts of the Southern Highlands with an Account of the Rural Handicraft Movement in the United States* (N. Y.: Russel Sage Foundation, 1937).

Eberlein, Harold Donaldson, "The Decorated Pottery of the Pennsylvania Dutch," *Arts and Decoration,* IV (1914), 109-112.

. . . ., and Roger Wearne Ramsdell. *The Practical Book of Chinaware* (Philadelphia: J. B. Lippincott, 1925). "American Chinaware," 293-299. The book stops at 1840.

Elliott, Charles Wyllys. *Pottery and Porcelain from Early Times Down to the Philadelphia Exhibition of 1876* (N. Y.: D. Appleton, 1877). "Pottery and Porcelain in the U S.," 331-342. The following extract was irresistable to quotation: Some twenty firms, mostly from Trenton, were collected in the southeast corner of the Main Building [of the Centennial Exhibition], where they made a creditable display of what is known as the "white granite" ware, so useful and so detestable; thick, that it may resist the hostility of the Milesian maiden, clumsy because of that, without color or decoration of any kind, and cheap: can we expect or demand much?

Elliott, Maud Howe (ed). *Art and Handicraft in the Woman's Building of the World's Columbian Exposition, Chicago, 1893* (Chicago: Rand McNally, 1894). Elizabeth W. Perry, "The Work of Cincinnati Women in Decorated Pottery," 100-106.

Elzner, H. O., "Rookwood Pottery," *Architectural Record,* XVII (1905), 295-304.

Emerson, Gertrude, "Marblehead Pottery," *The Craftsman,* XXIX, vi, 671-673.

Emery, N., "The Stevensons of Staffordshire," *Antiques,* LXVII, vi (June 1955), 494-495.

Evans, Paul F., "The Roberson Saga: Creative Years, 1866-1889; Commercial Years, 1891-1943," *Western Collector*, V, iv (April 1967), 7-12; V, v (May 1967), 7-12.

.............., "Victorian Art Tiles," *Western Collector*, V, xi (November 1967), 18-22. "A permanent exhibition of decorative art tiles is a portion of the decorative arts department at the Smithsonian Institution. What is probably the country's most outstanding collection of tiles was given to the Smithsonian Institution by E. Stanley Wires." Also, a group of ladies in West Philadelphia has been saving tiles from houses in the University district scheduled for demolition. Perhaps there are similar efforts elsewhere.

Fennelly, Catherine. *Something Blue: Some American Views on Staffordshire* (Sturbridge, Massachusetts: Old Sturbridge Village, 1955).

................., "Staffordshire on American Tables: The Collamore Evidence," *Antiques*, LXXXIV, i (July 1963), 75-79.

Fitzpatrick, Nancy R., "The Chesapeake Pottery Company," *Bulletin of The Maryland Historical Society* (March 1957).

Fox, Eleanor J. and Wedward G. Fox. *Gaudy Dutch.*

Frackleton, Susan Stuart, "Our American Potteries: The Gates Pottery," *Sketchbook*, V (1905), 73-80.

......................, "Rookwood Pottery," *Sketchbook* (1906), 273-277.

......................, *Tried By Fire: A Work on China Painting* (N. Y.: D. Appleton, 1892).

"Frackelton Collections of Ceramics Acquired," *Wisconsin Magazine of History*, XLII, p. 155.

Franchet, Louis. *Ceramic Decoration: Its Evaluation and Its Application* (1909).

Franco, Barbara. *White's Utica Pottery* (Utica, N. Y.: Munson-Williams-Proctor Institute, 1969).

Freeman, John C. and Judith S. Freeman. *Blue-decorated Stoneware of New York State* (Watkins Glen, N. Y.: American Life Foundation, 1966).

Freeman, Larry. *China Classics: Ironstone China* (Watkins Glen, N. Y.: Century House, 1954).

.............., *China Classics: Majolica* (Watkins Glen, N. Y.: Century House, 1949). Reprinted in 1967.

Galloway, George D., "The Van Briggle Pottery," *Brush & Pencil,* IX (1901), 1-11.

Gates, Burton N., "Boston Earthenware: Frederick Mear, Potter," *Antiques,* V, vi (June 1924), 310-311.

Gerry, Roger and Joseph T. Butler, "Japanese Export Porcelain for the American Market," *Antiques,* XCV, iv (April 1969), 544-546.

Gibson, Gerald G., "American Ceramics from the McKearin Collection," *Antiques,* LXXIV, i (July 1958), 62-65.

Gottesman, Rita Susswein. *The Arts and Crafts in New York, 1726-1804* (N. Y.: New York Historical Society, 1938/1954/1965). Three volumes.

Graham, John Meridith, II, "The Earthenware of Bonnin and Morris," *Antiques,* XLV, i (January 1944), 14-16.

Green, Charles, "The Identification of Bennington Cameo Parian," *Antiques,* XVI, iii (September 1929), 197-199.

. . . ., "Pond Lily Pitchers of Bennington," *Antiques,* XXI, i (January 1932), 26-27.

. . . ., "Some Bennington Pitchers," XVII, v (May 1930), 431-433.

Guthman, Patricia R., "Castleford Pottery for the American Trade," *Antiques,* XCII, iv (October 1967), 552-554.

Haddon, Rawson W., "Early Slip-decorated Canister," *Antiques,* IX, iii (March 1926), p. 166.

Hall, H. Byng. *The Bric-a-Brac Collector; or, Chapters on Chinamania* (Philadelphia: J. B. Lippincott, 1875).

Halsey, Richard Townley Haines. *Pictures of Early New York on Dark Blue Staffordshire Pottery . . .* (N. Y.: Dodd, Mead, 1899).

Hammerslough, Philip H., "Rarities in Tucker Porcelain," *Antiques,* LXXIV, iii (September 1958), 240-241.

Harrington, J. C., "Some Delft Tiles Found at Jamestown," *Antiques,* LIX, i (January 1951), 36-37.

Harrington, Virginia S., "Mysterious Staffordshire—and the Mormons?," *Antiques,* XCII, ii (February 1968), 238-239.

Harris, W. S. *The Potter's Wheel and How it Goes Around: A Complete Description of the Man of Pottery in America* (Trenton, N. J.: Burroughs and Mountford, 1886).

Harrison, Constance Cary. *Woman's Handiwork in Modern Homes* (N. Y.: Scribner's, 1881). "China Paintings," 99-114. Color plate.

Haskin, Leslie L., "Three Early Oregon Potteries of Barnet Ramsey," *Oregon Historical Quarterly,* XLIII (1942), 175-193.

Haviland & Company. *The White House Porcelain Service: Designs by an American Artist, Illustrating Exclusively American Fauna and Flora* (N. Y., 1879).

Hawes, Lloyd E. *The Dedham Pottery and the Earlier Robertson's Chelsea Potteries* (Dedham, Massachusetts: Dedham Historical Society, 1968).

Heckman, Albert W., "Pennsylvania Slipware," *Keramic Studio,* XXIII (1922), 208-219.

Heesey, M. Luther, "The Makers of Pottery in Lancaster County," *Lancaster County Historical Society Papers,* L, iv-v (1946), 117-128.

Hettinger, E. L., "Early Pennsylvania Potters," *American German Review* (December 1942), 23-26.

Hill, Nola O., "American History on Liverpool and Staffordshire," *Antiques,* LXIV, iv (October 1953), 290-293.

Holden, Marian L., "The Pewabic Pottery," *American Magazine of Art,* XVII (January 1926), 22-27.

Holmes, George Sanford. *Lenox China: The Story of Walter Scott Lenox* (Trenton, N. J.: Lenox Incorporated, 1924).

Holmes, W. H., "Origin and Development of Form and Ornament in Ceramic Art," *Annual Report of the U. S. Bureau of Ethnology,* IV (1882-1883), 437-465. (Published in Washington, D. C. in 1886).

Hood, Graham, "New Light on Bonnin and Morris," *Antiques,* XCV, vi (June 1969), 812-817.

Hooker, Frances Hopkins. *Afternoons with Ceramics* (Syracuse, N. Y.: The Portfolio Club, 1896). "United States," 152-142; mostly about Rookwood.

Horney, Wayne. *Pottery of the Gelena Area.*

Hornor, W. M., Jr., "Tucker & Hempmill Porcelain Works," *Antiques,* XIII, vi (June 1928), 480-484.

Hough, Walter, "An Early West Virginia Pottery at Morgantown," *Annual Report of the Smithsonian Institute* (Washington, D.C., 1899).

Hudson, J. Paul, "Earliest Yorktown Pottery," *Antiques,* LXXIII, v (May 1958), 472-473.

Hull, William. *Some Notes on Early Robineau Porcelains* (Syracuse, N. Y.: Everson Museum of Art, 1960).

Hume, Ivor Noel. *Here Lies Virginia* (N. Y.: Knopf, 1963).

............., "A Late Seventeenth-Century Pottery Kiln Site Near Jamestown," *Antiques,* LXXXIII, v (May 1963), 550-552.

............., "Rhenish Gray Stonewares in Colonial America," *.Antiques,* XCII, iii (September 1967), 349-353.

............., "Rouen Faience in Eighteenth-century America," *Antiques,* LXXVIII, vi (December 1960), 559-561.

Humphreys, Gregor Norman, "Clews' 'Picturesque Views' " *Antiques,* XVI, vi (December 1929), 483-486.

Jackman, Rilla Evelyn. *American Arts* (Chicago: Rand McNally, 1928). "Industries and Modern Crafts," 25-50.

James, Arthur E. *The Potters and Potteries of Chester County, Pennsylvania* (West Chester, Pennsylvania: Chester County Historical Society, 1945).

............., "Tucker & Hemphill China," *American Antiques Journal* (August 1947), 14-15.

Jarvie, Lillian Gray, "The Markham Potteries," *Sketchbook,* V (1905), 123-129.

Jayne, Horace H. F. *Tucker China, 1825-1838* (Philadelphia: Museum of Art, 1957).

............., "Tucker Porcelain: Thomas Tucker's Share," *Antiques,* LXXII, iii (September 1957), 237-239.

Jervis, W. P. *A Book of Pottery Marks* (Newark, N. J., 1897). "United States," 74-97.

............., *China Classics: European China* (Watkins Glen, N. Y.: Century House, 1953).

............., *The Encyclopedia of Ceramics* (N. Y.: Blanshard, 1902). Of value for its marks and entries for Art potteries.

............., *A Pottery Primer* (N. Y., 1911). "United States," 168-186.

............., *Rough Notes on Pottery* (Newark, N. J.: W. P. Jervis, 1896).

Joor, Harriet, "Pottery-Making Without a Wheel," *The Craftsman,* XIX, ii, 172-180.

Kahle, Katherine Morrison, "American Shaving Mugs," *Antiques,* XXXIII, v (May 1938), 268-270.

Kamm, Minnie Watson. *Old China* (Watkins Glen, N. Y.: Century House, 1951).

Keyes, Homer Eaton, "American Eagle Lowestoft," *Antiques*, XVII, vi (June 1930), 530-533.

...................., "American Ship Lowestoft," *Antiques*, XIX, vi (June 1931), 441-446.

...................., "The Boston State House in Blue Stafford-shire," *Antiques*, I, iii (March 1922), 115-120; I, vi (June 1922), 250-251.

...................., "The Chinese Lowestoft of Early American Commerce," *Antiques*, XVI, v (November 1929), 381-385.

...................., "The Cincinnati and Their Porcelain," *Antiques*, XVII, ii (February 1930), 132-136.

...................., "The 'Cupid and Psyche' Pattern," *Antiques*, XXIV, iv (October 1933), 132-133.

...................., "Lowestoft: Exclusively American," *Antiques*, XXI, iv (April 1932), 171-175.

...................., "Perplexities in Pottery," *Antiques*, XXIII, ii (February 1933), 54-55.

...................., "Spatter," *Antiques*, XVII, iv (April 1930), 332-337.

...................., "State Arms on Chinese Lowestoft," *Antiques*, XVIII, iv (October 1930), 321-323.

...................., "Wedgwood: English Friend of American Liberty," *Antiques*, LXXVI, v (November 1959), 446-449.

Keyser, C. Naaman. *Pennsylvania German Pottery* (Plymouth Meeting, Pennsylvania, 1945). Number two in the "Pennsylvania German Home Craft Series."

Kindig, Joe, Jr., "A Note on Early North Carolina Pottery," *Antiques*, XXVII, i (January 1935), 14-15.

Kircher, Edwin J. *Rookwood Pottery: An Explanation of Its Marks and Symbols* (Privately printed, 1962).

..............., *Rookwood, Its Golden Era of Art Pottery, 1880-1929.*

Klapthor, Margaret Brown, "White House China of the Lincoln Administration," *U. S. National Museum Bulletin*, 250; Contributions from the Museum of History and Technology, Paper 62, 109-120.

Knittle, Rhea, "Early Decorative Arts in Ohio," *Antiques,* XLIX, i (January 1946), 32-33.

............, "English China in Midwestern Advertisements," *Antiques,* XXVI, i (July 1934), p. 17.

............, "Henry McQuate, Pennsylvania Potter," *Antiques,* VIII, v (November 1925), 286-287.

............, "Muskingum County, Ohio Potters," *Antiques,* VI, i (July 1924), 15-18.

............, "Ohio Pottery Jars and Jugs," *Antiques,* XXIV, iv (October 1933), 144-145.

............, "Speciments of Ohio Pottery," *Antiques,* XXXII, iv (October 1937), p. 192.

Koch, Robert, "Rookwood Pottery," *Antiques,* LXXVII, iii (March 1960), 288-289.

LaGrange, M. J. *Pottery and Porcelain Bibliography* (Indianapolis: Indiana State Library, 1938).

Laidacker, Sam. *Anglo-American China During the Period from 1815 to 1860* (Bristol, Pennsylvania: Sam Laidacker, 1951).

............, *Auction Supplement to the Standard Catalogue of Anglo-American China from 1810-1850: A Record During the Period from May, 1938 to June, 1944* (Scranton, Pennsylvania: Sam Laidacker, 1944).

............, *Auction Supplement for the Period, June 1944 to January, 1949* (Bristol, Pennsylvania: Sam Laidacker, 1949).

............, *The Standard Catalogue of Anglo-American China from 1810 to 1850* (Scranton, Pennsylvania: Sam Laidacker, 1938).

Langenbeck, Karl. *The Chemistry of Pottery* (Easton, Pennsylvania: Chemical Publishing Co., 1895). The first ceramic chemist in America and a superintendent of Rookood Pottery and the Mosaic Tile Company.

Lardner, Dionysius. *A Treatise on the Origin, Progressive Improvement, and Present State of the Manufacture of Porcelain and Glass* (Philadelphia: Cary & Lea, 1832). Part of the Cabinet Cyclopaedia.

Larsen, Ellouise Baker. *American Historical Views on Staffordshire China* (N. Y.: Doubleday, Doran, 1939).

............, "History on Staffordshire," *Antiques,* LII, ii (August 1949), 114-116.

...................., "Identifying Makers of Historic Blue," *Antiquarian*, XII, i (February 1929), 34-35.

...................., "New Contacts with Old Staffordshire and the Potteries," *Antiques*, XXXVIII, v (November 1940), 222-224.

...................., "New Notes on Historical China," *Antiques*, XLI, vi (June 1942), 362-364.

...................., "Staffordshire Records of Early Modes of Travel," *Antiques*, XXIX, iv (April 1936), 147-151; XXIX, vi (June 1936), 254-258.

...................., "Thomas Godwin, Staffordshire Potter," *Antiques*, XXIII, iii (March 1933), 93-94.

...................., "Three Rare Staffordshire Pitchers," *Antiques*, LXXII, i (July 1957), 64-65.

...................., "Unlisted Views of America on Staffordshire China," *Antiques*, LXV, iii (March 1954), 210-213.

Laughlin, Gerald F. *The Clays and Clay Industries of Connecticut* (1905).

Leach, Mary James, "Louisville Potters and Potteries Before 1850," *Antiques*, LII, v (November 1947), 320-322.

LeBoeuf, Randall J., Jr., "Staffordshire and Steam," *Antiques*, LXXXV, vi (June 1964), 666-670.

Lee, Albert, "A Footnote to Staffordshire Lore," *Antiques*, XXVII, iv (April 1935) 136-139.

Leed, Gretal. *New York Crafts, 1700-1875: An Historical Survey* (Ithaca, N. Y.: Ithaca College Museum of Art, 1967). "Ceramics," 11-15.

Little, Nina Fletcher, "English Pottery and Porcelain In Colonial America," *Antiques*, LV, iv (April 1949), 268-271.

...................., "The Identification of Staffordshire Ladles," *Antiques*, LXXXVIII, ii (August 1965), 212-215.

Little, Ruth. *Painting China for Pleasure and Profit* (Lubbock, Texas: Brack, 1963).

Little, W. L. *Staffordshire Blue.*

Lockwood, Mary Smith. *Hand-book of Ceramic Art* (N. Y.: G. P. Putnam, 1878).

Low, John G and John F. Low. *Illustrated Catalogue of Art Tiles* (Chelsea, Massachusetts, 1884). Another issue in 1885.

.............., *Plastic Sketches (Tiles)* (Boston: Wellington, 1882). Another issued by Lee & Shepard in 1887. Listed in Watkins.

MacArthur, Arthur. *Education in its Relation to Manual Industry* (N. Y.: D. Appleton, 1884).

McCauley, Robert H., "American Importers of Staffordshire," *Antiques*, XLV, v (June 1944), 295-297.

.... *Liverpool Transfer Designs on Anglo-American Pottery* (1942).

McDougal, Taine Gilbert. *Casting of Clay Wares* (Washington, D. C.: GPO, 1916).

MacFarlane, Janet R., "Nathan Clark, Potter," *Antiques* LX, i July 1951), 42-44. Of note is the quotation of a *mss.* on "Rules for Making & Burning Stone Ware."

McKearin, George S. *Catalogue of a Loan Exhibition of Early American Pottery and Early American Glass from the Private Collection of* . . . (Hoosick Falls, N. Y., 1931).

McKearin, Helen, "The Launching of Henderson's Flint Stoneware," *Antiques*, LV, vi (June 1949), 432-433

McLaughlin, M. Louise. *China Painting: A Practical Manual for the Use of Amateurs in the Decoration of Hard Porcelain* (Cincinnati: Robert Clarke & Co., 1877). Re-copyrighted in 1883, 1894, 1904, and 1911. The 1911 edition advertises that it is the 21st thousand.

...................., "Losanti Ware," *The Craftman*, III, iii, 186-187.

.... *Pottery Decoration Under the Glaze* (Cincinnati: Robert Clarke & Co., 1880).

.... *Suggestions to China Painters* (Cincinnati: Robert Clark & Co., 1890). Revised edition.

MacMillan, Donald D., "Some Notes on English Delft in the American Colonies," *Antiques*, XLVII, iii (March 1945), 150-153.

Mason, George Champlin. *The Application of Art to Manufactures* (N. Y.: G. P. Putnam, 1858). "Porcelain, Chinese Porcelain, and Terracotta," 194-248.

Mason, M. M. *Illustrated Catalogue of Overglaze Colors and Other Materials for Porcelain Decoration* (N. Y., nd.).

.... *Overglaze Colors, Relief Enamels, and Other Materials for Porcelain Decoration* (N. Y., nd.).

Mercer, Henry Chapman, "An American Potter: Mercer and Moravian Tiles," *House & Garden*, I, iii (August 1901), 12-19.

.... *The Bible in Iron: Pictured Stoves and Stoveplates of the Pennsylvania Germans* (Doylestown, Pennsylvania: Bucks County Historical Society, 1961). Third edition This was the source of many of Mercer's Moravian tiles.

.... *Guidebook to the Tiled Pavement in the Capitol of Pennsylvania* (Doylestown, Pennsylvania, nd.). The State Capitol in Harrisburg is tiled with Mercer's Moravian titles.

....................., "The Pottery of the Pennsylvania Germans," *Pennsylvania German*, II (1901), 86-88.

....................., "Pottery of the Pennsylvania Germans," *Bucks County Historical Society Papers*, IV (1917), 187-191.

Mercer, William, "Cement Casting at Aldie: William Mercer," *House & Garden*, IV, iv (October 1903), 174-180. (Henry's brother)

Merrit, Arthur H., "Staffordshire Views of American Universities," *Antiques*, XXIV, iv (October 1933), 127-131.

Middleton, Jefferson. *Statistics of the Clay-Working Industries in the United States in 1912* (Washington, D.C.: GPO, 1913).

Miller, J. Jefferson, III, "The Larsen and McCauley Collections at the Smithsonian," *Antiques*, LXXXVIII, iv (October 1965), 522-525.

Millet, F. D., "Some American Tiles," *The Century Magazine*, XXIII, vi (April 1882), 896-904.

Minton, LeRoy H., "New Jersey's Part in the Ceramic History of America," *The Ceramist*, II, iv (Winter-December/February, 1922/1923), 270-289.

Mitchell, Elmer C., "The Art Industries of America: The Making of Pottery," *Brush and Pencil Bulletin and Record*, XV, iv (April 1905), 67-76.

Monachesi, *Mrs.* Nicola di Rienzi. *A Manual for China Painters* (Boston: Lee & Shepard, 1896). Revised and enlarged edition in 1907.

Montague, William E., "Early Pennsylvania Potters," *Bucks County Historical Society Collections*, V (1926), 197-202.

Moore, N. Hudson. *The Old China Book, Including Staffordshire, Wedgwood, Lustre, and Other English Pottery and Porcelain* (N. Y.: Frederick A. Stokes, 1903).

Moravian Tiles, "Picture Fireplaces: Illustrating Stories for Sitting Room, Library, and Nursery," *The Craftsman,* XXXI, iii (December 1916), 247-253.

Morley, Henry. *Palissy the Potter* (Boston: Ticknor, Reed and Fields, 1853). Two volumes.

Morey, Churchill & Morey. *Handbook of Ideas in China, Crockery, Silver, and Art Pottery* (1888).

Mosaic Faience Tiles (Zanesville, Ohio: Mosaic Tile Company, 1929).

Mudge, Jean McClure. *Chinese Export Porcelain for the American Trade, 1785-1835* (Newark, Delaware: University of Delaware, 1962). Extensive bibliography, especially periodical references.

Neaton. *On the Origin, Progressive Improvement and Present State of the Manufacture of Porcelain and Glass* (Philadelphia, 1846).

Nelson, Marion John, "Indigenous Characteristics in American Art Pottery,"*Antiques,* LXXXIX, vi (June 1966), 846-850.

New Jersey Pottery. *Early Arts of New Jersey: The Potter's Art, 1680-1900* (Trenton, N. J.: New Jersey State Museum, 1956).

.... *The Pottery and Porcelain of New Jersey, 1688-1900* (Newark, N. J.: The Newark Museum, 1947).

.... *Some Vanishing Phases of Rural Life in New Jersey: Pottery* (New Jersey Department of Agriculture, Circular 327).

New Jersey Stoneware (Monmouth County Historical Association, 1955).

New York Pottery. *Census of the State of New York for 1855* (Albany, 1857). p. 387. Lists potteries by counties and town, number of articles manufactured, and capital invested. Other years and similar valumes for other states should be valuable, too.

Nichols, George Ward. *Art Education Applied to Industry* (N. Y.: Harper, 1877). "Art Education in the United States," 126-131. He was the first husband of Maria Longworth, founder of Rookwood Pottery. Although their mutual interest in art pottery was beneficial to American ceramics, it was detrimental to their marriage; it was "not a happy one," Herbert Peck reports.

.... *Pottery: How it is Made; Its Shape and Decorations* (New York: G. P. Putnam, 1878).

Norman-Wilcox, Gregor, "American Historical Staffordshire Cup Plates," *Antiques*, XVIII, v (November 1930), 393-398.

...................., "American Historical Staffordshire Rarities," *Antiques*, XXV, v (May 1934), 178-182.

...................., "Staffordshire Views of the Boston State House," *Antiques*, XX, vi (December 1931), 363-366.

...................., "Staffordshire Ware in a Nutshell," *Antiques*, XXIX, iii (March 1936), 106-110.

Norton, F. H. "The Crafts Pottery in Nashua, New Hampshire," *Antiques*, XIX, iv (April 1931), 304-305.

............, "The Exeter Pottery Works," *Antiques*, XXII, i (July 1932), 22-25.

Norton, F. H. and V. J. Duplins, Jr., "The Osborne Pottery at Gonic, New Hampshire," *Antiques*, XIX, ii (February 1931), 123-124.

Onondaga Pottery Company. *Little Romances of China* (Syracuse, N. Y.: Privately printed, 1919).

Ormsbee, Thomas H., "Poughkeepsie Was Also a Jugtown," *American Collector* (February 1936).

Orton, Edward, "The Progress of the Ceramic Industry," *Bulletin, University of Wisconsin* (Engineering Series), II, ix (1903).

Osgood, A. H. *Complete Catalogue and Price List of Material for China Decoration* (N. Y.: Osgood Art School, 12 East 17th Street, nd.). Revised, enlarged, and illustrated.

Osgood, Adelaide H. *How to Apply Royal Worcester, Matt, Bronze, LaCroix, and Dresden Colors to China* (N. Y.: A. H. Osgood, 1891). The 18th edition was published in 1905.

Parloa, Maria. *Pocket Guide to Crockery and Silver Settings for the 1880 Table* (Watkins Glen, N. Y.: Century House, 1969).

Peck, Herbert. *The Book of Rookwood Pottery* (N. Y.: Crown, 1968). Winner of the American Life Foundation's Decorative Art Book Award.

Perry, (Mrs.) Aaron F., "Decorative Pottery of Cincinnati," *Harper's New Monthly Magazine*, LXII, ccclxxii (May 1881), 534-545. Covers china painting.

Phillips, John G. *China-Trade Porcelain; an Account of Its Historical Background, Manufacture, and Decoration* (Cambridge, 1956).

Phillips, Louisa, "Decorative Art: A Nation of Spoopendykes and a Land of Bric-a-Brac," *Good Housekeeping*, VI, xii (April 14, 1888), p. 287. So delightful that it is a pity we cannot quote the whole, so a part will have to suffice: ". . . the universal Mrs. Spoopendyke pacidly proceeds in the prosecution of her art labors, transfixing 'Japanese monsters on Yankee stone jars,' . . . And the universal Mr. Spoopendyke continues to fall over [them] . . .until even masculine human nature can endure it no longer, and one day he arises in his might and turns the whole menagerie out of doors, and once more the house of Spoopendyke is a home instead of an amateur museum or old curiosity shop."

Phoenixville Majolica. *Catalogue of Majolica, White Earthenware, etc.* (Phoenixville, Pennsylvania: Griffen Smith & Co., 1884).

Pitkin, Albert Hastings. *Early American Folk Pottery* (Hartford, Conn.: Case, Lockwood & Brainard Co., 1918).

Piton, Camille. *A Practical Treatise on China Painting in America with Some Suggestions as to Decorative Art* (N. Y.: Wiley, 1878). 12 mo. text & folio album of plates.

Porter, G. R. *A Treatise on the Origin, Progress, Importance, and Present State of the Manufacture of Porcelain and Glass* (Philadelphia, 1845).

Potter, Jeanne O., "The Uptons: Potters at East Greenwich," *American Collector* (November 1939), 8-9.

Poucher, J. Wilson, "The Caire Pottery at Poughkeepsie," *Yearbook of the Dutchess County Historical Society*, XXVI (1941), 73-77.

Practical Working Designs in Color (N. Y.: Osgood Art School, 1881). Size: 11½ x 18 (18 studies).

Priestman, Mable Tuke, "Rose Valley [Philadelphia]: A Community of Disciples of Ruskin and Morris," *House and Garden*, X, iv (October 1906), 159-165.

Prime, Alfred Coxe. *The Arts & Crafts in Philadelphia, Maryland, and South Carolina, 1721-1800* (Walpole Society, 1929/1932). Two volumes.

Prime, Phoebe Phillips (comp.). *The Alfred Coxe Prime Directory of Craftsmen Compiled from Philadelphia City Directories, 1785-1800* (Philadelphia, 1960).

Prime, William Cowper. *Pottery and Porcelain of all Times and Nations* (N. Y.: Harper & Brothers, 1879). Third edition. First issued in 1877.

Purviance, Louise and Evan and Norris F. Schneider. *Zanesville Art Pottery in Color* (Leon, Iowa: Mid-America Book, 1968).

Ramsay, John. *American Potters and Pottery* (Clinton, Massachusetts: Hale, Cushman, and Flint, Colonial Press, Inc., 1939). Another edition in 1947 by Tudor.

............, "American Rockingham Tableware," *American Antiques Journal* (October 1947), 4-5.

............, "Early American Pottery: A Resumé," *Antiques*, XX, iv (October 1931), 224-229.

............, "East Liverpool *versus* Bennington: Notes on Some Distinctive Ohio Pottery," *Antiques*, XLIX, i (January 1946), 42-44.

Raymond, W. Oakley, "The Remmey Family: American Potters," *Antiques*, XXXI, vi (June 1937), 296-297; XXXII, iii (September 1937), 132-134; XXXIII, iii (March 1938), 142-144; XXXIV, i (July 1938), 30-31.

.................., "Colonial and Early American Earthenware," *Antiquarian*, IX, vi (January 1928), 38-41.

.................., "Unmarked New York Pottery: Crolius and Remmey," *Antiquarian*, XIV, i (January 1930), 54-55.

Reinert, Guy F., "Slip-decorated Pottery of the Pennsylvania Germans," *American German Review* (March 1936), 12-14.

Remensnyder, John P., "The Potters of Poughkeepsie," *Antiques*, XC, i (July 1966), 90-95.

Revere Pottery. "The Story of Paul Revere Pottery," *The Craftsman*, XXV, ii (November 1913), 205-207.

Rhead, Frederick H. *Studio Pottery* (1910).

Rice, A. H. and John Baer Stoudt. *The Shenandoah Pottery* (Strasburg, Virginia: Shenandoah Publishing House, 1929).

Ries, Heinrich, "Clays of New York," *Bulletin of the New York State Museum*, VII, xxxv (June 1900).

.... *Clays of the United States East of the Mississippi* (Washington, D. C.: U. S. Geological Survey, 1903).

.... *History of the Clay-Working Industry in the United States* (N Y.: Wiley, 1909).

Ripley, Mary Churchill, "Historical Wares of the Future," *Old China*, II, xii (August 1903), 237-243; III, i (September 1903), 2-4; III, vii (March 1904), 116-117. An interesting series that attempts to predict which pieces of contemporary transfer-printed ware will be collectible in the future.

.................., "White House Porcelain," *Old China*, II, x (July 1903), 193-200.

Rookwood Catalogues (referenced in Peck). *Architectural Faience* (1907, 1909, 1919); *Garden Pottery and Ornaments* (undated); *The Rookwood Book* (1904).

Roseville Pottery Catalogues can be consulted at the Ohio Historical Society in Columbus, Ohio.

Sammis, *Mrs.* Irving S., "The Pottery at Huntington, Long Island," *Antiques*, III, iv (April 1923), 161-165.

...................., "The Pottery at Huntington, Long Island," *Huntington Historical Society* (1939).

Sargent, Irene, "An Art Industry of the Bayous: The Pottery of Newcomb College," *The Craftsman*, V, i, 70-76.

..............., "Chinese Pots and Modern Faience: Van Briggle Pottery," *The Craftsman*, IV, vi (September 1903), 415-425.

..............., "Potters and Their Products: The Low Art Tile Company," *The Craftsman*, IV, iii (June 1903), 149-160.

..............., "Some Potters and Their Products: McLaughlin's Losanti Ware," *The Craftsman*, IV, v (August 1903), 328-337.

..............., "Some Potters and Their Products: The Merrimac Pottery," *The Craftsman*, IV, iv (July 1903), 248-251.

Scheetz, Grier, "Bucks County Potters," *Bucks County Historical Society Collections*, IV (1917), 192-197.

Schleiger, Arlene. *Haviland China Pattern Books*.

Schneider, Norris. *Zanesville Art Pottery*.

Schwartz, Marvin. *Collector's Guide to Antique American Ceramics*.

..............., "Fine American Ceramics of the Victorian Period," *Antiques*, LXXVII, iv (April 1960), 386-389.

.... *A History of American Art Porcelain*.

Scoon, Carolyn, "New York State Stoneware in the New York Historical Society," *New York Historical Society Quarterly Bulletin*, XXIX, ii (1945), 83-91.

Seaman, Frank. *The Pottery and Porcelain at the Hut, Yama Farms, Napanoch, New York* (1918).

Shackleton, Philip. *Potteries of Nineteenth-Century Ontario* (Ottawa, 1964).

Shelton, William Henry, "The Unique Art Sale of America: The Salmagundi Club Mug Sale," *Brush and Pencil*, XV, iv (April 1905), 245-250. Begun in 1899; Charles Volkmar was the Club Potter.

Sherman, Frederick F. *Early Connecticut Artists and Craftsmen* (N. Y.: Privately printed, 1925).

Shirley, Bernice, "Rookwood Pottery," *American Antiques Journal* (November 1948), 10-12.

Shoemaker, Henry Wharton. *Early Potters of Clinton County* (Altoona, Pennsylvania: Tribune Publishing Company, 1916).

Sim, Robert J. *Pages From the Past of Rural New Jersey* (Trenton: New Jersey Agricutural Society, 1949).

Singleton, Esther. *Dutch New York* (N. Y.: Dodd, Mead, 1909). "China," 113-117.

.... *Social New York Under the Georges, 1714-1776* (N. Y.: D. Appleton, 1902). "China, Useful and Ornamental," 119-132.

Slosson, Annie Trumbull. *The China Hunter's Club* (Boston, 1878). "It was a charming idea to make a book like this, in which the romance of domestic potteries in New England homes serves to illustrate the history of Ceramic Art in connection with the early use of its products in America."

Smith, Chetwood. *Rogers Groups* (Boston, 1934).

Smith, G. Hubert, "Minnesota Potteries, from Pioneer Craft to Modern Factory," *Minnesota History*, XXX, vi (Summer 1953), 229-235.

Smith, H. L., "Cortland County, New York, Pottery," *Ceramic Age* (October 1935).

Smith, Mable Woods. *Anglo-American Historical China: Descriptive Catalogue, with Prices for which the Pieces were sold at the New York Auction Art Galleries in the Years 1920, 1921, 1922, and 1923* (Chicago: Robert O. Ballou, 1924).

Smith, Walter. *Art Education* (Boston, 1872).

Snow, Julia D. Sophronia, "Delineators of Adams-Jackson American Views," *Antiques*, XXX, v (November 1936), 214-219; XXXI, i (January 1937), 26-30; XXXII, i (July 1937); XXXVI, i (July 1939), 18-21; XXXVIII, iii (September 1940), 112-115.

...................., "Evidence Implicating a Staffordshire Potter," *Antiques*, XXVIII, v (November 1935), 188-191.

...................., "New Studies in Old Staffordshire," *Antiques*, XXXVI, v (November 1939), 242-244; XXXVI, vi (December 1939), 301-302.

...................., "Pottery Postscripts," *Antiques,* XL, iv (October 1941), 218-220.

Solon, Louis Marc Emmanuel. *Ceramic Literature* (London: Griffin, 1910). The standard reference bibliography.

...................., "List of Books on the History and Technology of the Ceramic Art: A Supplement to Ceramic Literature," *Ceramic Society Transactions,* VI (1911-1912), 65-104.

Spargo, John. *The A.B.C. of Bennington Pottery Wares: A Manual for Collectors and Dealers* (Bennington, Vermont: Bennington Historical Museum, 1948).

............, "Burlington Pottery," *Antiques,* VI, v (November 1924), p. 254.

.... *Early American Pottery and China* (N. Y.: Century, 1926). Reprinted in 1948.

............, "The Facts About Bennington Pottery: The Stoneware of the Norton Potteries and The Work of Christopher Webber Fenton," *Antiques,* V, i (January 1924), 21-25; V, v (May 1924), 230-237.

............, "The Fentons—Pioneer American Potters," *Antiques,* IV, iv (October 1923), 166-169.

.... *Potters and Potteries of Bennington* (Boston: Houghton-Mifflin, 1926). Reprinted in 1970.

Sparkes, John C. L. *A Handbook to the Practice of Pottery Painting* (N. Y.: Harper & Brothers, 1878).

Spinney, Frank O., "The Pottery Collection at Old Sturbridge Village," *Antiques,* LXVII, iii (September 1955), 250-251.

Stallknecht, F. *Two Papers on Artistic Pottery and Porcelain, New & Old.* (N. Y.: J. Miller, 1876).

Standard American Price List, Dale & Davis, Prospect Hill Pottery (Trenton, N J., 1884).

Stern, Anna M. P., "Phoenixville Majolica," *American Antiques Journal* (August 1947), 10-12.

Stiles, Helen E. *Pottery in the United States* (N. Y.: E. P. Dutton, 1941).

Stillwell, John E, "Crolius Ware and its Makers," *New York Historical Society Quarterly Bulletin,* X (1926), 52-66.

Storey, *Mrs.* Bellamy, "Rookwood Pottery," *National Cyclopedia of American Biography,* XI, p. 338.

Stoudt, John Baer, "Inscriptions on the Pottery of the Pennsylvania

Germans," *Bucks County Historical Society Collections,* IV, (1917), 587-599.

Stout, W. H., "History of the Clay Industry of Ohio," *Ohio Geological Survey: Coal Formation Clays of Ohio* (Columbus, Ohio, 1923).

Stow, Charles Messer, "The 'Deacon Potter' of Greenwich," *Antiquarian,* XIV, iii (March 1930), 46-47.

.................., "Pennsylvania Slip Ware," *Antiquarian,* XIII, iv (November 1929), 46-47.

Swan, Mabel M., "The Dedham Pottery," *Antiques,* X (August 1926), 116-121.

Swift, Samuel, "American Garden Pottery," *House & Garden,* IV, i (July 1903), 28-40.

Taylor, D. R. and Patricia Taylor. *The Hart Pottery, Canada West* (Picton, Ontario: Picton Gazette, 1966).

Taylor, Marjorie, "Stoneware of Ripley, Illinois," *Antiques,* LVI, v (November 1949), 370-371.

Taylor, William Watts, "Rookwood Pottery," *Forensic Quarterly,* I (1910), 203-218.

Teall, Gardner, "The National Arts Club of New York: Its Position as a Factor in the Encouragement of the Fine Arts, and Why It is Worth While, *The Craftsman,* XV, v (February 1909), 604-613. Illustrates many examples of American art pottery.

Teller, Barbara Gorely, "Ceramics in Providence, 1750-1800," *Antiques,* XCIV, iv (October 1968), 570-577.

Thomas, W. Stephens, "Major Samuel Shaw and the Cincinnati Porcelain," *Antiques,* XXVII, v (May 1935), 176-179.

Tiffany & Co. *Hints to Lovers of Ceramics* (1901-1903).

Tilton, Stephen, W. *Designs and Instructions for Decorating Pottery in Imitation of the Greeks, Romans, etc.* (1876).

Treadwell, John H. *A Manual of Pottery and Porcelain for American Collectors* (N. Y.: G. P. Putnam, 1872).

Tripps, Oscar Lovell. *Chapters in the History of the Arts and Crafts Movement* (Chicago: Bohemia Guild of the Industrial Art League, 1902).

Truax, William J., "Early Pottery Lighting Devices of Pennsylvania," *Antiques,* XXXVII, v (May 1940) 246-247.

Tudor-Craig, Sir Algernon, "Chinese Armorial Porcelain," *Antiques,* XIV, ii (August 1928), 124-128.

Van Briggle, "A Colorado Industry: Van Briggle Pottery," *House & Garden*, IV, iv (October 1903), 165-168.

Vance-Phillips, L. *Book of the China Painter: A Complete Guide for the Keramic Decorator* (N. Y.: Montague Marks, 1896). Appendices B & C discuss and illustrate two sets decorated by Charles Volkmar.

Van Ravenswaay, Charles, "Missouri Potters and Their Wares," *Missouri Historical Society Bulletin* (1951), 453-472.

Varnum, William H. *Industrial Arts Design* (Chicago: Scott, Foresman, 1916).

Wallis, George, "Report of Porcelain and Ceramic Manufacture," *General Report of the British Commissioners on the New York Industrial Exhibition* (London: Harrison, 1854). Listed in Watkins.

Waterhouse, Dorothy S. "Presidential China," *Antiques*, LIV, v (November 1948), 330-332.

Watkins, C. Malcolm, "North Devon Pottery and its Export to America in the 17th Century," *United States National Museum Bulletin*, 225; Contributions from the Museum of History and Technology Paper 13, pp. 17-59 (Washington, D. C.: Smithsonian, 1960).

...................., "North Devon Pottery in the Seventeenth Century," *Antiques*, LXXXII, i (July 1962), 58-61.

.... and Ivor Noël Hume, "The 'Poor Potter' of Yorktown," *United States National Museum Bulletin*, 249; Contributions from the Museum of History and Technology, Paper 54, pp. 73-112 (Washington, D. C.: Smithsonian Institution, 1967).

.... and J. Paul Hudson, "The Earliest Known English Colonial Pottery in America," *Antiques*, LXXI, i (January 1957), 51-54.

Watkins, Lura Woodside, "The ABC's of American Pottery," *Antiques*, XLIII, iii (September 1942), p. 134; XLIII, iv (October 1942), p. 196.

...................., "American Pottery Lamps," *Antiques*, LXIV, ii (August 1953), 108-110.

...................., "The Bayleys: Essex County Potters," *Antiques*, XXIV, v (November 1938), 253-255; XXXV, i (January 1939), 22-27.

...................., "Beans and Bean Pots," *Antiques,* XLVI, v (September 1944), 276-277.

...................., "The Brooks Pottery in Goshen, Connecticut," *Antiques,* XXXVII, i (January 1940), 29-31.

...................., " 'Catskill Moss' Earthenware," *Antiques,* XVIII, iii ,September 1930), 212-215.

...................., "A Checklist of New England Potters," *Antiques,* XLII, ii (August 1942), 80-82.

...................., "Colorful Ceramics of the 1880's in a Family Collection," *Antiques,* XCIII, i (January 1968), 100-103.

.... *Early New England Potters and Their Wares* (Cambridge: Harvard University Press, 1950). Coverage is extended to the end of the 19th century: "The Art Potteries," pp. 222-233. Reprinted in 1969.

...................., "Henderson of Jersey City and His Pitchers," *Antiques,* L, vi (December 1946), 388-392.

...................., "Low Art Tiles," *Antiques,* XLV, v (May 1944), 250-252.

...................., "New England Pottery in the Smithsonian Institution," *Antiques,* LXXII, iii (September 1957), 232-236.

...................., "Pratt's Color Prints on Staffordshire Ware," *Antiques,* LXII ii (August 1952), 122-125.

...................., "Some Unrecorded Pottery: American Molded Pitcher," *Antiques,* LXXIV, ii (August 1958), 135-137.

...................., "The Stoneware of South Ashfield, Massachusetts," *Antiques,* XXVI, iii (September 1934). 94-97.

...................., "Unlisted Subjects in 'Catskill Moss' Ware," *Antiques,* XXII, ii (August 1932), 54-56.

Watson, John F. *Annals of Philadelphia and Pennsylvania* (Philadelphia, 1856). Two volumes. Frank Sommer calls him "The First Historian of American Decorative Arts," *Antiques,* LXXXIII, iii (March 1963), 300-303.

Weygandt, Cornelius, "Jacob Mendinger: A Maker of Pennsylvania Redware," *Antiques,* XLIX, vi (June 1946), 372-373.

Webb, Judson Thomas. *Pottery Making* (Chicago: Lewis Institute, 1914).

Webster, D. B. *American Decorated Stoneware.*

.... *The Brantford Pottery, 1847-1907: History and*

Assessment of the Stoneware Pottery at Brantford, Ontario, Including Results of Excavations and Analysis of Products (Toronto: Royal Ontario Museum, 1968). Published as occasional paper, 13.

Wheeler, Robert G., "Checklist of Albany, N. Y. Potters," *New York History* (October 1944).

. . . . , "The Potters of Albany," *Antiques,* XLVI, vi (December 1944), 345-346.

White, Mary. *How to Make Pottery* (N. Y.: Doubleday Page, 1904). "Modern American Pottery," 167-179.

Williamson, Scott Graham. *The American Craftsman* (N. Y.: Crown, 1940).

Willis, Katharine, "Founders of Early American Pottery," *Antiquarian,* XI, i (August 1928), 33-35.

Winsor, Justin. *The Memorial History of Boston, Including Suffolk County, Massachusetts, 1630-1880* (Boston: James R. Osgood, 1880). Four volumes.

"Wisconsin Potters," *Wisconsin Magazine of History,* XXI, 375-396.

Wood, Richard and Virginia Wood. *Historical China Cup Plates.*

Wood, Ruth Hawe, "Memories of the Fenton," *Antiques,* VIII, iii (September 1925), 150-154.

Wood, Serry. *China Classics: English Staffordshire* (Watkins Glen, N. Y.: Century House, 1959).

. . . . *China Classics: Haviland-Limoges* (Watkins Glen, N. Y.: Century House, 1953).

. . . . *China Classics: Haviland-Limoges* (Watkins Glen, N.Y.: Century House, 1951).

Woodhouse, Samuel W., Jr., "The First Philadelphia Porcelain," *Antiques,* XXIV, iv (October 1933), 134-135.

. . . . , "Martha Washington's China and 'Mr. VanBraam'," *Antiques,* XXVII, v (May 1935) 186-188.

. . . . , "Punch and Punchbowls," *Antiques,* XXIX, ii (February 1936), 56-59.

Works Progress Administration. *Hands That Built New Hampshire: The Story of the Granite State Craftsmen, Past & Present* (Brattleboro, Vermont: Stephen Daye, 1940).

Young, Jennie J. *The Ceramic Art: A Compendium of the History and Manufacture of Pottery and Porcelain* (N. Y.: Harper & Brothers, 1878). "United States," pp. 442-487.

INDEX.